The Gavel and Sickle

The Supreme Court, Cultural Marxism, and the Assault on Christianity

Anthony Walsh

Boise State University

Critical Perspectives on Social Science

VERNON PRESS

www.vernonpress.com

In the Americas:
Vernon Press
1000 N West Street,
Suite 1200, Wilmington,
Delaware 19801
United States

In the rest of the world:
Vernon Press
C/Sancti Espiritu 17,
Malaga, 29006
Spain

Critical Perspectives on Social Science

Library of Congress Control Number: 2017957521

ISBN: 978-1-62273-378-1

Table of Contents

Acknowledgments

I would like to thank commissioning editor, Carolina Sanchez, PhD for her faith in this project. Thanks also to the remarkably able and efficient Argiris Legatos, editorial manager, for his guidance, and to Rosario Batana, director, and Javier Rodriguez, marketing coordinator.

I want to acknowledge also the input of Michael Johnston for his helpful comments. Thanks also to my co-authors on books and articles, Ginny Hatch and Craig Hemmens, for reading parts of the manuscript, and to my very special indexer, Hailey Johnson, who spots a number of mistakes while going through the indexing process—Cheers, girl! Whatever errors or omissions remain is entirely my fault.

Most of all, I would like to acknowledge the love and support of my drop-dead gorgeous wife, Grace (AKA, the Face). She is the center of my universe and the one who keeps me going year after year—what a treasure!

Foreword

Dr. Anthony (Tony) Walsh has a long history of scholarly inquiry, and much of this inquiry has not only produced a massive amount of published scholarships – over 35 published books and approximately 150 journal articles. Dr. Walsh is a leading scholar in the area of biosocial criminology and was recognized for a lifetime achievement award by its association. Biosocial criminology is at the forefront of the study of criminology today in marrying the offender's biology/genetics with his/her social environment. Dr. Walsh is a leading author in this field.

Dr. Walsh is also interested in the study of law and justice, having written one of the leading law and justice books in the field entitled *Law, Justice, and Society: A Sociolegal Introduction.* He has written several projects about the law and how it operates within the social world and provides justice.

This work, in particular, displays the context of law and justice as it relates to the First Amendment's Free Expression of Religion. In this book, Dr. Walsh describes how this component of the First Amendment may not be as free as it once was. This book argues how the First Amendment Freedom of Religion (and closely regarded Freedom of Political Expression) has been eroded over time by the political intrusion. The book discusses *private* business owners in doing *private* business yet retaining their public right to one of their inalienable rights – right to free exercise of one's faith. The book digs into difficult balances in our American jurisprudence in such dialogues as the establishment clause and the notion of separation of church and state. The book establishes clear lines in the sand when it comes to hot-button items such as gay rights and conservative, faith issues.

Readers should know what they are getting themselves into. This book is more of a position piece than it is a balanced treatise, but then, one can't say that it's alright to attack Christianity just a little bit to balance some scale or another. It relies on clear links to the socio/political/legal vantages points. Dr. Walsh is not shy in hitting issues that are not politically correct. In fact, in some respects, he addresses issues that are politically NOT correct. It's a smash-mouth workup of the crux between politics, law and civil liberties. The main issue with this piece is where does political correctness go too far?

Whether one believes in the author's stance that the government should not regulate behavior that encumbers on the free exercise of religious expression, or that should do so to protect sexual liberty, this piece can evoke good conversation. Readers should "give it a chance" and use it as a talking piece in the discussion of these and other politically-charged topics. Readers should use this as a beginning point for good, academic discussion. Dr. Walsh is not shy in addressing politically charged topics but also isn't shy in basic the argument on solid case law and relevant historical documents.

Dr. Walsh and I have had several conversations over the years ranging from the leftist sociologist "clever-sillies" of the postmodern era to the biological underpinnings of biosocial criminology. Many of our conversations are lively with significant disagreements with different approaches to the concepts discussed. This topic was not absent its own lively discussion between two scholars with different viewpoints. Even in that lively debate, Dr. Walsh is to be commended for providing a clear foundation and perspective on the unmistakable fact that Christianity is under assault in the United States.

Jeremy Ball. JD, PhD.

Southeast Missouri State University

Preface

After the thirteen colonies declared their independence from Great Britain in 1776, the Continental Congress adopted the Articles of Confederation in 1777. Under this document, the states retained full sovereignty, and the national government, such as it was, was weak. Although it was strong enough to bring the Revolution to a successful conclusion, it lacked many vital powers, such as issuing a national currency, raising taxes and troops, and forging a viable union between the states. Thus in 1787 delegates from all the states except Rhode Island met in Philadelphia and proposed a stronger central government under a new constitution that would assume many of the powers formerly exercised by the independent states. This effort produced a constitution, but also fierce opposition from some who feared that the rights they had fought for were insufficiently provided for by the new constitution. Those who opposed ratification of the constitution were called Anti-Federalists, and they demanded another convention to draft a Bill of Rights before they would ratify the constitution. Although the Federalists prevailed and the constitution was ratified without a Bill of Rights, the demand for one was so strong that after reviewing the rights guaranteed in state constitutions, the Ten Amendments to the Constitution comprising the Bill of Rights were added to it and ratified in 1791.

These rights were to protect individuals from violations by the federal government and were laid out in order of how the Framers viewed their importance. The most fundamental of these rights were expressed in the First Amendment: freedom of religion, speech, and press, the right peaceful assembly, and the right to petition the government for the redress of grievances. As to the nature of these fundamental rights, Alexander Hamilton wrote in 1775: "The sacred rights of mankind are not to be rummaged for, among old parchments, or musty records. They are written, as with a sunbeam, in the whole volume of human nature, by the hand of the divinity itself; and can never be erased or obscured by mortal power."[1] In other words, the rights laid out in the First Amendment were not dreamt up in the human mind, rather they are rights demanded by our human DNA, planted therein by the Creator.

As with everything that is natural and good, these sacred rights have to be guarded and cultivated. Christianity was to be the kindly guardian and cultivator of our rights against the many vices of the world that would destroy them. To this end, the Founders believed that non-denominational Christianity was to be respected, promoted, and extensively accommodated, for they knew that if Christianity withers, so will our precious rights. This is precisely why the Founders placed liberty in the exulted position of America's "first liberty." As President Calvin Coolidge remarked in his address celebrating the 150 anniversary of the Declaration of Independence; our rights "have their source and their roots in the religious convictions." and he warned that "Unless the faith of the American people in these religious convictions is to endure, the principles of our Declaration will perish."[2]

This book looks at how the very first right enumerated in the First Amendment—religious liberty—has been systematically eviscerated from the 1940s to the present. I initially thought of titling this book "The War on Christianity," taking my cue from President Obama's former Health and Human Services Secretary, Kathleen Sebelius, who told a cheering crowd at a Pro-Choice America fundraiser in 20011 "we are in a war" with religious dissenters.[3] Hillary Clinton also influenced my initial choice of title when she said in her 2015 *Women* in the *World s*peech: "Laws have to be backed up with resources and political will, and deep-seated cultural codes, *religious beliefs*, and structural biases have to be changed."[4] Add to this the 2016 Commission on Civil Rights report in which Commissioner Martin Castro maintained that religious liberty is nothing but "code words" for a string of nasty things such as discrimination and intolerance.[5] In other words, Sebelius' war must be waged on religious dissenters until they change their religious beliefs to conform to Clinton's notion of what they should be because, after all, Castro says they are nothing but shields hiding nefarious practices. This is how far our debased culture has departed from the very principles on which it was founded.

Who would have thought a couple of generations ago that a day would come in the United States when high-ranking government figures would declare "war" on citizens of faith who disagree with government policy? However, the "war" metaphor has been so abused by both the left (the "war on women") and the right (the "war on guns") that I chose the gentler term "assault" to describe government policies that attempt to strip institutions and individuals of their Christian identity if they actively dissent from those policies. These institutions and individuals believe that to assent to the dictates of a certain state, and federal policies would be a violation of their religious consciences.

As an ex-military man (marines) whose sons (army) and grandsons (air force) have served proudly, I am particularly outraged about the attacks on our Christian heritage that have been taken place in the military. An anti-Christian activist named Michael Weinstein has been doing everything in his power to purge Christianity from the military, and he has found powerful allies within the military itself, including Air Force Chief of Staff Norton A. Schwartz. Weinstein said in an interview with the *New York Times* that Schwartz "acknowledged that there [was] a problem" regarding religious freedom in the military.[6] For Schwartz and Weinstein, the problem was not that the military was allowing too little religious freedom, but that it was allowing too much!

A publication of the Family Research Council lists 39 egregious assaults on religious liberty from 2005 to 2013, and there are many, many, more.[7] Because attacks on religious freedom substantially increased during the Obama administration, I will address just one that lays bare Obama's attitude toward America's heritage which he infamously promised his liberal supporters that he would "fundamentally transform." In an effort to protect the religious liberty of members of the armed forces, especially military chaplains who are facing increasingly hostile environments, the United States Congress included a section (section 530) in its *National Defense Authorization Act for Fiscal Year 2014*. Section 503 would have required the Armed Forces to "accommodate actions and speech reflecting the conscience, moral, principles or religious beliefs of the member." Naturally, the Obama administration strongly objected to anything protective of Christianity or moral principles, as evidenced in its response to this proposal:

> The Administration strongly objects to section 530, which would require the Armed Forces to accommodate, except in cases of military necessity, "actions and speech" reflecting the "conscience, moral principles, or religious beliefs of the member." By limiting the discretion of commanders to address potentially problematic speech and actions within their units, this provision would have a significant adverse effect on good order, discipline, morale, and mission accomplishment.[8]

Christian principles are having "a significant *adverse* effect on good order, discipline, morale, and mission accomplishment"! Contrast this statement with that of George Washington, a man who sits head and shoulders, and even ankles above Obama, and in every way Obama's intellectual, moral, and spiritual antithesis: "Purity of Morals being the only sure foundation of public happiness in any Country and highly conducive to order, subordination and success in an Army, it will be well worth the Emulation of Officers of every rank and Class to encourage it both by the Influence of Example and the penalties of Authority."[9] Washington not only accommodated the "conscience, moral principles, or religious beliefs" of his troops, he strongly promoted them.

However, the war on Christianity began before Obama was born with the dim beginnings in the 1940s. I began with the United States Supreme Court's use of the Establishment Clause of the First Amendment to effectively silence the Free Exercise Clause as if the two clauses were in opposition. Far from treating religious freedom as something that cannot be "erased or obscured by mortal power" as Alexander Hamilton said, on many occasions the Supreme Court has treated it as though it was of no greater consequence than the right to wear pajamas to the prom. The Court has used the tactic of opposing the two religious clauses to purge the schools and the public square of anything remotely connected to the religious foundations of America. The Supreme Court's relentless assaults have allowed Barack Obama's executive branch, state courts, and administrative courts, to attack religious conscience on every front from the mighty Catholic Church on down to small family owned businesses. Small businesses have been decimated by ruinous fines for refusing to abide by government policies they oppose on religious grounds, and the Catholic Church has had to withdraw from offering some of its charitable services for the same reason.

The Court's slow and steady removal the Christian guardian of our rights and our morality from the public square has had the result of the debasement of American culture. While this debasement is certainly not the result of a conscious Supreme Court effort to do so, it is just as certainly a key part of the clearly stated cultural Marxist agenda. Cultural Marxism is a toxic anti-Christian, anti-capitalist, and anti-morality philosophy that has infected major portions of our most important social institutions, particularly the universities. Its ultimate goal is plainly stated in its own literature, particularly by its most famous apostle, Antonio Gramsci: "Marxists must change the residually Christian mind." [We need] "to alter the mind—to turn it to its opposite—so that it would become not merely a non-Christian mind but an anti-Christian mind."[10] It is the twin assaults by the courts and the warriors of cultural Marxism that led to the title of this book—The Gavel and Sickle.

During his presidential campaign, Donald Trump promised to defend religious freedom against the growing number attacks actively. His appointments to important government posts during his first 150 days as president have so far revealed that he was serious, but he still has a long way to go to fulfill his promise to protect Americans' most fundamental right. He has signed the *First Amendment Defense Act* barring the federal government from discriminating against individuals and organizations based upon their religious beliefs or moral convictions, but an executive act is only good as long as the president who signs it remains in office. It is not at all surprising that Democratic congresspersons and various anti-Christian groups have mounted a campaign against the Act; what is surprising is that an act to protect the First Amendment would be necessary in the 21st-century America. When a Constitution right needs an executive order to back it up, you know American freedom is on the line.

This book is an effort to explain the legal and cultural circumstances that have transpired over the last 80-odd years that have made the unthinkable necessary. The first chapter examines the slow decline of Christian morality in the United States and how the poisonous philosophy of cultural Marxism has played its part in bringing it about through what it terms the "long march through the institutions." The second chapter explores the many benefits that Christianity has delivered to the institutions and people of United States and to the Western world in general. The third chapter explores the liberal insistence that the United States is a not and has never been a Christian nation, and the fourth examines the awesome power of the United States Supreme Court. The fifth and sixth chapters examine the Establishment and Free Exercise clauses of the First Amendment, and subsequent chapters examine the sad results of the anti-Christian agenda in the United States.

Endnotes

1. Hamilton, A., *The Farmer Refuted*, pp. 97-98.
2. Coolidge, C., Speech on the 150th Anniversary of the Declaration of Independence.
3. Cited in Olson, Cardinal George criticizes Sebelius' declaration of "war on citizens."
4. Brennan, Hillary's infamous women in the world talk.
5. U.S. Civil Rights Commission. *Peaceful Coexistence*, p. 29.
6. Lichtblau, E., Questions raised anew about religion in military, p. 14.
7. Perkins, & Boykin, *Clear and present danger.*
8. Executive Office of the President (2013). Statement of Administration Policy.
9. Dean et al., *The Historical Magazine*, p. 57.
10. Quoted in Malachi, *Keys of this blood*, p. 250.

This book is dedicated to the First Liberty Institute and its President, CEO and Chief Counsel, Kelly J. Shackelford. First Liberty Institute is the largest legal organization in the United States dedicated exclusively to protecting religious freedom for all. It has fought lawsuits in every court system from the local level to the United States Supreme Court in defense of our precious "first liberty."

Chapter 1

Christianity under Fire: Capture the Culture; Capture the Soul

American Culture in the Mid-Twentieth Century

At the end of WWII, former British Prime Minister Winston Churchill remarked to Parliament that "America at this moment stands at the summit of the world," and few doubted his words. The United States emerged from the war as the wealthiest, freest, and most powerful nation on the planet, and the late 1940s through to the 1960s was America's "golden age." It was a time of unprecedented prosperity and social conservatism defined the cultural ethos. Families were intact and attended places of worship in their Sunday best, Billy Graham crusades drew millions, and a single mother was assumed to be a widow. Drugs were something you got from the pharmacy when you were sick, and sexually transmitted diseases were something sailors brought home from the fleshpots of the Far East. Elvis Presley's gyrating hips shocked older generations, and "darn" was just about the only expletive heard on the big screen. Self-reliance was a cardinal virtue, and reliance on welfare was a cardinal vice. In shows like *Leave it to Beaver* and *Father Knows Best,* the family was depicted as wholesome and churchgoing with children who respected their elders and said "sir" and "ma'am." Crime rates were low and punishment swift. Education was the serious business of mastering the three R's. Children were disciplined, and teachers emphasized patriotism, character, and Christian morality.

But a liberal worldview was gestating in the cracks of culture that eventually spouted up to undermine traditional values and morality. Hard leftists preach that America will progress more and more as it discards the "superstitions" of religion and the constrictions of the traditional family. They are doing their best to make this happen as the rest of us watch in silence as our culture careens over the cliff into moral anarchy. The post-war culture that emphasized self-control, discipline, and God and country, has slowly been replaced by a leftist culture that trumpets moral relativism and insidious permissiveness. What is most galling is that the nation's highest court, the United States Supreme Court, has been (no doubt unwittingly) a major player in advancing the far left agenda.

But I don't wish to romanticize the post-war period or choke the reader with unrealistic nostalgia. There were problems with racism and sexism, and homosexuals were imprisoned in their closets. But are blacks, women, and gays better off today? It depends on what we mean by "better off." According to a 2013 Urban Institute report, by all objective measures of well-being the African Americans community fares less well today than it did then. Among the findings were that in 1950, 53 percent of African-American women were married and living with a spouse, but by 2010 only 25 percent were. The percentage of black children born out-of-wedlock rose from 15 percent in 1950 to 73 percent in 2009.[1] This means there are more fatherless children running wild in gangs and perpetuating the cycle of welfare, poverty, prison, and early death. Blacks have a homicide rate almost 13 times higher than the white-non-Hispanic rate, and the vast majority of the victims are other blacks.[2] Some may point to a higher rate of graduation from high school among blacks today than in the 1950s as a positive, but does it really mean anything in the context of lowered standards, "social" promotion, teaching to the test, and any number of other shenanigans schools employ to push barely literate kids out of the door with a relatively worthless piece of paper?

What about women? A National Bureau of Economic Research report tells us that: "By many objective measures the lives of women in the United States have improved over the past 35 years, yet we show that measures of subjective well-being indicate that women's happiness has declined both absolutely and relative to men."[3] Otherwise put; today's women are wealthier and better educated and have more material things than their grandmothers, but they are a lot less happy. What is the use of all those material benefits if they don't make you happy? In the 1950s, the report notes, women reported greater happiness than men, but today men report greater happiness than women. This could well be because feminism encouraged women to "free" themselves from the power of men, and (in Gloria Steinem's famous quip) to "become the kind of man we wanted to marry." Younger women have become more like men in many respects; their use of the "F-word" is almost as great as men's, and their level of promiscuity not far behind. By freeing themselves from patriarchy, women have also freed men from their traditional roles as husbands and providers. The deterioration of women's moral behavior had led to a decline in male respect for women, which in turn has resulted in a "love 'em and leave 'em" attitude, huge increases in out-of-wedlock births, divorce, and the "feminization of poverty."[4]

The lot of homosexuals is probably the exception. In the 1950s, homosexuality was viewed as a mental illness and homosexuals as disturbed or evil. Gays were targeted for abuse, risked getting fired from work if "outed," and homosexual acts could result in imprisonment. Being gay today is accepted and even exalted in such shows as *Will and Grace* and *Queer Eye for the Straight Guy*. We even had the White House lit up in rainbow colors to celebrate the legalization of same-sex marriage in 2015. The downside is that after gay liberation won the day closets emptied and were remodeled into bathhouses where gays and bisexuals engaged in sexual activity without restraint or inhibition. This led to an epidemic of sexually transmitted diseases, the most deadly being AIDS. According to a 2014 U.S. Department of Health & Human Services report, men who engage in homosexual behavior represent about 4 percent of the male population, but in 2010 they accounted for 78 percent of new HIV infections among males and for 54 percent of all people (male and female) with HIV infection.[5]

American Culture Circa 2016

In the late 1960s, American culture began, in Judge Robert Bork's telling phrase, "slouching toward Gomorrah." During this period we saw the ascent of liberalism and its politics of blanket equality, entitlement, and envy. We saw the rejection of the values of conventional society previously limited to a few exotic beatniks spill over to a flood of hippies. Leftist intellectuals lauded the hedonistic hippy lifestyle in books and articles as signaling liberation from "bourgeois capitalism." In the hippy "Age of Aquarius", all sorts of weird ideas such as postmodernism, political correctness, and moral relativism emerged. Formerly confined to America's pony-tailed professoriate in the social sciences and humanities with little else to do than think up such ideas, they have oozed out of the ivory tower to infect a significant proportion of the general population. These unhappy and disaffected hippie drop-outs took to swallowing, sniffing, and injecting everything in sight to dull their empty lives until taking that last "trip too far." A 2015 Substance Abuse and Mental Health Services Administration report reveals that 22 percent (more than 1 in 5) of young adults aged 18 to 25 were current users of illicit drugs. This corresponds to about 7.7 million young adults potentially ruining their lives for a few moments of escape from reality.[6]

Hippies were the vanguard of the so-called sexual revolution, which assured that STDs were no longer the retribution suffered by sailors and slappers. A 2015 American Sexual Health Association report reveals that more than half of all Americans will suffer that penalty at some point in their lives. The report estimates that 19.7 million new STD cases are reported every year in the U.S. costing the economy $15.6 billion in 2010 dollars ($17.2 billion in 2016 dollars) annually. It also notes that one in four teens contracts an STD each year and that half of all sexually active persons will contract an STD by age 25.[7] We're not slouching toward Gomorrah; we're sprinting toward it like Olympic athletes.

Entertainment Then and Now

In the 1950s TV music shows such as the Ed Sullivan and Lawrence Welk shows featured wholesome songs. We saw Pat Boone with his hand over his heart, crooning to his sweetheart that "Every star's a wishing star that shines for you," in *April Love,* and Elvis loving his sweetheart tenderly in *Love me Tender.* Fast forward to 2012 and see that paragon of sleaze, Lil Wayne, hand on crotch, caterwauling in *Every Girl:* "I wish I could f**k every girl in the world," and the equally obnoxious Pitbull howling that his "ho" has "got an ass like a donkey, with a monkey (vagina), look like King Kong," in *I know you want me.* Thinkers from Plato to John Steinbeck have noted that popular music expresses a culture's values and beliefs better than any other factor. To the extent that this is true, the violence, filth, and nihilism featured in much of modern teen pop music is a damning indictment of our modern culture.

Not to be outdone, 21st century TV cartoons are also wallowing in muck. Cartoons in the 1950s featured shows mainly for children such as *Bugs Bunny,* but the most wildly popular cartoon show today (hopefully not watched by children) is the toilet humor of *South Park.* Nothing is sacred in *South Park.* Songs that are supposed to celebrate the birth of Christ are turned into the most blasphemous filth imaginable, such as "Merry F#*king Christmas." The most obnoxiously depraved "Christmas" song of all, *Howdy Ho!* features the Virgin Mary engaging in oral sex with the three wise men.

Mocking Christianity is also fashionable in the arts. Andres Serrano's notorious photograph *Piss Christ* depicted a crucifix submerged in a glass of his urine. To add insult to injury, Serrano received $5,000 from National Endowment for the Arts to come up with this loathsome "creation." We also have the deeply offensive painting by Chris Ofili called *The Holy Virgin Mary* partly created from elephant dung and liberally collaged with pornography. New York Mayor Rudy Giuliani objected to public money used to display this obscenity but lost the battle to such paragons of virtue as Hillary Clinton and other prominent leftists.

Our cities are now dotted with "adult" bookstores, and pornographic sites are the most visited sites on the Internet. Every year we have three-day Exxxotica expos around the country (since 2006) drawing crowds as large as 26,000 and featuring pornography, sex toys, and lots of lewd conduct. Scantily clad women (and some men) are on hand to sing the praises of loveless sex, even solitary sex with the toys they want to sell. There is even a dungeon where a visitor can "experiment" with sadomasochism. Exxxotica is sold as a venue where we can improve our sex lives, but all it does is substitute meaningful lovemaking for the soulless and mechanistic achievement of orgasms.

Photographer Robert Mapplethorpe also received government grants to display his homoerotic and sadomasochistic pictures, including one with a man urinating into another man's mouth. Another photo was a self-portrait with a whip planted deep into his anus, and another depicted naked minor children with a graphic focus on their genitals. The works of these depraved individuals were defended by the anointed ones on the left on First Amendment grounds as free speech. My libertarian streak does not lead me to favor censorship, but I do object to tax dollars being used to support anti-Christian filth masquerading as art. Government support for this garbage smacks of royal patronage; that is, state-sponsored art stamped with an official seal of approval. Leftist feel that it is just fine to use tax dollars to display the products of these degenerates in the public square attacking Christian morality while at the same time demanding tax dollars to remove from the public square, crucifixions, crèches, the Ten Commandments, and other religious symbols that exalt Christianity. The Supreme Court is their ally, issuing ruling after ruling aimed at outlawing anything smacking of Christianity from the public domain.

A 2016 report edited by Kelly Shackelford of the First Liberty Institute highlights a relentlessly growing pattern of hostility toward Christianity in the United States. The report lists more than 600 incidents over the previous 10 years in all areas of public life from public schools, to the workplace, to the military which have prevented people from living the lives according to their faith and conscience. In Shackelford's words: "It is eroding the bedrock on which stand vital American institutions such as government, education, the military, business, houses of worship, and charity. It has the potential to wash away the ground that supports our other rights, including freedom of speech, press, assembly, and government by consent of the people.[8]

First Liberty and other organizations supporting religion and the family such as the Alliance Defending Religious Freedom and the American Family Association have actually been designated, along with the KKK and the American Nazi Party, as hate groups, by the Southern Poverty Law Center (SPLC). The SPLC is an ultra-liberal organization dedicated to "Keeping an eye on the radical right," as their official website puts it. It seems like every group in the United States except those who share the SPLC's agenda is a hate group. Putting religious and family values groups in the same box as Klansmen and Nazis serves the purpose of demonizing them, thus making attacks on them more acceptable to more people. American culture has certainly transformed

from a culture founded on Christian principles to a culture in which government actively supports actions hostile to Christianity and where Christians
must keep their faith in the closet and may be punished by law for exercising
it in the public square. How in the world did we get so debased?

Cultural Marxism: The Origins of the Rot

Culture can move individuals to greatness or leave them wallowing in muck
because it informs our worldview and serves as a guide for what is right or
wrong. We are all coated in culture because it is the cloth from which we
weave our values, attitudes, beliefs, and behaviors. There are many different
subcultures within mainstream American culture, but we all acquire the lessons of the broad culture via parents, education, and the media as if by osmo-
sis. Some may reject it, but it influences us all for better or for worse. Because
Americans have been fed a steady diet of leftist propaganda vilifying or mocking traditional values of morality and personal responsibility, far too many of
them support politicians who promise them everything at someone else's
expense. I attended a Bernie Sanders presidential campaign event in April
2016 where I witnessed him promise an audience of mostly young people all
kinds of "free stuff" to their enthusiastic whoops, cheers, and chants. They do
not realize that that have to be willing to sacrifice freedom to get their government free stuff, and by the time they do it is too late.

Given that they were at a Bernie Sanders event as enthusiastic supporters,
perhaps they are not too concerned with freedom anyway. The way they were
talking and behaving, as well as the way they were dressed, liberally adorned
with tattoos and rings, stuck all over the place, it is obvious that they are the
ones who have taken in the worst aspects of our culture. They are ignorant of
the sad history of socialism and of the realities of economics. I imagine if
someone were to mention old-fashioned virtue to them they would be highly
amused. They would scoff at Ben Franklin's warning that: "Only a virtuous
people are capable of freedom, as nations become corrupt and vicious, they
have more need of masters." One wonders if the United States will reach the
stage when Christianity and the family have been so defiled and corrupted
that Americans will be "in need of masters?"

Make no mistake; the radical left knows that it needs to destroy American
foundations if it is to build its utopia. Karl Marx taught his followers that if the
socialist revolution is to be successful, it must first spiritually disarm the people by ridding a country of its two epicenters of morality—religion and the
family. In his *Feuerbach Thesis # 4*, Marx wrote: "Once the earthly family is
discovered to be the secret of the heavenly family, the former must be destroyed in theory and in practice."[9] True to Marxist philosophy, after the Rus-

sian Revolution, the Soviet Union first went after religion. Atheism became its established religion, and it embarked on a program of ridiculing religion, harassing believers, and propagating atheism in schools. After declaring Soviet state officially atheist, it then went after Marx's "earthly family" by passing legislation legitimizing the offspring of the unmarried, making divorce available on demand, and encouraging "free love" as the "essence of communist living."[10]

The Soviet government's agenda resulted in Ivan's abandoning their Natasha's from Riga to Vladivostok and to millions of father-absent children roaming the streets who "formed into gangs, and who would rob and attack people in the street, or even invade and ransack apartment blocks."[11] After assessing the damage, the Soviet government responded by extolling the family, the sanctity of marriage, the evils of divorce, and the joys of parenthood, as well as by passing laws making divorce more difficult and restoring the legal concepts of legitimacy and illegitimacy. The powerful state apparatus of the Soviets could legislate and strictly enforce radical and counter-radical changes fairly swiftly, but it has taken decades of slow cultural debasement in the United States to see millions of father-absent children wreaking similar havoc. Millions of Americans are on some form of welfare, languishing in existential despair and frittering their time away in mindless pursuits. All of this makes them dependent on Big Brother government rather than on the traditional family structure for their sustenance, which is exactly what socialists and "progressives" want (more votes for the Democrats). The more people there are feeding at the public trough—and that includes the teachers and professors (yes, I'm one of them) to whom we entrust our children's minds—the more people there will be who are susceptible to leftist propaganda and control.

The same undermining of Christianity and the family occurred in the United States by a slow process of piecemeal cultural change helped along by anti-religious Supreme Court decisions. The pace has been so slow that the rot has hardly been noticed. Unmarried motherhood does not carry the moral stigma it once did; most states have "no-fault" divorces, and free love is the "hip" thing that drives both processes. As Christianity has become less embedded in our country, our moral compasses have gone haywire, and many behaviors once considered unacceptably deviant have been "normalized," or at least trivialized. Our culture has become overwhelmed with deviance, and since society can tolerate only so much deviance, says former Senator and sociologist Daniel Moynihan, we respond by "defining deviance down."[12] Physician and columnist Charles Krauthammer added his own notion to Moynihan's claiming that it is not enough to normalize deviance there must be a counter strategy to define the formerly normal (such as Christian morality) as deviant to achieve moral leveling.[13] Moynihan and Krauthammer provide numerous examples of defining deviance downwards or upwards in ways that advance the leftist agenda.

The Frankfurt School and Cultural Marxism

The poisonous philosophy behind the ongoing degradation of the "shining city on the hill," as we used to call the United States, can be traced indirectly to the establishment of the Hungarian Soviet Republic in March 1919, under Bela Kun. As with all leftist-inspired revolutions, this one proceeded to engage in an orgy of death and destruction known as the "Hungarian Terror." It seems farfetched to trace the modern condition of American culture to a small nation tucked away in south-central Europe, but what was spawned as a cancerous educational philosophy in that tiny country has metastasized and found its way into the vital organs of our own educational system. I do not claim that this was a conscious conspiracy to undermine the moral foundation of America. Hungarian communists were concerned only with Hungary, but these programs and thinking started a meandering chain of events that eventually led to Marxist ideas quietly finding a welcome home in American education via European socialist emigres.

Following WWI, socialists, and progressives were puzzled by the failure of the working classes of Europe to respond to Marx's call to rise and destroy their capitalist states and embrace utopian communism. They came to realize that it was cultural and not economic factors that stood in the way of secular salvation and that violent revolution would never succeed in Western societies as long as they maintained the cultures they were built upon. Cultural Marxists dumped many of orthodox Marxism's ideas such as "surplus value" and the "inevitability of history," retaining only Marxism's animus for everything moral and everything Western.

Because it was the cultural superstructure that supported capitalism, it must be the focus of attack. A gradual evolutionary approach to communism through cultural debasement was deemed a more viable approach than violent revolution. The biggest obstacle to implementing socialism was Christianity—the foundation of Western morality—and so it had to be destroyed. Historians Will and Arial Durrant describe the absolute opposition of Christianity and utopian communism: "Heaven and utopia are buckets in a well: when one goes down the other goes up; when religion declines Communism grows."[14] The Durrants are supported by none other than Karl Marx himself, who wrote: "communism begins where atheism begins."[15]

The educational philosophy in the Hungarian Soviet Republic was the brainchild of Marxist philosopher Georg Lukacs, who was the People's Commissar for Education and Culture. In this position, he was able to define what was politically correct and incorrect in Hungarian Education from kindergarten to university. Raymond Raehn explains that Lukacs launched what became known as "Cultural Terrorism." As part of this terrorism, he instituted a radical sex education program in Hungarian schools. Children were instructed in "free love, sexual intercourse, the archaic nature of middle-class family codes, the out-datedness of monogamy, and the irrelevance of religion, which deprives man of all pleasures."[16] These are exactly the values the Russians foisted on their culture with such disastrous results, and the values being foisted on American students today in more subtle (and sometimes not so subtle) fashion.

The Hungarian Soviet Republic lasted only 133 days before Bela Kun was ousted by an invading Romanian army aided by Hungarian workers who wanted no part of the stench of communism, but it began the sequence of events that led to the Institute for Social Research—better known as the Frankfurt School—in Germany. When the Hungarian counter-revolution occurred, Lukacs fled to the Soviet Union, and subsequently to Germany in 1923, and became a member of the Frankfurt School. The Frankfurt School was a kind of Marxist think tank financed by the son of an Argentine-German millionaire named Felix Weil. The School studied ways to deconstruct the economic and revolutionary basis of Marxism and to reconstruct it with an evolutionary cultural basis. Michael Minnicino writes that Lukacs' believed that the political movement capable of turning Western societies toward socialism would have to be "demonic."

By this Lukacs meant that "it could only succeed when the individual believes that his or her actions are determined by 'not a personal destiny, but the destiny of the community' in a world '*that has been abandoned by God.*'"[17]

Lukacs' strategy was fashioned on the Italian Marxist Antonio Gramsci's theory of "cultural Marxism." Cultural Marxism refers to a theoretical synthesis of Marxist and Freudian thought dedicated to the idea that communism can be achieved incrementally by cultural evolution. The agents of cultural revolution are the intellectual wordsmiths in academia and the news media, and marginalized groups such as radical activists in the black, feminist, and gay communities, as well as others, alienated from mainstream society. Marginalized groups are recast from alienated malcontents to victims of racism, sexism, homophobia, religious bigotry, and capitalism, and it is the task of wordsmiths to convince them of the benefits to be gained by their destructive agenda.

Cultural Marxism had its beginning as an effort to explain why communism was not possible in Western societies. Gramsci, who yearned for the "suicide of Catholicism" and the "execution of God," believed that it was because the proletariat shares the Christian religion with the bourgeoisie that socialist revolutions had not occurred in the West. It was, therefore, essential to capture the mind of a society by capturing its culture. In other words, it is necessary to quietly and incrementally debase the culture by undermining Western traditions and values by using the media, the law, and education to weaken Christianity and the family.

This was termed "the conquest of the system" by a process described as "the long march through the institutions." Capturing and reshaping institutions such as the schools, universities, the media and entertainment industries, and the courts, and even seminaries and political parties would lead to people abandoning capitalism and embracing socialism without them barely noticing it had happened. Once you have control of the movie and music industries, you have an open pipeline to pump messages into the minds of impressionable young people, and thus promote as much sleaze as you want while simultaneously casting aspersions on Christian morality and practices. Gain access to the press, schools, and universities, and you have much the same opportunities through more cerebral pipelines to distort American history and vilify capitalism and the nasty white males whose values made the unparalleled success of the West possible. Best of all, capture a political party that rewards sloth and penalizes success, that turns the races, sexes, and sexual orientations against each other to gain political power, and you have the perfect cultural Marxist recipe for turning this nation into a second-rate bloated socialist state incapable of doing anything except foisting further degradation and ruin on its people.

It is impossible not to see this moral deterioration occurring, but leftists know that their goal requires it. Gramsci knew that religion stood in the way of this goal and thus attacks on Christianity must be waged relentlessly and comprehensively: "Marxists must change the residually Christian mind. He needed to alter the mind—to turn it into its opposite—so that it would become *not merely a non-Christian mind but an anti-Christian mind.*" [18] Thus, it is the disaffected journalists, entertainers, artists, teachers, and professors of society rather than its workers who would be instrumental in establishing communism.

How ironic it is that after defeating the tyranny of political and economic Marxism around the world in the Cold War we are losing to cultural Marxism in our own backyards. The left has no love for Western civilization, as it showed with its meltdown over President Trump's affirmative defense of it in his speech in Poland prior to the G20 summit in Hamburg in 2017. Trump asked whether the West has the will to survive and if we have the confidence in our Christian values to defend them. Having lived in the clutches of communism for so long, the Poles were thrilled when Trump sprinkled his determined defense of Western culture with references to Christianity and family values. In America, however, leftist journalists started pulling out their hair. Peter Beinart wrote a piece in *The Atlantic* titled "The Racial and Religious Paranoia of Trump's Warsaw Speech." The title starkly reveals the hard left's mindless preoccupation with race and with its anti-Christian bias.

Although Gramsci never acknowledged it, he owed a debt to the British Fabian Society, founded in 1884, for many of his ideas. Its founders were a bunch of eccentric socialists who steered away from calling themselves by that name lest they aroused suspicion. Their first coat of arms was a wolf in sheep's clothing, which says a lot about Fabian duplicity. This logo was later abandoned because of its negative connotations and has been replaced by a tortoise, representing the Fabian's goal of a slow, imperceptible transition from capitalism to socialism. One of Fabianism's most famous members, George Bernard Shaw, described the Fabian strategy as "methods of stealth, intrigue, subversion, and the deception of never calling socialism by its right name."[19] Using these tactics, socialism could take hold by slowly debasing the culture until its dumbed-down population, obsessed only with Juvenal's "bread and circuses" to keep them superficially happy and docile, no longer has the wit to notice or care. This insight is nothing new; Norman Thomas, a six-time Socialist Party candidate for U.S. president, said as much in a 1944 speech: "The American people will never knowingly adopt socialism. But, under the name of 'liberalism,' they will adopt every fragment of the socialist program, until one day America will be a socialist nation, without knowing how it happened." [20]

As if to prove that Thomas knew what he was talking about, the 2016 Democratic National Convention in Philadelphia opened with a prayer by Christian minister, the Rev. Cynthia Hale. Almost immediately the crowd of limousine liberals booed and jeered her, as they booed God during the 2012 Democratic convention. Not only that, during her invocation the crowd began chanting "Bernie, Bernie," rooting for Sanders the socialist savior, leaving little doubt that socialism is now mainstream in the Democratic Party, and how far it has sunk into the moral sewer. The only truly surprising thing about this is that a Christian minister was invited to offer a prayer at a Democratic Party event in the first place.

Coming to America

When the Nazis shut the Frankfurt School down and started persecuting Jews, who constituted the core of the School, it moved to Columbia University in New York. Notable Frankfurters were appointed to positions in other elite universities where they slotted in comfortably with the leftist professoriate. They immediately began to repay America's hospitality by applying "critical thinking" to every institution ordinary Americans hold dear because mass society has to reach a state of hopelessness and alienation to realize socialist revolution. "Critical thinking" conveys a positive message of being open to all points of view, but in reality, it is the unrelenting pursuit of the negative in order to vilify and obliterate any system of thought that runs counter to leftism. Michael Walsh aptly describes the critical theory as: "At once overly intellectualized and emotionally juvenile...When everything could be questioned, nothing could be real, and the muscular, confident empiricism that had just won the war gave way, in less than a generation, to a central-European nihilism celebrated on college campuses across the United States."[21]

You can readily see this influence in the missives of leftist academics. Their poisoned pens scribble nihilistic codswallop on acres of foolscap that is eagerly devoured by other privileged malcontents looking for meaning among Mephistophelean sewer rats. Like Mephistopheles, they cannot create, but they sure can destroy. Their philosophy of political correctness has spread like cancer in the ivory tower and beyond and regulates public debate by casting opposing (non-leftist) views as bigoted, racist, sexist, and homophobic, and therefore illegitimate. Political correctness is essentially a strategy of censorship that creates a deadening tyranny of speech regulation and thought anxiety in American education.

The most influential member of the Frankfurt School was Herbert Marcuse, the guru of free love. Marcuse was a typical leftist in his belief that tolerance is only for left-wing ideas and practices. He wrote: "Liberating tolerance, then, would mean intolerance against movements from the Right and toleration of movements from the Left."[22] Marcuse wanted a utopian socialist society which, he counseled, "is to be ruled *despotically* by an enlightened group whose chief title to do so is that its members will have realized in themselves the unity of Logos and Eros, and thrown off the vexatious authority of logic, mathematics, and the empirical sciences."[23] Marcuse's mandate has formed the intellectual foundation for the academic left and its machine of intolerant political correctness. In many social science and humanities departments around the country, he has achieved his goal of converting "illusion into reality and fiction into truth."[24] Marcuse's sophistry became so convincing to alienated minds that his Orwellian Newspeak defines much of the nonsense we see coming out of the liberal ivory tower. If you can convince people that censorship is tolerance, you can convince them of anything—freedom is slavery, ignorance is strength, black is white, $2 + 2 = 5$, and socialism is just great.

Marcuse channeled both Marx and Freud in his best-selling *Eros and Civilization*, the Bible of the New Left. In it, he explained his vision of individual freedom as being a life free of anxiety, by which he meant free of the constraints of morality. Marcuse wrote that man "is free only where he is free from constraint, external and internal, physical and moral—when he is constrained neither by law nor by need."[25] Just like Lukacs, Marcuse wanted to remove any and all constraints on sexual behavior, including behaviors most people consider perverse and which physicians consider harmful: "the perversions uphold sexuality as an end in itself."[26] The ultimate goal of this unbridled sexuality was honestly stated as the destruction of the family: "This change in the value of and scope of libidinal relations would lead to a disintegration of the institutions in which the private interpersonal relations have been organized, particularly the monogamic and patriarchal family."[27] Marcuse would have been very satisfied had he lived long enough to attend an Exxxotica convention, listen to Lil Wayne's foul mouth, watch *South Park*, or see a parade of sick artists receiving grants to ridicule, defile, and blaspheme Christianity.

Barack Obama's War on Christianity

I am not going to claim that Barack Obama consciously and malevolently waged a Lukacs-like war on Christianity while in office. Although attacks on religious freedom increased dramatically under his administration, efforts to purge religion from American public life began before he was born. What were previously quite, sneaky, attacks have now become much more open and robust. Obama made it his business in many places here and abroad to declare that "we are no longer a Christian nation," and he has demonstrated his contempt for Western culture on many occasions. Rather than celebrating all the United States has done for the world, Obama is fixated on the negative and rushes to apologize for America, indicating to foreign leaders who dislike America that he understands and "feels their pain."

The anti-Christian, anti-capitalism and anti-Western agenda Obama tried to implement is not surprising since he has many mentors and friends with a hatred of the United States, and who believe with him that Western nations are prosperous because they have exploited and oppressed people of color. Obama shamelessly tells us the kinds of disgruntled rabble-rousers he sought as mentors in college, particularly Marxists, radical feminists, and postmodernist types—in short, anyone that didn't make any sense. The friends he sought were fellow alienated students with values as far away from mainstream culture as possible and writes of their juvenile behavior: "When we ground out our cigarettes in the hallway carpet or set our stereos so loud that the walls began to shake, we were resisting bourgeois society's stifling constraints. We weren't indifferent or careless or insecure. We were alienated."[28]

Obama virtually marinated in radical leftist ideas in his formative years, surrounded as he was with people resembling hybrids of a Politburo comrade and a Black Panther. His parents were both ardent communists, and his mentors included Frank Marshall Davis, a communist and rabid anti-white racist, and Edward Said, a Columbia professor and supporter of Palestinian terrorism. Obama's "liberation theology" pastor, Jeremiah Wright, whose infamous remark—"No, no, no, not God bless America! God damn America"!—speaks for itself. Among his other friends and acquaintances are Derrick Bell, a rabid anti-white racist, and Bill Ayers, who is a professor of education despite his unrepentant domestic terrorism and self-description as a communist revolutionary. This bevy of alienated malcontents is united by radical leftist and racist politics and a visceral hatred of the West, and it would be naive to believe that their philosophy has not rubbed off on Obama. He has voiced support for the virulently toxic, racist, and anti-police group Black Lives Matter, whose members chant such despicable hatred as "What do we Want? Dead Cops! When do we want them? Now!" When Micah Johnson opened fire on July 7, 2016, killing five police officers and injuring nine others and two civilians during a Black Lives Matter demonstration, they got what they wanted, but no words of condemnation of this group from Obama for fermenting hatred and violence were ever heard.

Obama's Czars

Ample evidence that Obama is contaminated by radical leftism was his appointments of a number of like-minded individuals to be special advisors ("czars") on everything from A to Z. Almost all these czars were unconfirmed by congress and unaccountable to it, which is a violation of the Constitution's Article II, Section 2 of the Appointment Clause. This clause states that officers of the United States may be appointed by the president only with the advice and consent of the Senate, yet in true autocratic fashion Obama made end-runs around Congress on almost all of them; so much for the "transparency", he promised for his administration. In a letter to Obama, Senator Robert Byrd voiced deep concerns over the proliferation of unconstitutionally appointed czars (more than 40): "The rapid and easy accumulation of power by White House staff can threaten the constitutional system of checks and balances... At the worst, White House staff has taken direction and control of programmatic areas that are the statutory responsibility of Senate-confirmed officials."[29]

The *Judicial Watch Report* lists a litany of corruption and scandals among almost all of Obama's czars, but I am only interested in the extent to which the record shows their values and behavior the consistent with cultural Marxism. Attorney General Eric Holder is so obsessed with anti-white animus that he refused to prosecute Black Panthers who intimidated whites at the voting polls to prevent them from voting in the 2007 elections or members of the Puerto Rican terrorist group FALN. The Deputy Attorney General, David Ogden, spent much of his career outside the administration defending pornographers. Diversity czar Mark Lloyd wants to remove all white people from powerful positions in the media in favor of minorities; to use licensing rules to bring a more liberal voice to talk radio, and has on many occasions praised the "incredible revolution" of Venezuelan president Hugo Chavez, who brought his oil-rich country to ruin with his socialist policies. Science czar John Holden wants to control population growth by such Maoist solutions as forced abortions and involuntary sterilization and suggests that a "planetary regime" is necessary to implement the policies. Safe and Drug-Free Schools czar Kevin Jennings has made successful efforts to promote homosexuality in schools, has held education seminars to expose children to "unorthodox" sexual practices (shades of Georg Lukacs), wrote a forward to a book called *Queering Elementary Education,* and praised a prominent member of the North American Man-Boy Love Association.

Other czars are members of various socialist organizations. Manufacturing czar Ron Bloom voiced the opinion that "We know the free enterprise market is nonsense," and was associated with Obama's former communications director, Anita Dunn, who gushes over the sadistic Chinese dictator Mao Zedong, her "favorite philosopher." Energy and Environmental czar Carol Browner is one of the prominent members of the world-wide Socialist International. And finally, Green Jobs czar Van Jones, a self-admitted anarchist/communist and anti-white racist, is infamous for showing strong support for Mumia Abu-Jamal, convicted of murdering a white police officer in Philadelphia. Given enough rope, this cabal of corrupt leftists was capable of putting Obama's promise to "fundamentally transform America" into practice; but thankfully could not. Obama and his clique may not call themselves cultural Marxist, but Lukacs and Gramsci's DNA is written all over their actions.

The Obama Cult of Personality

In 2008, economist Paul Krugman (himself very left-wing) stated that: "I'm not the first to point out that the Obama campaign seems dangerously close to becoming a cult of personality." A cult of personality is associated with totalitarian regimes such as Hitler's Germany, Stalin's Russia, Mao's China, and Kim Il-Sung's North Korea. Personality cults are a kind of substitute political religion, and therefore flourish where religion has been decimated. Charismatic leaders cultivate an idealized, heroic, and worshipful image of themselves via the controlled use of the media and education, although in Obama's case the media have done it of their own volition.

Obama was barely in the White House when he was awarded the Nobel Peace Prize for doing absolutely nothing. Perhaps they were overly impressed by his inaugural speech when he promised to perform miracles and opined that future generations would say of him "This was the moment when the rise of the oceans began to slow and our planet began to heal." Writing in the *San Francisco Gate* in 2008, Mark Morford characterized Obama "as a Lightworker, that rare kind of attuned being who has the ability to lead us not merely to new foreign policies or health care plans or whatnot, but who can actually help usher in *a new way of being on the planet.*"

Chris Matthews, the news anchor for the ultra-liberal MSNBC, compared Obama to Jesus and gushed "This is bigger than Kennedy. [Obama] comes along, and he seems to have the answers. This is the New Testament...I feel this thrill going up my leg." Louis Farrakhan, the leader of the racist Nation of Islam and another member of Chicago's corrupt crowd that spawned Obama, said in a speech to his followers: "Brothers and sisters, Barack Obama to me, is a herald of the Messiah. Barack Obama is like the trumpet that alerts you something new, something better is on the way...[when Obama talks] "the Messiah is absolutely speaking." At the Soul Train Awards, actor Jamie Foxx blasphemously said: "It's like church in here. First of all, give an honor to God and our Lord and Savior Barack Obama." Finally, in June of 2012, Newsweek magazine celebrated Obama's endorsement of same-sex marriage with an image of him on the cover sporting a rainbow halo above his head.

These are just a few of the many examples of the quasi-religious nature of Obama's cult of personality that allowed him to ignore the Constitution and the Congress and get away with it. That there was such a cult is an indication of how far left the media have drifted. Any opposition to Obama's policies and actions were condemned as racist, which tends to silence timid souls. But now that he has gone, I believe that the best thing Obama did for this country with his leftist policies was to decimate the Democratic Party in the 2016 elections. Dissatisfaction with his policies put Republicans in charge of the White House and both Houses of Congress, elected a record number of Republican governors and legislative bodies around the country, and gave us the prospect of appointing a Supreme Court Justice or two who actually respect the Constitution.

Wacky Right-Wing Conspiracy Theory?

Leftists are masters of destroying an argument in their own minds with hissing epithets such as racist, sexist, or fascist, which are sure conversation stoppers that relieve them of the necessity of discussion. This was very much in evidence during the 2016 Democratic campaign. Almost every issue was turned into one of race or gender, and dire warnings were issued about what will happen if Republicans were gaining power, such as Joe Biden's remark that the GOP wants to "put Y'all Back in Chains." The GOP was also accused of "waging war on women." and hating homosexuals. Likewise, leftists do not want the issue of attacks on Christianity discussed in public, so they claim that criticism of cultural Marxism and its agenda is anti-Semitism because the original members of the Frankfurt School were Jews. This is about as absurd as saying that a person is anti-German, Russian, or Chinese because he or she abhors Nazism, Stalinism, or Maoism.

If the anti-Semitism charge won't stick, then they will put books such as this down to a wacky right-wing conspiracy theory. It is by such sophomoric name-calling that leftists often win the day because people tend to quickly get bored with documented arguments while they are easily animated with emotional appeals. If the attacks on religious liberty is nothing more than a conspiratorial fantasy in the mind of right-wing nuts, why do we see the caseload of First Liberty Institute, the nation's largest legal organization dedicated exclusively to defending religious liberty, grow almost exponentially from 63 cases in 2010 to 388 in 2016; a 516% increase? [30] If it is a conspiracy, why was the *First Amendment Defense Act* barring the federal government from discriminating based on religious beliefs or moral convictions necessary? When President Trump signed the Act on May 4th, 1917, he remarked: "No American should be forced to choose between the dictates of the federal government and the tenets of their faith. We will not allow people of faith to be targeted, bullied or silenced anymore." Was he making all this up? It is also difficult to see how leftists can claim that cultural Marxism is just a right-wing illusion with no basis in reality because cultural Marxism is a well-developed school of thought so named by its founders and articulated in their own writings in many books and articles.

Leftists trashed W. Cleon Skousen's prophetic 1958 book *The Naked Communist* as a wacky right-wing conspiracy theory.[31] Skousen, a former FBI agent, police chief of Salt Lake City, and professor listed 45 strategies communists want to implement to gain a foothold in this country. Among those listed by Skousen were the breakdown cultural standards of morality by promoting pornography and obscenity all formats; to present sexual degeneracy and promiscuity as normal, natural, and healthy, and to eliminate prayer or any religious expression in the schools. Readers can judge for themselves the extent to which of Skousen's "wacky" predictions made in 1958 is a sad reality some 60 years later. Skousen based his predictions by examining the writings of Marxists and the information he came across as an FBI agent. If his book is a wacky conspiracy theory, then the voluminous Marxist literature revealing its views on religion and the family, and how they must be attacked and destroyed to make socialism successful in the West, was nothing more than an intellectual exercise. I don't think anyone believes that.

Every year, an organization called International Christian Concern (ICC) publishes the *Hall of Shame Report* listing the nations that are persecuting Christians. The 2016 report included the United States for the very first time, citing events that occurred from 2012 to 2015. Although persecution in the United States is mild compared to Christian persecution in Islamic countries, the: "ICC sees these worrying trends as an alarming indication of the decline in religious liberty in the United States."[32] With Obama gone and Donald Trump signing the *First Amendment Defense Act* we may see a reverse of a situation that would have been unthinkable 50 years ago. However, such acts are only good as long as the president who signs it remains in office, and Democratic congresspersons and other anti-Christian groups will be tirelessly campaigning against the Act. People who care about the future of America and who know the value of Christianity in all spheres of life must just as tirelessly fight to preserve the inalienable right to religious exercise as guaranteed by the First Amendment to the Constitution.

Endnotes

1. Acs, Braswell, Sorensen, and Turner.
2. Steffensmeier, Feldmeyer, Harris and Ulmer.
3. Stevenson and Wolfers, p. 3.
4. Hunnicutt and Broidy.
5. U.S. Department of Health & Human Services, 2014.
6. Substance Abuse and Mental Health Services Administration, 2015.
7. American Sexual Health Association, 2015.
8. Shackelford, K., Undeniable, p. 5.
9. Quoted in Jal, M. Interpretation, p.136.
10. Hazard, Butler and Maggs, p. 470.
11. Hosking, *The First Socialist Society*, p. 213.
12. Moynihan, D., Defining deviancy down.
13. Krauthammer, C., Defining deviancy up.
14. Durrant & Durrant, *The Lesson of History*, p. 51.
15. Quoted in Sheen, F. *Communism and the Conscience of the West*, p. 69
16. Raehn, R. The historical roots of political correctness, p. 2.
17. Minnicino, The Frankfurt School, p. 6.

18. Quoted in Malachi, *Keys of This Blood,* p. 250; emphasis added.
19. Quoted in Stormer, *None Dare Call It Treason,* p. 26.
20. Quoted in Miller, M. *The Book and the right.* P. 264.
21. Walsh, M., *The Devil's pleasure palace,* p. 1.
22. Marcuse, *An essay on liberation,* p.109).
23. Quoted in Kolakowski, *Main currents of Marxism,* p. 416; emphasis added.
24. Marcuse, *One dimensional man,* p. 252.
25. Marcuse, *Eros and Civilization,* p. 187.
26. Ibid, p. 50.
27. Ibid, p.201.
28. Obama, *Dreams from My Father,* 101.
29. Judicial Watch, p. 7.
30. First Liberty, 2017
31. Skousen, *The Naked Communist.*
32. International Christian Concern, p. 11.

Chapter 2

The Many Blessings of Christianity

> "No Human society has ever been able to maintain
> both order and freedom, both cohesiveness and liberty
> apart from the moral precepts of the Christian religion
> applied and accepted by all classes."
> John Jay, first Chief Justice of the United States Su-
> preme Court

The Success of the West

Secularist leftists bent on destroying Christianity morality are fond of asserting that religion and science have forever been at odds; the former claiming
absolute truth based on faith and the latter seeking tentative truths based on
empirical evidence. There are a number of specific examples that they can
draw on to support their claims, such as the Catholic Church's trial of Galileo
for his heliocentric views and the rift between Biblical literalist and scientists
over evolution. Although we do see conflicts from time to time when religious
literalists assert something at odds with empirical science, they pale in comparison to the many instances that the Church has actively funded and encouraged learning of all kinds. The Church founded the first Western university—the University of Bologna—in 1088 as well as many others and made
mathematics and science compulsory parts of the education of anyone wanting to study theology.

Almost all of America's early universities such as Harvard, Yale, and Princeton were founded as religious institutions designed to cultivate the spiritual
and moral nature of their students. Secularists claim that Thomas Jefferson
would have none of this and that he founded the first secular university: the
University of Virginia.[1] However, Jefferson did not found a secular Godless
university; in the spirit of Constitutional non-preferentialism, he founded a
non-denominational Christian university. In his 1818 Report of the Commissioners for the University of Virginia, Jefferson made it quite plain that religious instruction was vital, and directed that the teaching of: "the proofs of
the being of a God – the Creator, Preserver, and Supreme Ruler of the Universe—the Author of all the relations of morality and of the laws and obligations these infer—will be within the province of the Professor of Ethics."[2]

In his *Protestant Ethic and the Spirit of Capitalism,* first published in 1905, the famous German sociologist/economist Max Weber set out to discover why Western civilization is the only one where science and capitalism became the rational, systematic, and specialized institutions that they are. In his own words: "Only in the West does science exist at a stage of development which we recognize today as valid. Empirical knowledge, reflection on problems of the cosmos and of life, philosophical and theological wisdom of the most profound sort, are not confined to it, though in the case of the last the full development of a systematic theology must be credited to Christianity."[3] While not denying the impetus of the great Catholic universities and the musings of the early theologians related to discovering the footprints of God in nature, his thesis was that the "overdrive" was engaged by the new religions of Calvinism and Puritanism. These religions exhorted followers to pursue earthly vocations with enthusiasm (the Protestant work ethic) with success being an indication that God favored them for salvation.

More than a century later, two books, one by physicist/philosopher James Hannam,[4] and the other by sociologist/historian Rodney Stark,[5] added to the long line of scholarship that traces the success of the West to Christianity. They assert that Christianity's encouragement of science was the spark behind the success of capitalism, and the economic and political freedoms generated by capitalism culminated in the dominance of the West in all major spheres of human endeavor. Both authors suggest that the West's success in the sciences is traceable to its belief in a God of order and reason who designed a predictable universe intelligible to the human mind. For example, physicist Paul Davies writes of the influence of this belief on Isaac Newton, stating that "Isaac Newton first got the idea of absolute, universal, perfect, immutable laws from the Christian doctrine that God created the world and ordered it in a rational way." [6]

From the very earliest days of Christianity, the Church taught that reason is a gift of God, and that we must use this gift to come to know Him through incrementally coming to understand his creation. St. Albertus Magnus, the 13th century patron saint of science, stated that: "In studying nature we have not to inquire how God the Creator may, as He freely wills, use His creatures to work miracles and thereby show forth His power; we have rather inquire what Nature with its immanent causes can naturally bring to pass."[7] In another work, Magnus wrote: "It is the task of natural science not simply to accept what we are told but to inquire into the causes of things."[8] Ultimately, the great contribution of these theologians lay in their conviction that there are laws of nature front-loaded by God at the beginning of time and await discovery so we may better understand His creation.

We also see the scientific spirit Solomon's prayer in Wisdom 7: 17-22 in which we are invited to use our God-given reason to hound nature in its nooks and crannies until we discover what God has hidden for us to find:

For He gave me sound knowledge of what exists, that I might know the structure of theuniverse and the force of its elements, The beginning and the end and the midpoint of times, the changes in the sun's course and the variations of the seasons, Cycles of years, positions of stars, natures of living things, tempers of beasts, Powers of the winds and thoughts of human beings, uses of plants and virtues of roots— Whatever is hidden or plain I learned, for Wisdom, the artisan of all, taught me.

There are many examples of Christian theologians extolling science so that we may fully appreciate God's work. In their insistence that God has invested nature with natural laws that enable it to organize and elaborate itself, the ancient theologians insisted that the universe is lawful. It is this insistence on a lawful universe that led to Darwin's theory of evolution through natural selection. Darwin believed that evolution by natural selection does not preclude a Creator. Arguing only against the notion of the independent creation of each species, Darwin wrote: "To my mind it accords better with what we know of *the laws impressed on matter by the Creator,* that the production and extinction of the past and present inhabitants of the world should have been due to secondary causes, like those determining the birth and death of the individual."[9]

Darwin's use of the words "secondary causes" recalls St. Augustine's words in *De Genesi ad Literam* (V.4:11): "It is therefore, *causally* that Scripture has said that *earth* brought forth the crops and trees, in the sense that *it received the power of bringing them forth.* In the earth from the beginning, in what I might call the roots of time, God created what was to be in times to come." That is, the properties of the earth that make crops and trees possible are secondary to the primary cause that has been immanent in the laws of nature from the very beginning of the universe. The matter was given the power to act directly on other matter; hence the idea of secondary causation, without such a guiding idea no science would be possible.

Of course, no one claims that Christianity is a necessary and sufficient cause of Western success, only that it was a highly decisive factor. It is hardly a coincidence that of all the 88 countries designated "free" in the 2015 Freedom in the World Index, 80 (90.9%) are Christian.[10] Non-Christian countries that have successfully transitioned to free status such as Singapore, Japan, and South Korea have ridden the West's coattails. Rodney Stark quotes a leading Chinese scholar's opinion as to why the West has been so preeminent. After looking at all sorts of other possibilities (cultural, historical, political, and economic), the scholar writes: "But in the past twenty years, we have realized that the heart of your culture is your religion: Christianity. This is why the West is so powerful. The Christian moral foundation of social and cultural life was what made possible the emergence of capitalism and then the successful transition to democratic politics. We don't have any doubts about this."[11]

To the extent that capitalism has led to the success of the Western World relative to the non-Western world—and it is without question that it has lifted billions of people around the world out of poverty (even Marx agreed with this)—we have to acknowledge its connection to science. And to the extent that this is true, we have to acknowledge the role of Christianity's commitment to reason and progress. "Could modern science have arisen outside the theological matrix of Western Christendom?" asks Peter Harrison, professor of science and religion. He answers: "It is difficult to say. What can be said for certain is that it did arise in that environment and that theological ideas underpinned some of its central assumptions. Those who argue for the incompatibility of science and religion will draw little comfort from history."[12]

Science Rediscovers God

Despite this evidence, atheists claim that science and religion are in conflict. However, Elaine Ecklund and Jerry Park surveyed 1,646 scientists at 21 elite universities and asked if they see such a conflict. Among those who did see a conflict, 17.1 percent "strongly agreed" and 19.5 "agreed somewhat." Among those who disagreed that there is a conflict, 33.1 percent "strongly disagreed" and 23.8 percent "disagreed somewhat" (6.4% had no opinion). Thus the plurality of elite scientists (56.9%) did not believe that there is a conflict between science and religion. Furthermore, 68 percent said that they were "spiritual" to some degree, and 46.6 percent said they attended a place of worship at least a few times a year.[13] According to the doyen of science, Albert Einstein: "A legitimate conflict between science and religion cannot exist. Science without religion is lame, religion without science is blind."[14] Science and religion complement one another because science is an attempt to understand the nature and mechanisms of the universe, and religion is an attempt to understand its meaning and purpose.

It is probably true that there are many more scientists today who see no conflict between science and religion that was the case 100 years ago. The tremendous advances in science and technology over the last century have enabled scientists to plumb the depths of creation and to stand in awe. The literature abounds with examples of scientists who have been dragged by their science to faith. Jim Holt quotes Albert Einstein in a 1997 *Wall Street*

Journal article titled "Science Resurrects God:" "The more I study science, the more I believe in God."[15] Einstein also notes: "Everyone who is seriously involved in the pursuit of science becomes convinced that a spirit is manifest in the laws of the Universe-a spirit vastly superior to that of man, and one in the face of which we with our modest powers must feel humble."[16]

Not far behind Einstein in the pantheon of great scientists is Max Planck, the founder of quantum theory, who said in his Nobel Prize acceptance speech: "All matter originates and exists only by virtue of a force which brings the particle of an atom to vibration and holds this most minute solar system of the atom together. We must assume behind this force the existence of a conscious and intelligent mind. This mind is the matrix of all matter."[17] It is thus no mystery why prize-wining mathematical physicist Robert Griffiths has said: "If we need an atheist for a debate, we go to the philosophy department. The physics department isn't much use."[18] What has occurred to move so many physicists from atheism or agnosticism to their belief in God?

Prior to the 1930s, almost all physicists believed that the universe was static, uncaused, and eternal. Despite this scientific consensus, the Church maintained for centuries that the universe had a beginning and a cause, and it was right. The discovery of the "Big Bang" that brought matter/energy, time, and space into being in a split-second flash some 13.7 billion years ago revolutionized scientific, philosophical, and religious thinking. The universe had a beginning and a cause after all, and that cause has to be an entity that transcends time, space, and matter/energy since these things did not exist before the creation. As astronomer George Greenstein put it: "As we survey all the evidence, the thought insistently arises that some supernatural agency, or rather Agency, must be involved. Is it possible that suddenly, without intending to, we have stumbled upon scientific proof of the existence of a Supreme Being? Was it God who stepped in and so providentially created the cosmos for our benefit?" [19]

Greenstein's statement calls on the so-called "anthropic principle" of physics. The anthropic principle maintains that the universe contains so many fundamental constants that if changed even by one part in a trillion it could not accommodate conscious life or even an inhabitable planet. In an interview with physicist and philosopher Stephen Meyer, Lee Strobel quotes Meyer's take on the theological implications of the Big Bang and the anthropic principle. He believes that the fine-tuning of constants of the universe all the way back to the first millisecond suggests an intelligent cause: "Theism affirms the existence of an entity that's not only transcendent but intelligent as well--namely God. Thus theism can explain Big Bang cosmology and the anthropic fine-tuning."[20]

Biology has its own "big bang" in the form of the Cambrian explosion, which is a phenomenon describing the discovery that all the modern body plans of various animal types (phyla) came online almost at once. In evolutionary time, the Cambrian explosion represents a huge jump in complexity without any transitional forms. In one of the top textbooks on invertebrates, its authors write: "Most of the animal phyla that are represented in the fossil record first appear, 'fully formed,' in the Cambrian some 550 million years ago ...The fossil record is therefore of no help with respect to the origin and early diversification of the various animal phyla."[21] In other words, we have no fossils assignable to any putative ancestors of the fossilized phyla found in Cambrian and pre-Cambrian sediments, and their absence is striking. Their absence is striking since Darwinism is based on tiny stepwise changes over multiple generations that should show up in the fossil record. However, they are nowhere to be found; there are no transitional intermediaries leading to these "fully formed" creatures. Every phylum with a fossil record is represented in the Cambrian strata, and *none* have appeared since. This sudden geological infusion of massive amounts of new biological information needed to create a wide variety of phyla is difficult to explain materialistically and is affirmative evidence for intelligent design. The Cambrian explosion does not, of course, preclude the subsequent process of natural selection, or any other evolutionary process that produces "descent with modification."

My intention is, however, not to provide scientific evidence for the existence of God; there are many hundreds of books and articles available written by first-class scientists who will do that for you. I merely want to show that Christianity and science, far from being in conflict, are intimately related. There have been rifts, sometimes serious rifts, but these tend to be between zealots in both camps; fundamentalist religious believers in one camp and adherents of scientism (the belief that science is the only reasonable worldview and the one and only path to useful knowledge) in the other. The Christian exhortation to explore the fingerprints of God in the natural world—absent in the theology of other religions—means that Christianity and science are the warp and woof of the spiritual and material progress of the Western world. My intention in this chapter is to provide evidence from history and the social sciences of the many great benefits of adhering to Christianity both to society and to individuals.

Christianity Promotes a Moral Society

It has been noted by many people on many occasions that religion is a prerequisite for morality. Moral people obviously act in more virtuous and principled ways than amoral or immoral people, which benefits both themselves and society, and whatever benefits society benefits atheists as well. A free society is not held together only by the muscular arms of law enforcement, but more importantly by the voluntary obedience of its citizens to unwritten rules of right and wrong. These unwritten rules are seriously compromised without the force of morality and righteousness behind them supplied by religion. With religious beliefs being pushed ever further to the background in our culture, the secularist's relativistic "values" just can't cut it.

A mountain of medical, psychological, and social research, as well as history and common sense, shows that Christianity promotes healthy societies, families, and individuals in many different ways. If Christianity did not supply these benefits, there would be no point in Marxists trying to destroy it. Cultural Marxists know that it is only America's Christian heritage that stands in the way of their totalitarian dreams. In his farewell address to the nation upon leaving his second term as President of the United States, George Washington stressed the importance of religion to this new republic and warned that national morality and social cohesion cannot be maintained without religion:

> Of all the dispositions and habits which lead to political prosperity, Religion and Morality are indispensable supports. In vain would that man claim the tribute of Patriotism who should labor to subvert these great Pillars of human happiness-these firmest props of the duties of Men and citizens...Let it simply be asked, where is the security for property, for reputation, for life, if the sense of religious obligation desertthe oaths, which are the instruments of investigation in Courts of Justice? And let us with caution indulge the supposition that morality can be maintained without religion. Whatever may be conceded to the influence of refined education on minds of peculiar structure, reason and experience both forbid us to expect that National morality can prevail in exclusion of religious principle.[22]

The great French social philosopher of American life, Alexis Tocqueville, commented over 175 years ago that America's bounty rested on its religion: "there is no country in the world where the Christian religion retains a greater influence over the souls of men than in America, and there can be no greater proof of its utility and of its conformity to human nature than that its influence is powerfully felt over the most enlightened and free nation of the earth."[23] Even skeptics such as historians Will and Ariel Durant know the value of religion and what happens in its absence: "It has conferred meaning and dignity upon the lowliest existence, and through its sacraments has made for stability by transforming human covenants into solemn relationships with God...*There is no significant example in history, before our time, of a society successfully maintaining moral life without the aid of religion.*[24]

In an earlier book published in 1935, Will Durant echoed George Washington's fears about what happens when to a nation's morality when it abandons religion, telling us that it begins with the self-absorbed chattering classes. When we stop believing in God, we will believe in anything and do anything as morality is sucked out of society. What follows is that "Conduct, deprived of its religious supports, deteriorates into epicurean chaos; and life itself, shorn of consoling faith, becomes a burden alike to conscious poverty and to weary wealth. In the end, a society and its religion tend to fall together, like body and soul, in a harmonious death." [25]

Russia: Defender of Religious Freedom?

We have seen how the Soviet Union descended into a moral cesspool after declaring atheism its official religion, destroying churches, impugning the traditional family, and encouraging "free love." Americans used to describe Russia, the central power of the old Soviet Union, as the Godless "evil empire" wallowing in misery and tyranny. Who would have thought some 30 years later that the current president of Russia and former KGB officer, Vladimir Putin, would turn the tables on us to describe the United States as morally bankrupt because it has turned its back on its traditional Christian values? In his 2014 state of the nation address to the Russian people, Putin said: "Many Euro-Atlantic countries have moved away from their roots, including Christian values...Policies are being pursued that place on the same level a multi-child family and a same-sex partnership, faith in God and a belief in Satan. This is the path to degradation." He further said that social and religious conservatism is the only key to preventing the world from slipping into "chaotic darkness." The head of the Russian Orthodox Church, Patriarch Kirill I, also noted that laws preventing the display of religious symbols in many Western countries represent a "spiritual disarmament" of their people. He further noted that: "The general political direction of the elite bears, without doubt, an anti-Christian and anti-religious character...We have been through an epoch of atheism, and we know what it is to live without God...We want to shout to the whole world, 'Stop!'" [26]

Putin and Kirill know better than any American politician how important Christianity is because they lived most of their lives in Godless Russia and experienced its social and spiritual malaise. Skeptics will view Putin's and Kirill's statements as self-serving attempts to return to the pre-Soviet unity of church and state. Putin certainly needs help in confronting the corruption and organized crime rampant in modern Russia during the difficult business of transforming a command economy to a free market. He has a realistic and pragmatic understanding of the fact that culture must have a stable moral compass to survive that a secularist worldview cannot provide. It is for this reason that Putin's Russia has seen a vast construction and restoration of churches destroyed by the communists, and has encouraged the teaching of religion in schools.

When asked in 2007 by *Time Magazine* in his "Person of the Year" interview what role faith plays in his leadership and the role it should faith play in government and society, he replied: "First and foremost we should be governed by common sense. But common sense should be based on moral principles first. And it is not possible today to have morality separated from religious values. You could say that it is my deep conviction that the moral values without which humankind cannot survive cannot be other than religious values" [27] Whatever you may think of Putin, he is the only reliable defender of Christian civilization among the world's leaders, and even if he is doing so to advance Russian interests, his statements regarding the West's moral decline as it decouples itself from its Christian heritage ring loud and true.

Christianity and Democracy

In a 1947 speech in Parliament, Winston Churchill remarked that: "Many forms of Government have been tried, and will be tried in this world of sin and woe. No one pretends that democracy is perfect or all-wise. Indeed, it has been said that democracy is the worst form of Government except for all those other forms that have been tried from time to time." The problems of democracy are obvious to those who live in one. In America, a huge chunk of the electorate has no clue about the realities of economics and has no stake in society. They vote for anyone promising them the biggest portion of other people's money, and living from day to day and indulging in the pleasures of the moment. Yet for all its many faults, as Churchill said, there is none better. Only in a mature democracy with checks and balances and the rule of law (republicanism, if you will) do all have a chance to have their say, and democracies tend to be places where freedom reigns and one's material needs are best met. People in mature democracies can do with impunity what the vast bulk of humankind has not dared to do throughout history—criticize their government. But the great British writer, philosopher, and poet G. K. Chesterton tells us that it is difficult to criticize the government when there is no higher power than it, who tells us that without God Big Government becomes the Almighty. "Wherever the people do not believe in something beyond the world, they will worship the world. But, above all, they will worship the strongest thing in the world.[28]

Chesterton's point was made many years earlier by Alexis de Tocqueville. He argued that religion protects liberty by guarding against what he considered the greatest danger to democracy—the thirst for equality—which he believed led to despotism. If someone lacks religion "each man gets into the way of having nothing but confused and changing notions about the matters of greatest importance to himself and his fellows." Thus by giving order to the lives of its adherents, religion promotes democracy. Tocqueville further states that if the individual, "has no faith he must obey, and if he is free he must believe."[29]

De Tocqueville was not impugning equality as the Founders viewed it; equality of political, social, and civil rights. Writing in the century before de Tocqueville, French philosopher Voltaire knew well the difference between equality of rights and equality of goods: "equality is at once the most natural and the most chimerical thing in the world: natural when it is limited to rights, unnatural when it attempts to level goods and power."[30] Socialists and liberals believe in equality of outcome, which is to be achieved by subjecting different people to different rules, and affording some special privileges such as provided by affirmative action programs or quotas. Because only the big government has the wherewithal to implement such programs, it becomes the God whom the left implores to implement its destructive agenda. Conservatives, on the other hand, believe that the distribution of resources should depend on a person's contribution (equity) in a process where everyone is subjected to the same rules and are judged by the same standards.

Having forsaken religion, the left-wing intelligentsia attaches itself with a religious fervor not only to socialism and its egalitarian dream, but also to postmodernism, radical feminism, and moral relativism because they have to believe in something greater than themselves. As G.K. Chesterton once remarked, "when a man does not believe in God he will believe in anything." Practicing Protestants, Catholics, and Jews are almost always conservatives because they already have a religion and have no need the destructive leftist secular alternatives. Leftists are aware someplace in the recesses of their mind of the principle, if not the words, of President John Adams when he wrote that the American "Constitution was made only for a moral and religious people" because "we have no government armed with power capable of contending with human passions unbridled by morality and religion."[31] Because socialists and many liberals support unbridled passion as "freedom of expression," that pesky Constitution must be rewritten, mangled by postmodern "interpretations," or replaced altogether.

Christianity Promotes Stable and Loving Families

There's a lot of truth in that old aphorism declaring that "The family that prays together, stays together." Not only does it stay together, but it also does so happier and healthier than non-religious families. A strong and stable marriage is positively associated with a bounty of benefits for the marriage partners and their children, including better physical, mental, and emotional health. A strong and stable marriage is itself related to religious practices such as church attendance and living one's faith on a daily basis. Of course, not all religious families are happy and stable, and many non-religious families are. Families in which males believe that their religion commands them to be lord and master over their wives and children are in all likelihood less stable and happy than non-religious families with a more egalitarian outlook on the relationship between the sexes. However, the literature on the topic shows (and does so consistently) that genuinely Christian marriages are significantly better than non-religious marriages on all measures.

A study of the marital well-being of 354 couples in the *Journal of Marriage and the Family* found that religiousness is related to marital well-being through what the authors called "relational virtues." [32] That is, religious practice is related to relational virtue (commitment, lower levels of conflict, forgiveness, emotional closeness, and sacrifice) and not at all to the promotion of "patriarchal inequality;" a favorite backhander thrown by radical feminists who are not at all fond of either religion or marriage. Another study found that the more married couples practiced their religious faith, the more satisfied they were with their marriages. Sixty percent of those couples who attended a place of worship at least once a month rated their marriages "very satisfactory" compared with only 43 percent who attended less often or not at all.[33]

Drawing on the National Survey of Families and Households sample of 3,336 respondents, the General Social Survey of 24,099 respondents, and the Survey of Adults and Youth (2,309 respondents), Bradford Wilcox found that the more husbands attended religious services, the happier their wives were with the level of affection, understanding, and quality time spent with them. He calls such men "soft patriarchs" because they define themselves as the head of their family and take a strict approach to needed discipline, but this approach is softened by a great deal of affection for, and involvement with, their wives and children.[34]

Further evidence is provided by data from over 9,000 subjects drawn from across the U.S. showing that adults who frequently attend religious services as children were significantly more likely to provide assistance to parents in their old age. Religious attendees also reported higher quality relationships and more frequent contact with parents. These results held after taking into account a large number of other factors, and reminds us of Proverbs 22:6: "Train up a child in the way he should go; even when he is old he will not depart from it." The researchers concluded, "It appears that the influence of religion in fostering early parent-child ties noted in prior research extends throughout the life course, influencing ties between adult children and their parents."[35]

It is uncontested that divorce is, in most cases, a plague on society and on children. Given the benefits of church attendance has for families it is not surprising that church attendance leads to a decreased likelihood of divorce. This has been established by numerous studies. Marriages in which both spouses attend church (the same church; spouses with different faiths are somewhat more like to divorce than a non-religious couple) with regularity are 2.4 times less likely to end in divorce than marriages in neither spouse attends a place of worship.[36] In fact, it has frequently found over more than six decades of studies that religious commitment is the most important predictor of stability and happiness in marriage.[37]

The Family, Religion, and Antisocial Behavior

In the Broadway musical *West Side Story* there is a scene in which two warring gangs belt out their explanation for their delinquent behavior saying they are they are "depraved on account I'm deprived" in the song "Gee, Officer Krupke:" "Our mothers all are junkies, Our fathers all are drunks. Golly Moses -- natcherly we're punks." A stable, loving, and committed two-parent family will not produce such offspring. An examination of 113 studies linking attendance at religious services to criminal offending and illegal drug use revealed that 97 studies found a significant negative relationship (church attendance was related to a lower frequency of offending) and 16 showed no significant relationship. No study found a positive relationship (church attendance leads to high rate of offending). The authors concluded: "attending religious services is the best-documented correlate of [the prevention of] crime."[38]

The moral and spiritual values of parents preclude the kinds of behavior, such as alcohol and drug abuse, divorce, and out-of-wedlock births that lead many children "natcherly" to engage in antisocial behaviors. Families with high levels of religious participation employ strict monitoring of their children's educational and extra-curricular behavior, providing them with moral guidance in the context of warmth and caring. Both parents and children in religious households rate the quality of their relationships with one another significantly higher than do parents and children in non-religious households.[39] A review of relevant research noted that: "The tendency of religious beliefs to place great value on children increases parental motivation to spend time and energy on their children. Not only are religious parents less likely to abuse or yell at their children but they are also more likely to hug and praise them often and to display better parent functioning."[40]

From a variety of sources, Edward Kruk paints a grim picture of the growing number of children in America being reared in amoral circumstances in unstable families by single, poor, and often isolated mothers:

Eighty-five percent of youth in prison have an absent father, 71% of high school dropouts are fatherless, 90% of homeless and runaway children have an absent father and fatherless children and youth exhibit higher levels of depression and suicide, delinquency, promiscuity and teen pregnancy, behavioral problems and illicit and licit substance abuse, diminished self-concepts, and are more likely to be victims of exploitation and abuse.[41]

One of the most glaring consequences of growing up in a fatherless home is poverty. According to the U.S. Census Bureau, in 2014 the median family income for Asians/Pacific Islanders was $74,297, for whites it was $60,256, for Hispanics $42,491, and for African Americans, it was $35,398.[42] These figures have a perfect *inverse* correlation with out-of-wedlock births. The U.S. Department of Health and Human Services reports rates of out-of-wedlock births of 73.5 percent for African Americans, 53.3 percent for Hispanics, 29 percent for whites, and 17 percent for Asian Americans.[43] A U.S. Census Bureau study broke down family types by race and income and found that white single-parent households were more than twice as likely as black two-parent households to have an annual income of less than $25,000 (46% versus 20.8%). In other words, a black two-parent family is less than half as likely to be poor as a white single parent family.[44] Liberals attribute black poverty to everything under the sun (racism is their favorite, of course) except that which is staring them in the face—a tragically high rate of single-parent households. It is no wonder that a huge survey of the benefits of family stability prepared for the U.S. Department of Health and Human Services noted that "children from two-parent families live longer and enjoy overall better health than children from single-parent families or whose parents divorced in childhood." [45]

A huge Swedish study of 986,342 children comparing children living in single-parent households with those living in two-parent households found that children with single parents showed greatly elevated risks of psychiatric disease, suicide or attempted suicide, injury, and drug and alcohol addiction. The study's authors concluded that growing up in a single-parent family has numerous disadvantages and poses increased risks for physical and mental problems.[46] Growing up in a fatherless home implies either divorce or out-of-wedlock birth (more rarely, father's death). A Fragile Families Research Brief found that "Mothers who attend religious services frequently are 73 percent more likely to be married at childbirth than mothers who attend services infrequently or not at all." [47]

Religion and Physical and Mental Health

Karl Marx once told his flock that religion is the opiate of the masses. Perhaps he was right, since all systems of belief that entail hope and counsel love are good for the health of body and spirit. Of course, he didn't mean it in this sense; he meant that it was a childish fairy tale with a hope of an afterlife whose soothing comfort that prevented believers from embracing his vision of a communist paradise on earth. Similarly, Sigmund Freud saw religion as mere superstition and a sign of psychological immaturity, but for Freud we all, atheist and theist alike, were a little neurotic and psychologically immature. There are doubtless aspects of religion and religious believers that fit into the schemes of Marx and Freud, but a reasoned Christianity can lead to personal and social enlightenment, psychological maturity, and most certainly, greater happiness and physical and mental health. This is not simply my opinion; it is the opinion of 96 percent of physicians who agreed in a *Journal of Family Practice* survey that spiritual well-being is important for physical and mental health.[48]

Let us take the issue of religion and longevity to start. Robert Hummer and his colleagues examined data from the National Health Interview Survey on cause of death to look at the role of religious involvement in adult mortality. After running all their mathematical models, they concluded: "We showed that religious involvement is strongly associated with adult mortality in a graded fashion. Those who never attend services exhibit the highest risk of death, and those who attend more than once a week exhibit the lowest risk."[49] The risk of death is 1.87 times greater for those who never attend services compared with those who attend more than once a week, which translates to a seven-year difference in life expectancy at age 20. This 1.87 figure was reduced after controlling for the effects of health status, socioeconomic status, and social ties, the researchers to 1.5 times greater. This is still a very positive impact of attending religious services on life expectancy and, besides, religion confers these positive effects on health status, socioeconomic status, and social ties the researchers controlled for. Another study followed an initial group of 5,286 adults for 28 years and found, controlling for a large number of health-related factors, that subjects who attended church one or more times a week were 23 percent less likely to die in follow-up periods than non-attenders.[50]

Religious worship is also a spiritual antibody against the number-one health scourge of modern America: hypertension and associated cardiovascular problems. Daniel Hall conducted a study comparing various mechanisms (exercise, diet, medication) that lower the risk of heart disease. He asked if the study could show if religious attendance is more cost-effective than Lipitor and answered affirmatively: "The real-world, practical significance of regular religious attendance is comparable to commonly recommended therapies, and rough estimates even suggest that religious attendance may be more cost-effective than statins [cholesterol lowering medication]."[51] This study was based on a review of a number of studies involving more than 21,000 subjects. A larger study of 36,000 Norwegians found that people who regularly attended religious services (despite being older on average than those who did not) had significantly lower blood pressure. Interestingly, there was a gradient in effect among churchgoers with increasing religious attendance being associated with decreasing blood pressure.[52] In one of my own studies of hypertension, after controlling for other health-related factors, I found that 30.9 percent of non-church attendees were hypertensive versus only 7 percent of church attendees.[53]

In addition to cardiovascular diseases, religious observance has been shown to have a positive effect on coping with many kinds of chronic diseases such as multiple sclerosis and cancer.[54] None of these studies introduce supernatural intervention as a cause (although it should not be dismissed out of hand). They seek the answers to these positive effects occur by analyzing ancillary practices associated with a religious outlook such as strong social support systems, increased self-esteem and self-efficacy, and healthy habits and practices stressed by many religious denominations. Some studies go further and examine the physiological processes associated with these ancillary practices such as their positive effects on the cardiovascular, hormonal, and immune systems. One mechanism is that religious involvement helps to reduce stress or makes coping with it easier. Studies have found lower levels of cortisol (a hormone released when under stress and known to be involved in high blood pressure) in religious than in non-religious people.[55] Religion thus acts as a buffer against stress and thus against elevated levels of blood pressure.

There are other processes identified by scientists called psychoneuroendocrinologists who investigate the complex routes by which positive and negative social and psychological experiences affect the body and mind, for better or for worse. They show how the experiences we have with the world leave their markers on the brain and on our hormonal and immunological systems. However, an examination of this literature is beyond the scope of this book, so I will conclude with the words of one such scientist: "Perhaps someday we will look back and wonder how we ever presumed that well-being is unrelated to the workings of the spirit. Just as the relation of mind and body was rejected by biomedicine until the weight of evidence made such a connection tacit, so, too, may the role of spirit become acknowledged fact."[56]

The Economic Benefits of Christianity

German sociologist and economist Max Weber and British economist and philosopher Adam Smith agreed with America's Founders that Christianity, morality, and economic prosperity are closely linked. According to Harvard's Kelly Mua, the link exists "mainly by fostering religious beliefs that influence individual traits such as honesty, work ethic, thrift, and openness to strangers."[57] Using data from 66 countries and encompassing the years 1981 through 1997, a team of economists augments Mua's observation when they write: "We find that on average, religious beliefs are associated with 'good' economic attitudes, where "good' is defined as conducive to higher per capita income and growth...Overall, we find that Christian religions are more positively associated with attitudes conducive to economic growth." [58]

We have seen how the rational mindset of Christianity led to the establishment of capitalism, but can we put a dollar amount on the benefits of Christianity to modern America? Rodney Stark says "yes, we can. In his book *America's Blessings: How Religion Benefits Everyone, Including Atheists,* Stark estimates that Christianity benefits the American economy to the tune of $2.6 trillion per year; that's $2.6 *trillion*! How did he arrive at such a figure? He does this by asking: "What would it cost if America suddenly were transformed into a fully secularized society?"[59] That is, if there were no practicing Christians in society holding the values they do and behaving in ways I have outlined in this chapter, how much would the additional costs to the U.S. economy/taxpayer be?

Because practicing Christians commit far less crime and less likely to be involved in drug and alcohol abuse, they provide massive savings for the criminal justice system. Happier intact homes figure means less divorce, illegitimacy, and parental abuse and neglect, leading to huge savings in welfare and other associated costs. Religious schools and homeschooling result in better grades and higher graduation rates, and thus to better job prospects. This means less unemployment, fewer deadbeats, and lower unemployment benefits being paid out. Better physical and mental health among Christians saves billions in health care costs. Regular religious attendees give more money to charity and volunteer their time much more than other, and more charitable giving and volunteering saves many millions of dollars in what otherwise would be a burden on the taxpayer. In addition to all these economic benefits (and Stark lists many others), the greater happiness and peace enjoyed by practicing Christians is something that cannot be quantified, but it surely adds to the economic benefits of Christianity in many away.

Some deeply religious souls may object to my arguments as offering only pragmatic and reasoned grounds for believing in God and. They may argue that belief in God comes from the depths of the heart and that one must voluntarily place Him there because he is God, and not because it is prudent or self-serving to do so. This has been a theistic argument ever since Pascal's Wager argument (it is wise to accept God and to live accordingly since you have eternal life to gain if you do, and eternal damnation if you don't). The suggestion is that some folks will feign belief in God's existence "just in case" on the basis of prudential rationality rather than faith, which is considered dishonest and immoral.

This argument strikes me as saying that one cannot accept the truth of anything based on rational analysis of the facts, and that emotion is the only valid path to knowing the truth. Think of all the scientists who rejected their atheism or agnosticism on their rational understanding of God's creation. Are they feigning or accepting the Creator involuntarily? Of course not; how can you feign belief to yourself? God would surely prefer honest seekers who come to their beliefs rationally over those who merely "go through the motions" because that's what they were taught to do as children. In any case, my intention here is to detail the benefits of Christianity and the adverse consequences of abandoning it and putting all faith in Big Brother, and not theological disputes about the nature of faith.

This chapter has provided a small number of examples of how Christianity benefits society and the body, mind, and spirit of individuals. Cultural Marxists and rabid atheists who love a good Christian-bashing will not let such facts stand in their way. But even they benefit because they are able to live their lives in a free and wealthy society, thanks to our Christian heritage. As noted by John Jay in the epigraph of the chapter: "No Human society has ever been able to maintain both order and freedom, both cohesiveness and liberty apart from the moral precepts of the Christian religion applied and accepted by all classes. Should our Republic ever forget this fundamental precept of governance, men are certain to shed their responsibilities for licentiousness, and this great experiment will then surely be doomed." [60] It is obvious that John Jay saw this nation as a Christian nation founded, forged, and sustained by Christian principles, but there are modern naysayers who deny this truth. It is to this topic we now turn.

Endnotes

1. Vickers, A., *The New Nation*, p. 74.
2. Jefferson, T. (1818). Report of the Commissioners.
3. Weber, M. The *Protestant Ethic*, p. 13
4. Hannam, J., *God's Philosophers*.
5. Stark, R., *The Victory of Reason*.
6. Davies, P., Taking science on faith.

7. Kennedy, D., *St. Albertus Magnus*, p. 265.
8. Ibid, p. 265.
9. Quoted in Dilley, S., Charles Darwin's use of theology. p. 31; emphasis mine.
10. Freedom in the World Index
11. Stark, *The Victory of Reason*, p. 235.
12. Harrison, *Christianity and the rise of modern science.*
13. Ecklund and Park, Conflict between religion.
14. Quoted in Wolpert, *The unnatural nature of science*, p. 146.
15. Quoted in Holt, J. Science Resurrects God.
16. Quoted in Marsh, J., p. 72.
17. Quoted in Olsen, *Future Esoteric*, p.382.
18. Quoted in Kainz, The *Existence of God and the Faith-instinct*, p. 21.
19. Quoted in In Strobel, *The case for a creator*, p. 189.
20. Ibid, p. 98.
21. Barnes, Calow, and Olive, *The Invertebrates*, pp. 9-10. Invertebrates are animals with no spine or backbone. About 97% of all animals are invertebrates.
22. Washington, Washington's farewell address.
23. Tocqueville, p. 199.
24. Durant, W. & Durant, A. *The Lessons of History*, pg. 43 & 51; emphasis mine)
25. Durant, *Our Oriental Heritage*, p. 71.
26. Bennetts, Who's 'godless' now?
27. *Time Magazine*, Person of the year.
28. Chesterton, *The Collected Works*, p. 57.
29. Tocqueville, *Democracy in America*, p. 444.
30. Quoted in Durant, *The story of philosophy*, p. 245).
31. Adams, letter to Massachusetts Militia, 11 October 1798.
32. Day and Acock, Marital Well-being.
33. Bahr and Chadwick, Religion and family.
34. Bradford Wilcox, *Soft patriarchs, new men.*
35. King, Ledwell, and Pearce-Morris, Religion and ties between adult children, p. 834.
36. Call and Heaton, Religious influence on marital stability.
37. Larson, Larson and Gartner, Families, Relationships and Health.
38. Ellis and Walsh, Criminology, p. 205.
39. Aquilino, Two views of one relationship.
40. Dollahite and Thatcher, p.5.
41. Kruk, Arguments for an equal parental responsibility, p. 49.
42. U. S. Census Bureau, 2015
43. U.S. Department of Health and Human Services, 2011.

44. McKinnon and Humes, *The Black Population.*
45. Wood, Goesling and Avellar, p. 48.
46. Weitoft, Hjern, Haglund and Rosén, p. 289.
47. Fragile Families Research Brief, p. 2.
48. Ellis, Vinson, and Ewigman, Addressing spiritual concerns of patients.
49. Hummer, et al., Religious involvement and U.S. adult mortality, p. 283.
50. Strawbridge, et al., Frequent attendance at religious services.
51. Hall, D., Religious attendance: More cost effective than lipitor? p.432.
52. Sørensen, et al., The relationship between religious attendance and blood pressure.
53. Walsh, Religion and hypertension.
54. See Mueller, Plevak and Rummans, Religious involvement, spirituality, and medicine; and. Koenig et al., Attendance at religious services, interleukin-6.
55. Dedert, et al., Religiosity may help.
56. Levin, Religion and mental health, p. 113.
57. Mua, Religion as a Tool for Economic/Political Transformation, p. 1.
58. Guiso, Sapienza, & Zingales, People's opium? Religion and economic attitudes, p.225.
59. Stark, *America's Blessings*, p. 163.
60. Jay, *John Jay, The Correspondence and Public Papers of John Jay.*

Chapter 3

The Christian Foundation of
the United States

"The general principles on which the fathers achieved independence were the general principles of Christianity. I will avow that I then believed, and now believe, that those general principles of Christianity are as eternal and immutable as the existence and attributes of God."
John Adams, second President of the United States.

America's First Freedom

Religious liberty is America's "first freedom," but this precious freedom been consistently under attack across our nation since the 1940s by left-wing atheist organizations that knowingly or unknowingly are carriers of the cultural Marxist's diseased ideology. Plainly, these folks are winning in the courtroom, the classroom, and the pressroom. In the past two decades, deeply religious Christians have been demonized as bigots, maltreated by secular activists, and penalized by the law for having the audacity to obey their religious consciences publicly. This would be seen by the Founding Fathers of our country as a most grievous abomination because to a man they were committed to religious liberty. Eminent scholar David Hall illustrates this by quoting George Mason's 1776 draft of Article XVI of Virginia's Declaration of Rights:

> That as Religion, or the Duty which we owe to our divine and omnipotent Creator, and the Manner of discharging it, can be governed only by Reason and Conviction, not by Force or Violence; and therefore that all Men should enjoy the fullest Toleration in the Exercise of Religion, according to the Dictates of Conscience, *unpunished and unrestrained by the Magistrate.*[1]

We will encounter numerous instances throughout this book in which religious believers have been unconscionably punished and restrained "by the Magistrate." Previous generations of Americans would have been infuriated, even to the point of armed resistance if we go back far enough if they were to witness the way Christians are being treated if they dare to practice their religion outside of their homes or churches. They might even be more incensed at the weak to the non-existent opposition this has generated from the current generation of Americans.

In the spirit of full disclosure, I should reveal my philosophy on religion and politics. I do not subscribe to any religious denomination, but I do believe in God as Creator of the universe. If forced to put a brand on my spiritual beliefs, I say I am a deist with a strong tendency toward theism. Deism comes from the Latin for God, and thus affirms the same belief in God that is fundamental to almost every religious creed. Organized theistic religion seeks to explain God in a concrete intelligible way in the form of rituals, sacred writings, and icons such as the Ten Commandments, the basis of morality and law of all three religions of "the book." These things bring belief in God "into the material world," so to speak, in a way that all can seek to understand the glory of God in simple, tangible terms through the institutionalized mechanism of rituals, faith, and fellowship. These things reify and focus people's emotional convictions which may otherwise be unintelligible abstractions. Christians who believe in an active, interventionist God, have a deep reverence for the mechanisms of religion, and believe that they have a right to promote them in the public square, are the people who are under attack.

As we saw in the previous chapter, atheists are keen to smugly denounce religious faith as at odds with science and reason, but deism is fully compatible with science, as numerous scientific luminaries have declared. Albert Einstein, the greatest of them all, proclaimed that: "My religion consists of a humble admiration of the illimitable superior spirit who reveals himself in the slight details we are able to perceive with our frail and feeble minds. That deeply emotional conviction of the presence of a superior reasoning power, which is revealed in the incomprehensible universe, forms my idea of God." [2]

Atheists believe that Darwin's theory of evolution put paid to the notion of Divine creation. Evolution by natural selection is supported by much empirical evidence, and fundamentalist Christians play into the hands of atheists when they deny it. Fundamentalists deny it because they believe that to accept it would be to deny God, but this is by no means true. Theodosius Dobzhansky, a giant of 20th-century biology, described himself as both a creationist and an evolutionist, as did former atheist Francis Collins, head of the National Human Genome Project. Recall that Charles Darwin himself talked about "laws impressed on matter by the Creator." Dobzhansky believed that science does not preclude the process of evolution having either an author or a goal: an Alpha and an Omega. He wrote: "It is wrong to hold creation and evolution as mutually exclusive alternatives. I am a creationist and an evolutionist. Evolution is God's, or Nature's, a method of Creation." [3] Dobzhansky's creationism was not a six-day affair presided over by a bearded giant who needed to rest on the seventh day. Rather, it implied a universe in which all the laws of nature were "front-loaded" by the Creator at the beginning of the universe with the Big Bang ("Let there be light") and then left alone to do what they were designed to do.

Many prominent scientists are coming to the same conclusion as Dobzhansky as science unlocks more and more of God's work. While we cannot deny the reality of evolution, no one understands how the process began. Natural selection is not a "force" that produces biological change, but a process that reacts to environmental pressures on genetic material within living organisms; that is, it requires the presence of self-replicating DNA contained in a living organism for it to take place. Without the complex information contained in the DNA code there can be no self-replication; without self-replication, there can be no reproduction, and without reproduction, the various mechanisms of evolution have nothing to work with. Natural selection does not, and cannot explain the origin of DNA; this is the real mystery of life. Origin-of-life biologist, Stephen Meyer, tells us that no expert in the field believes any longer that the absolutely mind-boggling complexity of the huge amount of information contained in DNA could have arisen by chance, putting the probability of that at 10^{25}; that's many, many trillions.[4] Furthermore, former atheist Dean Kenyon, one of the foremost biochemists of our time, after a long career trying unsuccessfully to determine how complex proteins and cells could self-organize naturalistically, came to the conclusion that: "We have not the slightest chance of a chemical evolutionary origin for even the simplest of cells...so, the concept of the intelligent design of life was immensely attractive to me and made a great deal of sense, as it very closely matched the multiple discoveries of molecular biology."[5]

Politically, I am a Jeffersonian small government, freedom-first-and foremost classical liberal (which makes me a conservative today), who believes strongly in Jefferson's words: "The policy [of America] is, to leave their citizens free, neither restraining nor aiding them in their pursuits." This, I suppose, makes me a conservative with a large libertarian streak. It is thus from a conservative/libertarian/deistic-tending-to-theism ideology that I examine the current assault on Christianity by left-wing organizations such as the American Civil Liberties Union (ACLU), the Freedom From Religion Federation (FFRF), Southern Poverty Law Center (SPLC), and the Gay, Lesbian & Straight Education Network (GLSEN). These groups love big government and have used state and federal governments to bludgeon Christianity. This growing trend is an atrocity that can only lead to ever greater cultural degradation, because we need a Christian moral backbone to the laws regulating society, as

Gouverneur Morris, a man whose role in crafting the United State Constitution was second only to James Madison, tells us:

> Religion is the only solid basis of good morals; therefore education should teach the precepts of religion, and the duties of man toward God. These duties are, internally, love and adoration: externally, devotion and obedience; therefore provision should be made for maintaining divine worship as well as education...For avoiding the extremes of despotism or anarchy ... the only ground of hope must be on the morals of the people. I believe that religion is the only solid base of morals and that morals are the only possible support of free governments. Therefore education should teach the precepts of religion and the duties of man towards God.[6]

In the Beginning

When the Founding Fathers met in Philadelphia in 1787, they were embarking on a grand but daunting task to create the philosophical and legal framework for the new nation they were forging out of thirteen independent former colonies. Newly independent from Great Britain, each new state shared the English common law and the English language, and unlike the future French and Russian Revolutions, they had no desire to fundamentally transform everything that went before: "The American Revolution was a reluctant uprising staged by men who were exceptionally dedicated to the English constitution."[7] This reluctance to part from the ways of their forefathers was well voiced by Thomas Jefferson in 1775: "Believe me, dear Sir: there is not in the British Empire a man who more cordially loves a union with Great Britain than I do. But, by the God that made me, I will cease to exist before I yield to a connection on such terms as the British Parliament propose; and in this, I think I speak the sentiments of America."[8] Most of the Founding Fathers took the position that the separation from Britain was a legal separation and that the Declaration of Independence was a political bill of divorce based on legal grounds found in the English constitution. In the minds of many of the leading figures of the American Revolution, they were loyal to the precedent established by their forefathers in England as a result of the Glorious Revolution of 1688.

The newly formed United States retained almost all the cultural and legal traditions, as well as the Christian traditions inherited from Great Britain. In many ways, in 1776 the United States was true to the traditions of the "old country" than Britain itself. At the time that the United States Constitution was gestating in Philadelphia, public displays of Christian faith were everywhere on display to remind people of God. The governments of the various states funded and fully supported religious displays, just as they enforced laws forbidding religious vilification. In short, beginning with the Mayflower, the settlers of this continent created a culture in which the moral authority of Christianity was taken for granted. Fast forward to the present, and we have a complete reversal. Religious displays are banned completely from the public square, as are prayers in schools and even the celebration of Christmas in some of them while, as we have seen, blasphemy of the vilest sort is funded by tax payer's dollars. That, to steal a phrase from Barack Obama again, is a "fundamental transformation of America."

Is the United States a Christian Country?

It is politically incorrect today to refer to the United States as a Christian country. Barack Obama has made it his business in many places here and abroad during his presidency to declare that we are not a Christian nation. He has said it to applause in Cairo, Paris, Istanbul, and in various locations in the United States. In a visit to Egypt he famously declared that the United States was "one of the largest Muslim countries in the world," but the U.S. Government's own statistics showed that in 2007 Muslims were 0.6% of the population, or about three million[9] Of course, Obama's math is deficient; after all, this is the man who claimed to have campaigned in "all 57 states, with, er, one or two left to go" and who claimed that his father, born in 1936 in Kenya, served in World War II, which ended in 1945.

Political correctness to the contrary, the United States is a Christian country in almost every sense of the term. Legal scholar Ashley Bell writes American law, politics, and culture are saturated with religious expressions and beliefs that reflect the deeply Christian nature of the United States. She notes that our currency is imprinted with "In God We Trust;" that the Supreme Court opens each session with "God Save the United States and this Honorable Court;" that Americans salute the flag with the words "one nation, under God," and so on.[10] Up until the attacks on religion gathered steam in the 20th century, American institutions and American life were saturated with reminders of our Christian traditions. Legal scholar John Witte writes of how religious symbols appear on state seals and state documents and how the Ten Commandments and Bible verses were inscribed on the walls of courthouses and other public buildings: "Crucifixes and other Christian symbols were erected in state parks and on statehouse grounds. Flags flew at half-mast on Good Friday and other high holy days. Christmas, Easter, and other holy days were official holidays. Sundays remained official days of rest." [11]

Despite all this, there are people, especially leftist academics, who become agitated when America is referred to as a Christian country and feel that if Americans value their Christian roots and endeavor to live in accordance with them, they are dangerous bigots set on offending people who are not Christians. They have come to feel this way despite the fact that: "not only did America have a Christian Founding, but virtually all of the Founders were devout, orthodox Christians who consciously drew from their religious convictions to answer most political questions."[12] Of course, radical leftist could care less about such historical facts; they have a built-in antipathy to Christianity because it is what stands in their way to achieving Big-Government utopia. Even if these facts were to be acknowledged they would be considered irrelevant because they were written by rich white men.

Much of the argument about the nature of this country rests with how "Christian country" is defined. A definition is an exercise in which we try to make something definite, distinct, or clear. This works well in science, where great care is taken to define its terms unambiguously by the use of objective and precise measurements. But this exercise is notoriously difficult in human endeavors where people are free to define something in a way that leads to their conclusion by cherry-picking evidence and engaging in verbal acrobatics (think of Bill Clinton's contorted definition of "sexual relations" regarding his interlude with Monica Lewinski). We can also define something so broadly and positively that almost everyone would agree with it, or we can define it so narrowly and negatively that almost no one would agree with it. In the business of discussing and writing about the law as it pertains to religion, we will see that the courts outdo Clinton substantially in their many confusing and contradictory definitions.

One definition offered by Americans United for Separation of Church and State (AUSCS) is that for the United States to be a Christian country if must be officially defined as such. The AUSCS relies on presumed claim attributed to the "religious right" that this country is indeed "officially" a Christian country: "Religious Right groups and their allies insist that the United States was designed to be officially Christian and that our laws should enforce the doctrines of (their version of) Christianity."[13] The AUSCS argument that the United States is not "officially" Christian, is absolutely true. It is also true that some members of the Constitutional Convention wanted Christianity designated as the official religion of the United States and were outraged when it was not. An attempt was made in 1864 to make America officially Christian by the National Reform Association. This group believed that the Civil War was God's punishment for failing to ordain the country as officially Christian and advocated for an amendment to atone for that omission. However, I am not aware of any group, "religious right" or otherwise, that has seriously advanced this cause since then. AUSCS should be reminded that many things are what they are without being "officially" defined as such.

Those who subscribe to the view that we are a Christian nation (albeit, not "officially") appeal to the ringing words of the Declaration of Independence:

> When in the Course of human events, it becomes necessary for one people to Dissolve the political bands which have connected them with another, and to assume Among the powers of the earth, the separate and equal station to which the Laws of Nature and of Nature's God entitle them... We hold these truths to be self-evident, that all men are created equal; that they are endowed by their Creator with certain unalienable rights; that among these are Life, Liberty, and the pursuit of Happiness.

In the final paragraph of the Declaration of Independence, the signatories noted they were "appealing to the Supreme Judge of the world for the rectitude of our intentions," and declared "a firm reliance on the protection of divine Providence, we mutually pledge to each other our Lives, our Fortunes, and our sacred Honor." The mention of "Nature's God" and "Creator" reveals Thomas Jefferson's busy hand in drafting the document. Jefferson was a deist and always resisted terminology that could be taken as favoring one Christian denomination over another. Just as some have taken the words of the Declaration as unequivocal evidence that we were born a Christian nation, those who deny it point to what they consider the vague and generic deistic phrasing. Yet orthodox Christians regularly made use of such terminology in those times and did not consider it vague, generic, and deistic.

Those with a distaste for the notion of the United States is a Christian nation grant that the Declaration mentions God, but take comfort that the Constitution is "Godless" They correctly point out that the Constitution contains no references to God, Jesus Christ, or Christianity, and that it does not proclaim the United States to be officially a Christian nation. It is difficult to see how this settles the argument for it edits out the nuances surrounding the drafting of the Constitution. The Constitution may only be fairly characterized as "Godless" insofar as it consciously deferred to the states on matters of religion and devotion to God. The Framers believed it inappropriate for the federal government to encroach upon the states' jurisdiction in such matters. At the very least, the Constitution is deistic, and deism is a natural religion whose adherents believe in the existence of God on rational grounds free of reliance on religious authority or holy books. Deists believe in God in the same way that Einstein did: "I believe in Spinoza's God, who reveals Himself in the lawful harmony of the world." [14] Thus, if we pay due regard to the rationale behind the wording of the Constitution, as well as its deistic flavor, it is far from "Godless."

The reason Constitution leaves out specific Christian references is that Founders created the document to form a national government composed of sovereign states. The representatives of the various states were fearful of a powerful federal government and thus wanted to specify what its powers were to be and what powers the states were to retain. The powers of the general (federal) government were to be limited to the purposes enumerated in Article I, Section 8 of the Constitution. The only religious clause in the document (Article VI) prior to the ten amendments in the Bill of Rights, added in 1791, forbids religious tests as qualifications for federal office. This clause was intended to defuse controversy and to prevent any claims of religious preferentialism. It was universally understood that any legislation or disputes relating to religious or moral matters were to be the sole purview of state and local governments and that the federal government was forbidden to interfere. As Thomas Jefferson observed: "Certainly, no power to prescribe any religious exercise or to assume authority in the religious disciple, has been delegated to the General Government. It must then rest with the States, as far as it can be in any human authority."[15]

Jefferson was a champion of state's rights because it was at that level where power was closest to "we the people." He wanted a limited federal government and was always on guard to ensure that its legislative, executive, or judicial branches did not encroach on state's rights. He earnestly believed that:

the true barriers of our liberty in this country are our State governments; and the wisest conservative power ever contrived by man, is that of which our Revolution and present government found us possessed. Seventeen distinct States, amalgamated into one as to their foreign concerns, but single and independent as to their internal administration, regularly organized with legislature and governor resting on the choice of the people, and enlightened by a free press, can never be so fascinated by the arts of one man, as to submit voluntarily to his usurpation.[16]

Another argument made by groups such as AUSCS against the idea that the United States is a Christian nation is that the Free Exercise of religion clause of the First Amendment does not indicate that the provision applies only to Christianity. This is correct, and it is the grandeur of the Constitution that it is religiously inclusive—a really radical notion at that time. Both Jefferson and Madison, its primary authors, were well-versed in history. They were thus aware of how officially religious governments crush human freedom and how religious rivalries had prompted numerous wars. Not favoring any one religion is the basis of religious freedom and social peace. They were also very much cognizant of Voltaire's 1733 *Letters Concerning the English Nation*. The most famous quotation from those letters reads: "If there were only one religion in England, there would be danger of tyranny; if there were two, they would cut each other's throats; but there are thirty, and they live happily together in peace."[17]

Yet another argument often voiced by those who deny our Christian heritage is the wording in the 1797 Treaty of Tripoli between the United States and the Barbary States written by a diplomat, John Barlow, approved by President John Adams, and ratified by the Senate. Article 11 of the Treaty reads: "the Government of the United States of America is not, in any sense, founded on the Christian religion." This is the *only* statement found in the literature in which a Founding Father expressed (more correctly "approved") a negative statement regarding the religious status of the United States, and those who gush over it conveniently omit the surrounding text and the circumstances that necessitated the Treaty.

The treaty with the Barbary States was of critical importance to the United States in order to protect its shipping in the seas around the Barbary coasts. At that time the U.S. was bargaining from a position of weakness. The United States had to pay tribute to the Barbary States to assure the safety of its ships from Barbary pirates. Tribute payment lasted until the treaty was renegotiated in 1815 when the United States negotiated from a position of strength. Article 11 was dropped from the renegotiated treaty, another fact that opponents of Christianity ignore.[18] It is instructive that in the year following the 1795 Treaty of Tripoli, Adams wrote the following words to the men of the Massachusetts Militia: "Our Constitution was made only for a moral and religious people. It is wholly inadequate to the government of any other." It is clear from this that his "approval" of Barlow's wording was meant only to appease the Islamic leaders of the Barbary States when the United States was weak.[19]

The United States was Founded Solidly on Christian Principles

The culture of what was to become the United States did not suddenly appear de novo in 1776; it began at least 250 years before. If we look at the language, laws, and customs of colonial America and compare them with the America of 1800 very little had changed. The earliest document in the American colonies, such as the Mayflower Compact, signed by the Pilgrims aboard the ship, acknowledged that they undertook to voyage from England: "for the Glory of God, and advancements of the Christian faith." The Fundamental Orders of Connecticut, adopted in 1639, made frequent references to Christianity such as the colonists were "to maintain and preserve the liberty and purity of the Gospel of our Lord Jesus," and " "Laws here established, and for want thereof, according to the Rule of the Word of God." The Massachusetts Body of Liberties of 1641 has among its many provisions the "Civil Authority hath power and liberty to see the peace, ordinances, and Rules of Christ observed in every church according to his word." The various charters of the colonies, and later the states, were saturated with such language; proof enough that the early settlers were Christian to the core and wanted their settlements to reflect their beliefs.

Nonetheless, we can agree that it is absolutely true that the United States is not a Christian country if by "Christian country" one means a Christian theocracy in which church dogma constitutes part of the legal landscape, or that Christians are privileged over followers of other religions. The United States is not a Christian nation in the sense that the Catholic, Baptist, Methodist and other churches are Christian. These denominations are Christian in that they were founded and existed to promote Christianity; the United States was not founded and does not exist, to promote Christianity. The United States exists to promote freedom, human rights, and "life liberty, and the pursuit of happiness," but it seems to have forgotten how Christianity has aided and abetted these noble goals. Neither is America a Christian nation in the sense that every citizen is a Christian or is required to be one and to live up to its precepts.

The United States is assuredly a Christian nation, however, if we define a nation by its character and articulated principles. The character and principles articulated by men instrumental in forming this nation were overwhelmingly Christians. If this nation is not Christian in a legal sense, it is most definitely a Christian nation in a philosophical, historical, and cultural sense. Writing of the influences of William Blackstone's *Commentaries on the laws of England* on the thinking of the Founding Fathers, Historian Daniel Bernstein says: "No other book *except the Bible* played a greater role in the history of American institutions."[20] In the *Federalist No.2* published in 1787, John Jay, the first Supreme Court Chief Justice, wrote under the *nom de plume* of "Publius": "With equal pleasure I have as often taken notice that Providence has been pleased to give this one connected country to one united people—a people descended from the same ancestors, speaking the same language, professing the same religion, attached to the same principles of government, very similar in their manners and customs."

Backing Jay's claim is the 1790 U.S. census reports showing that 67.5 percent of all white Americans or their ancestors came from the British Isles and the rest from other European countries such as Germany and Holland. Thus, if we define "Christian nation" terms of its foundational principles and of the faith of the vast proportion of its white inhabitants, both at the time of its founding and today, this is a Christian nation. The United States is not a Christian nation in the same sense that Saudi Arabia is a Muslim nation, but its Christian origins and character are everywhere to be seen. That the United States is no longer as homogeneously Anglo-Saxon as it was, does not detract from its heritage. This is not employing the "politics of exclusion," exercising religious bigotry, or claiming a privileged status for Christians: it is a valid historical claim that many great American statesmen have made.

A Supreme Court case making this same argument is *Church of the Holy Trinity v. United States* (1892). This case was an immigration case and not one about religion per se. The issue was whether or not hiring a foreigner (in this case an English pastor named E. Walpole Warren) violated the federal Contract Labor Act of 1885 passed with the intention of limiting immigration and preventing American companies from hiring cheap labor from overseas. In a unanimous decision remanding the case, the Supreme Court turned it into a religious issue by pronouncing that "no purpose of action against religion can be imputed to any legislation, state or national because this is a religious people. This is historically true. From the discovery of this continent to the present hour, there is a single voice making this affirmation." In support of its ruling, the Court cited numerous historical documents written by the Founding Fathers, court rulings and legal documents, and even went back to Ferdinand and Isabella's granting of a commission to Christopher Columbus and Queen Elizabeth's colonial grant to Sir Walter Raleigh on condition they establish Christian settlements. The Court also wrote:

> [T]he churches and church organizations which abound in every city, town, and hamlet; the multitude of charitable organizations existing everywhere under Christian auspices; the gigantic missionary associations, with general support, and aiming to establish Christian missions in every quarter of the globe. These, and many other matters which might be noticed, add a volume of unofficial declarations to the mass of organic utterances that this is a Christian nation.

The Rev. E. Walpole Warren kept his post.

Evidence that our Forefathers Considered America a Christian Nation

What follows is a few among a multitude of examples of famous Americans, beginning with George Washington's "Earnest Prayer," written at the close of the Revolutionary War in 1783 and sent to the governors of the newly freed states, asserting that we are a Christian nation.

- "I now make it my earnest prayer, that God would have you and the State over which you preside, in his holy protection, that he would incline the hearts of the Citizens to cultivate a spirit of subordination and obedience to Government--to entertain a brotherly affection and love for one another, for their fellow Citizens of the United States at large, and particularly for their Brethren who have served in the Field, and finally, that he would most graciously be pleased to dispose us all, to do Justice, to love Mercy, and to demean ourselves with that Charity, Humility, and Pacific temper of mind which were the Characteristics of the *Divine Author of our blessed Religion*, and without an humble imitation of whose example in these things, we can never hope to be a Happy Nation." [21]

- Celebrating July 4th in 1821, sixth president of the United States, John Quincy Adams, proclaimed that: "The highest glory of the American Revolution was this: it connected, in one indissoluble bond, the principles of civil government with the principles of Christianity." Although certain secular humanists claim this to be a fake quote, it sits innocently of that charge in the United States Congressional Record.[22] In a letter to Thomas Jefferson on June 28, 1813, second president of the United States, John Adams, wrote: "The general principles on which the fathers achieved independence were the general principles of Christianity. I will avow that I then believed, and now believe, that those general principles of Christianity are as eternal and immutable as the existence and attributes of God."[23]

- Asking for a day of national prayer in 1863, Abraham Lincoln wrote: "Whereas, the Senate of the United States, devoutly recognizing the Supreme Authority and just Government of Almighty God, in all the affairs of men and of nations, has, by a resolution, requested the President to designate and set apart a day for National prayer and humiliation. And whereas it is the duty of nations as well as of men, to own their dependence upon the overruling power of God, to confess their sins and transgressions, in humble sorrow, yet with assured hope that genuine repentance will lead to mercy and pardon; and to recognize the sublime truth, announced in the Holy Scriptures and proven by all history, that those nations only are blessed whose God is the Lord."[24]

- During a mid-Atlantic summit with British Prime Minister Churchill during World War II, Franklin D. Roosevelt described the United States as "The lasting concord between men and nations, founded on the principles of Christianity," and then led the crew of the American warship in singing "Onward, Christian Soldiers."[25]

- Writing to the Pope in 1947, President Truman declared "This is a Christian Nation." President Woodrow Wilson affirmed that "Ameri-

ca was born to exemplify the devotion to the elements of righteousness which are derived from the Holy Scriptures."[26]

- Addressing an annual prayer breakfast in 1954, Chief Justice Earl
  Warren said: "I believe no one can read the history of our country
  without realizing that the Good Book and the Spirit of the Saviour
  have from the beginning been our guiding geniuses whether we look
  to the first Charter of Virginia...or to the Charter of New England...or
  to the Charter of Massachusetts Bay...or to the Fundamental Orders
  of Connecticut...the same objective is present: a Christian land governed by Christian principles. I believe the entire Bill of Rights came
  into being because of the knowledge our forefathers had of the Bible
  and their belief in it: freedom of belief, of expression, of assembly, of
  the petition, the dignity of the individual, the sanctity of the home,
  equal justice under law and the reservation of powers to the people."[27]

- As late as 1983, the 97th Congress of the United States passed Public
  Law 97-280, which was signed by President Ronald Reagan. It reads
  as follows:
  WHEREAS the Bible, the Word of God, has made a unique contribution in shaping theUnited States as a distinctive and blessed nation
  and people;
  WHEREAS deeply held religious convictions springing from the Holy
  Scriptures led to the early settlement of our Nation;
  WHEREAS Biblical teachings inspired concepts of civil government
  that are contained in our Declaration of Independence and Constitution of the United States;
  WHEREAS many of our great national leaders--among them Presidents Washington, Jackson, Lincoln, and Wilson--paid tribute to the
  surpassing influence of the Bible in our country's development, as in
  the words of President Jackson that the Bible is "the Rock on which
  our Republic rests";
  WHEREAS the history of our Nation clearly illustrates the value of
  voluntarily applying the teachings of the Scriptures in the lives of individuals, families, and societies; WHEREAS this Nation now faces
  great challenges that will test this Nation as it has never been tested
  before; and
  WHEREAS that renewing our knowledge of and faith in God through
  Holy Scripture can strengthen us as a nation and a people: NOW,
  THEREFORE, be it Resolved by the Senate and House of Representatives of the United States of America in Congress assembled, That the
  President is authorized and requested to designate 1983 as a national

"Year of the Bible" in recognition of both the formative influence the Bible has been for our Nation, and our national need to study and apply the teachings of the Holy Scriptures.

- And finally, from the most astute observer of the American society of all: Alexis de Tocqueville. In his magisterial *Democracy in America*, he wrote:

  The sects that exist in the United States are innumerable. They all differ in respect to the worship which is due to the Creator, but they all agree in respect to the duties which are due from man to man. Each sect adores the Deity in its own peculiar manner, but all sects preach the same moral law in the name of God. If it is of the highest importance to man, as an individual, that his religion should be true, it is not so to society. Society has no future life to hope for or to fear; and provided the citizens profess a religion, the peculiar tenets of that religion are of little importance to its interests. Moreover, all the sects of the United States are comprised within the great unity of Christianity, and Christian morality is everywhere the same.[28]

The website "All about history" adds to this by listing a number of observations pointing to the conclusion that the Founding Fathers envisioned a state bathed in Cristian principles, albeit, not in the dogma of any one particular denomination. These include the use of the Bible as a textbook in early America; the Ten Commandments carved into many court buildings; the swearing-in practice, our currency, and the national anthem mentions God. We may also point to the numerous religious inscriptions on at various monuments In Washington, D.C., including the Jefferson Memorial which contains the following words from Jefferson himself taken from the Virginia Statute for Religious Freedom:

Almighty God hath created the mind free. All attempts to influence it by temporal punishments or burthens...are a departure from the plan of the Holy Author of our religion...No man shall be compelled to frequent or support any religious worship or ministry or shall otherwise suffer on account of his religious opinions or belief, but all men shall be free to profess and by argument to maintain, their opinions in matters of religion. I know but one code of morality for men whether acting singly or collectively.

The Left's Denial of our Christian Heritage

Many left-wing types are uncomfortable with our Christian heritage, and because they are uncomfortable, they want to deny it to the rest of us. They may be hard leftists imbued with cultural Marxism who know Christianity must be destroyed if their goal is to be attained, or they may be weak leftists who merely want to go along with the politically correct herd. Many have sunk so low as to dishonor the thousands of American soldiers killed in World War I who are honored by the World War I Veterans Memorial Peace Cross in Bladensburg, Maryland. This cross was dedicated in 1925, but the militantly anti-Christian group American Humanist Association (AHA) wants it removed. One of the plaintiffs in the suit seeking its removal, Steven Lowe, said that the cross upsets him whenever he passes it. Perhaps it does because it symbolizes self-sacrifice, suffering, and hope, and honors real men who gave their lives for milk-sops and snivelers like Lowe could live could live in peace and freedom. A United States District Court ruled that the Memorial is constitutionally permitted, but in late 2015 the AHA appealed the decision to the U.S. Court of Appeals, and thus the outcome is uncertain at the time of writing.[29] However, in a similar case in San Diego, the Mount Soledad Cross was ordered dismantled by the Federal Court of Appeals. This illustrates the lengths to which radical leftists will go in their efforts to rid us of our Christian heritage and to spiritually degrade us all.

Sometime in the distant future, even the Jefferson Memorial is sure to upset some left-wing soul who will cry to the government that he or she is offended. This delicate creature may enlist the American Civil Liberties Union (ACLU)— no friend of religious liberty—to take the complaint all the way to the Supreme Court. It is not without possibility that the Court may rule it unconstitutional, and someone will be ordered to take a sandblaster and obliterate yet another part of the American heritage. I say "distant future" because the Supreme Court, in its self-assumed infinite wisdom, has ruled (for now, at least) that public monuments such as the Jefferson Memorial are "secular," having, according to the Court in *Marsh v. Chambers* (1983), lost their "seemingly" religious meaning. Christians are appalled when judges and other public officials proclaim that crosses, crèches, and Christmas carols, and Christmas itself, no longer have religious significance and that the Ten Commandments are a secular code, but proclaiming they are not religious doesn't make it so.

If these things are merely secular remnants of a bygone age, why are atheists and leftists so bothered by them as to demand their removal? Professor Steven Epstein knows that they have religious significance, and he believes that because they do they should be removed. He has marshaled court cases from the past 50 years to support the position that religious icons, and even the references to God on monuments, coins, flags, courthouses, or wherever, are unconstitutional and should be abandoned. After making his case, Epstein declares that: "the Court should have the intellectual honesty and fortitude to recognize that ceremonial deism violates a core purpose of the Establishment Clause." [30]

Anti-religionists, therefore, demand the removal of reminders of our Christian heritage precisely because they believe they do have religious significance. These folks are so implacably anti-Christian and committed to the goals of cultural Marxism that they will not rest until all references to God or Christianity are obliterated from American life. If some people demanding the removal of Christianity are not cultural Marxist salivating for socialism, but rather patriotic atheists, they might ponder James Reston's trenchant question: "If religion was so important in the building of the Republic, how could it be irrelevant to the maintenance of the Republic?"[31]

It would be a mistake to view the assault on Christianity as an entirely a modern assault. There have been previous attacks, but what is new in the present day is the government response to them. In 1883, a petition was presented to Congress by an atheist group asking for the removal of Christianity from government institutions. This was something entirely novel and almost unthinkable by most Americans at the time. An incensed House Judiciary Committee in 1854 responded to the petition by noting that:

> Down to the Revolution, every colony did sustain religion in some form. It was deemed peculiarly proper that the religion of liberty should be upheld by a free people. Had the people, during the Revolution, had a suspicion of any attempt to war against Christianity, that Revolution would have been strangled in its cradle. At the time of the adoption of the Constitution and the amendments, the universal sentiment was that Christianity should be encouraged, not any one sect. Any attempt to level and discard all religion would have been viewed with universal indignation. ... That was the religion of the founders of the republic, and they expected it to remain the religion of their descendants.[32]

The weapon used to attack a religion that radical secularists of all stripes have been using for so long are the very religious clauses in the Constitution that were designed to protect it. It thus behooves us to examine the origin of these clauses and how they were viewed by their authors. I contrast the views of the authors of the Constitution on the clauses with the views of the haughty Justices sitting on the Supreme Court since the 1940s when the first legal salvoes aimed at marginalizing Christianity were fired. But I first look at the role of the United States Supreme Court in American life because it is this imperial body that is called upon to give Constitutional approval to the case by case destruction of our Christian heritage.

Endnotes

1. Hall, D. *Did America Have a Christian Founding?* p.10; emphasis mine.
2. New York Times. *Dr. Albert Einstein Dies in Sleep.*
3. Dobzhansky, Nothing in biology, p. 125.
4. Meyer, S. DNA and the origin of life.
5. Kenyon, D. *Unlocking the mystery of life*, p. 35
6. Oneil, T., *The Student manifesto*, p. 46.
7. Johnson, The rule of law in the realm, p. 3).
8. Quoted in Hazelton, *The Declaration of Independence*, p. 19.
9. Central Intelligence Agency. *The World Factbook.*
10. Bell, God Save this Honorable Court, pp. 1276-1277.
11. Witte, The essential rights and liberties, p. 406
12. Hall, Did America Have a Christian Founding? p.2.
13. Americans United for Separation of Church State. Is America a Christian nation? p.1.
14. Einstein, *The ultimate quotable Einstein.* P. 325
15. In Dreisbach and Hall, *Sacred Rights*, p. 531.
16. In Ford, *The Writings of Thomas Jefferson*, pp. 308-9.
17. In Durant and Durant. *The Age of Voltaire*, p. 119).
18. Lambert, *The Barbary wars.*
19. Adams, *The Works of John Adams*, p. 229.
20. In Locay, *Unveiling the Left*, p. 300, emphasis added.
21. U.S. History/Valley Forge, George Washington's Earnest Prayer.
22. Congressional Record, 2001, vol.147, p, 20222.
23. Barton, *The Founding Fathers on Jesus, Christianity and the Bible.*
24. Mathisen, *The Routledge Sourcebook of Religion and the American Civil War*, 236.
25. DeMar, p. 2.
26. Ibid, p. 3.
27. Black, J. *When Nations Die.*
28. de Tocqueville, *Democracy in America*, p.303.
29. First Liberty, Federal Court Declares Historic.
30. Epstein, 2174.
31. Reston, J., Faith of Our Fathers, p. 12a.
32. Congressional Record 108th Congress p. 21226.

Cases Cited

Church of the Holy Trinity v. United States, 143 U.S. 457 (1892).
Marsh v. Chambers, 463 U.S. 783 (1983).

Chapter 4

The U.S. Constitution and the Supreme Court: A Marriage Gone Sour

"The opinion which gives to the judges the right to decide what laws are constitutional, and what are not, not only for themselves in their own sphere of action, but for the Legislature & Executive also, in their spheres, would make the judiciary a despotic branch." Thomas Jefferson, third President of the United States.

The Constitution and the Court

Although Christianity is being attacked by a variety of organized groups; sometimes subtly and mildly, and sometimes overtly and harshly, the blows are most telling when they come from the muscular arm of the state, particularly from the United States Supreme Court. When the Supreme Court hands down a decision it must have at least the appearance of being based on the Constitution. It is thus important to examine the Court and its use of the Constitution when ruling on religious issues. Of course, not all Court decisions are hostile to religion. It has been quite protective in some periods, and quite hostile in others. When it is protective it simply preserves the status quo as intended by the Founders; when it is hostile, however, it mangles their intentions in ways hard to repair and impossible to justify.

A constitution is a formal document that creates (constitutes) a government. The document lays out the mode in which a government is organized and the manner in which sovereign power is distributed to its various branches. It enumerates national goals and aspirations according to the system of beliefs and values existing at the time it was written; regulates institutional and social behavior, and sets forth the rights of individuals living under it. Of course, constitutions are just words on paper; it is up to individuals with the power to do so to give them life.

Nineteenth-century British Prime Minister, William Gladstone once said: "The American Constitution is, so far as I can see, the most wonderful work ever struck off at a given time by the brain and purpose of man."[1] This country has lived up to the promises of this "wonderful work" in the main but is too often mauled by activist courts acting as a super-legislature into something quite different from the original. In *Hurtado v. California* (1884), the Court distinguished between the protections afforded the people in the United States and Great Britain:

> The actual and practical security for English liberty against legislative tyranny was the power of a free public opinion represented by the Commons. In this country, written constitutions were deemed essential to protect the rights and liberties of the people against the encroachments of power delegated to their governments and the provisions of Magna Charta were incorporated into Bills of Rights. They were limitations upon all the powers of government, legislative as well as executive and judicial.

The Supreme Court claims for itself the role of Captain America providing protection against legislative and executive tyranny, but who guards the guardians? Not "we the people" because Supreme Court justices enjoy lifetime tenure, no matter how offensive to public sensibilities their decisions may be. For all intents and purposes, the Supreme Court is a law onto itself with virtually no check on its power to run the lives of all Americans regardless of their will. The Court has the power to overturn anything passed by elected bodies almost at its whim (a case has to be brought before it before it can exercise that whim, but the justices chose the cases they will hear). Activist justices have found all sorts of ideas lurking in the penumbras of the Constitution that its Framers could never have imagined or approved.

The power of the Supreme Court to do this is an unintended consequence of the Framers profound distrust of both the rule of aristocratic monarchy and of the rule of majoritarian democracy. To avoid either, they founded a constitutional republic with three co-equal branches: executive, legislative, and judiciary. A republic and democracy are seemingly identical, but they are not. In a republic, the sovereignty is supposed to reside in each individual person, while in a democracy the sovereignty is invested in the majority. The Framers set out to form a national government of limited powers to protect the God granted inalienable rights of every individual. These inalienable rights are enumerated in the Constitution and have plain meanings which were only meant to be changed by the stringent process of a Constitutional amendment. In an aristocratic monarchy or direct democracy, there is no protection for the individual dissenter or for a minority, because decisions made in either case are un-appealable. In our American republic, we may appeal violations of inalienable rights all the way to the Supreme Court, upon which we rely on reading the Constitution's plain words as they are written. We shall see, how-ever, that the Court has rejected God-given rights contained in the Free Exer-cise Clause of the First Amendment in favor of statutory rights granted by man. These novel statutory rights are commendable in themselves, but they have clashed with Constitutional rights on many occasions, and they have prevailed over those rights. The basis for this aberration has been decisions handed down by the Supreme Court enfeebled the role of Christianity in American life.

Mark Pulliam notes how the Supreme Court became emboldened during the 1960s and 1970s and set out advance the liberal agenda in an orgy of judi-cial activism, which included madding, "obscenity and pornography protect-ed expression; expanded the supposed "wall of separation" between church and state; interfered in the operation of public schools; authorized race-conscious affirmative action in higher education; and generally advanced a liberal political agenda at every opportunity.[2] Others may run the country on a day-to-day basis, but when important social and moral issues are contested, the unelected and life-tenured members of the United States Supreme Court have the highest governing authority. If you believe in a representative repub-lic—"government for the people, by the people"—this should alarm you, as it did federal appeals judge and legal philosopher, Learned Hand, who declared: "For myself it would be most irksome to be ruled by a bevy of Platonic Guard-ians, even if I knew how to choose them, which I assuredly do not."[3]

Congress and Legislating

Legislating is the process of making laws governing conduct by a body of people duly elected by the people to engage in that task. The Constitution explicitly assigned the role of lawmaking to Congress in Article 1, Section 1: "All legislative powers herein granted shall be vested in a Congress of the United States, which shall consist of a Senate and House of Representatives." Article 1 lists the enumerated powers of Congress, and it is clear that the Founding Fathers meant this branch to be the first among equals simply be-cause, unlike the executive and judicial branches, its members sit closest to the wishes of the people. As James Madison put it in *Federalist Paper No. 51*: "In a republican government, the legislative authority necessarily predomi-nates." But the "Platonic Guardians" sitting on the Supreme Court has usurped the role of the legislature on many matters on many occasions by legislating from the bench, which I find more than "irksome."

I am not alone. A 2005 survey conducted by the American Bar Association found that 56 percent of respondents agreed with the statement that "judicial activism" has reached a "crisis" and that judges who "routinely overrule the will of the people, invent new rights and ignore traditional morality and ignore voters' values should be impeached. Nearly half agreed with a congressman who said judges are "arrogant, out-of-control and unaccountable."[4] Constitutional scholar Jeremy Waldron also abhors this arrogant activism; quoting Ronald Dworkin, Waldron says that on, "'intractable, controversial, and profound questions of political morality that philosophers, statesmen, and citizens have debated for many centuries,' the people and their representatives simply have to 'accept the deliverances of a majority of the justices, whose insight into these great issues is not spectacularly special.'"[5]

The Constitution does not provide the federal judiciary with the power to invalidate acts of Congress. According to James Madison's notes, only 11 of the 55 delegates to the Constitutional Convention expressed an opinion on the desirability of judicial review of legislative matters. Only one, James Wilson, argued that the courts should have the power to strike down federal or state legislation. Alexander Hamilton's statement in *Federalist Paper No. 78* is often taken as supposing that the Court has this power: "The interpretation of the laws is the proper and peculiar province of the courts. A constitution, is, in fact, and must be regarded by the judges, as a fundamental law. It, therefore, belongs to them to ascertain its meaning, as well as the meaning of any particular act proceeding from the legislative body." In order to dispel notions of judicial supremacy over the legislature, however, he added:

> Nor does this conclusion by any means suppose *a superiority of the judicial to the legislative power.* It only supposes that the power of the people is superior to both; and that where the will of the legislature, declared in its statutes, stands in opposition to that of the people, declared in the Constitution, the judges ought to be governed by the latter rather than the former. They ought to regulate their decisions by the fundamental laws, rather than by those which are not fundamental...It can be of no weight to say that the courts, on the pretense of a repugnancy, may substitute their own pleasure to the constitutional intentions of the legislature...The courts must declare the sense of the law; and if they should be disposed to exercise will instead of judgment, the consequence would equally be the substitution of their pleasure to that of the legislative body.[6]

Hamilton's point was that the judiciary should be subordinate to the legislature if it is responding to the will of the people, but that the legislature should be subordinate to the judiciary when legislation stands in opposition to the Constitutional rights of the people (the principle of "Government of the people, by the people, for the people."). He was also adamant that the Court should judge strictly according to the Constitution, and not substitute "their pleasure."

Hamilton was a strong Federalist committed to a strong central government; anti-federalists committed to small government and state's rights maintained that each branch of government should determine for itself the constitutionality of its actions. Robert Yates, writing under the pseudonym "Brutus" in the *Anti-Federalist Papers*, wrote with prophetic insight that the Court will indeed rule according to "their pleasure." He wrote that the Court:

> will not confine themselves to any fixed or established rules, but will determine, according to what appears to them, the reason and spirit of the constitution. ..They have therefore no more right to set aside any judgment pronounced upon the construction of the constitution, than they have to take from the president, the chief command of the army and navy, and commit it to some other person. The reason is plain; the judicial and executive derive their authority from the same source, that the legislature do theirs; and therefore in all cases, where the constitution does not make the one responsible to, or controllable by the other, they are altogether independent of each other.[7]

If Congress passes a law and the president signs it, why should unelected judges be the ones that determine its constitutionality? After all, if according to Chief Justice Charles Hughes' famous dictum that the Constitution is "what the Supreme Court says it is," we are stuck with the rule of the majority of nine unelected lawyers who can, and who have, told us that the Constitution means one thing at one time and quite another thing at another time. Thus we have a body of "Constitutional law" which is derived from the actual Constitution only occasionally. The Court often appears to consider the Constitution to be a blank slate on which it can scribble anything it likes and then justify it with legal sophistry. You may argue that someone has to decide contentious issues with finality, to which I would reply that it should be "we the people" through duly enacted legislation promulgated by *elected* legislators who are subject to recall.

The Quasi-Religious Nature of the Supreme Court

One may wonder how it is possible that the Supreme Court majority has become a juristocracy imposing its will on "we the people." After all, it has neither the power of the purse (legislative branch) nor the sword (executive branch). Some believe that the Supreme Court justices are servants of the Constitution as priests and pastors are the servants of the gospels, but the Constitution often becomes a servant of the Court, just as the gospels have often been the servant of priests and pastors. Whether we think of the Court as an almost divinely inspired creator and guardian of American rights or as "at once the most powerful, and the most irresponsible of all the men in the world who govern other men,"[8] the concept of legitimacy is central to understanding how nine unelected and life-tenured lawyers have come to rule over our social and moral lives.

Like priests and pastors, Supreme Court Justices are legitimated by traditional and rational authority, and these forms of authority may be maintained in the face of heavy criticism if it is buttressed by charismatic authority. Charismatic authority is "generated by exceptional, unusual, and even quasi-supernatural qualities attributed to individuals or institutions."[9] Robert Taylor, who describes the Supreme Court as "a priesthood that governs," paints a dramatic picture of the process of the justices' decision-making and of the awesome consequences of those decisions. All this occurs after the Court has decided for itself, in true autocratic manner, which of the numerous petitions (about 2%) brought before it that it wants to hear.

> No public hearings are then held, only arguments for the various sides, and these are strictly timed and can, at the Court's pleasure, be dispensed with altogether. Then follows secret deliberations . . . and finally, the promulgation of an entirely new law, valid across the nation and virtually immune to repeal. A law may upset the established customs and practices of an entire culture; it may abruptly make criminal conduct legal or render criminal what has previously been permitted; or it may force upon lower jurisdictions policies radically at odds with those that have the support of the people and with what had been long established there—and all this without warning . . . as in the most rigid despotism.[10]

The legitimizing effect is in evidence when these aloof justices in their marble palace interpret the Constitution: "Just as the magisterial statements of the Papacy are more compelling for Roman Catholics when they come ex-cathedra, the Supreme Court's rulings have more legitimacy when symbolically connected to the U.S. Constitution." [11] Of course, the Court's business is always somehow connected to the Constitution, although these connections are often tenuous at best.

Political Ideology and the Court

If it is true that Supreme Court justices are servants to the Constitution, then the ideological composition of the Court should not matter. But it does; presidents are not known for nominating judges hostile to their ideology. Presidents are aware there is nothing short of asking Congress to declare war that has such far-reaching effects on the nation than the appointment of a Supreme Court justice to forward their agendas long after they have left office. In matters of social morality, the ideological composition of the Court is more important than the content of the "gospel." This is so because the Justices interpret the written words, and often do so in ways diametrically opposed to the interpretations offered by previous Courts with a different ideological stance. The heated and often hostile interrogations of Supreme Court nominees plainly speak to the fact that senators are well aware of the ideological nature of Court decisions having to do with moral issues. Commenting on this hostility, economist and philosopher Thomas Sowell opines: "If judges confined themselves to acting like judges, instead of legislating from the bench, creating new 'rights' out of thin air that are nowhere to be found in the Constitution, maybe Senate confirmation hearings for Supreme Court nominees would not be such bitter and ugly ideological battles."[12] Of course, "inventing new rights" is fine if old ones are not pushed aside and crushed to make way for them.

Of course, judges must always make rulings that accord with written law, but they can always find the right law and "interpret" it in such a way that it satisfies their vision of "right." Note the honesty of the great American 19th century Judge Chancellor James Kent as he tells us how he made use of law to make decisions that accorded with his personal views:

> My practice was first to make myself master of the facts. . . . [B]y the time I had done this slow and tedious process I was master of the cause [case] & ready to decide it. I saw where justice lay and the moral sense decided the cause half the time, & I then set down to search the authorities until I had exhausted my books, & I might once & a while be embarrassed by a technical rule, but I almost always found principles to suit my views of the case.[13]

This strategy amounts to judges sending their clerks to the legal stables to find a horse that will take them from where they are to where they want to go without breaking a leg. Many studies show that judicial decisions are highly predictable by judges' political ideology, race, gender, and religion if the case before them involves their ideological predilections. Justice Thurgood Marshall was notorious for this, explaining his legal philosophy as: "You do what you think is right and let the law catch up."[14] Marshall's former clerk (and now U.S. Supreme Court Justice herself), Elena Kagan, admits that she struggled to write opinions for Marshall because she could often find no legal basis for the decisions that he asked her to write.

Another example is Justice Sonia Sotomayor's actions when she was a federal appeals judge hearing a discrimination claim against the city of New

Haven, Connecticut. The city Fire Department held strictly job-related exams for promotions to captain and lieutenant, but the city threw out the test results when all who qualified for promotion were white (with two white-Hispanics). The city feared suits filed by black firefighters claiming the results had a disparate impact on them if it allowed the test results to stand. This was evidently sufficient grounds to ignore the results of the test, which had, of course, a "disparate impact" on those who passed the test and were denied their due. The white firefighters filed suit claiming they were unfairly denied promotions because of their race (imagine how students would feel if a professor threw out their tests because no black student passed). Sotomayor, along with her two liberal colleagues, rejected their claim, disposing of it in an unsigned opinion consisting of a single paragraph of 135 words stating that the firefighters did not have a viable Title VII claim (a claim of intentional discrimination). She thus undermined the concept of a merit-based system for deciding who gets what while promoting the liberal notion that whites cannot claim protection from discrimination based on race, or at least they should be gracious enough not to.

How the Supreme Court took the Power to Legislate

The Supreme Court is provided for in Article III, Sections I and II of the Constitution: "The judicial power of the United States shall be vested in one Supreme Court, and in such inferior courts as the Congress may from time to time ordain and establish...The judicial power shall extend to all cases, in law and equity, arising under this Constitution, [and] the laws of the United States." It is difficult to see from this just how far its power was intended to stretch. As we have seen, some legal scholars assert that the Framers intended some form of judicial review of the constitutionality of federal and state legislation, while others assert that it is clear that they never meant the Court to have the power to void legislative acts. Charles Beard, one of the most influential historians of the 20th century, analyzed the intentions of the Framers on the power of the Supreme Court to overturn legislature and concluded:

> Not only is the power in question not expressly granted, but it could not have seemed to the framers to be granted by implication. Of the members of the Convention of 1787, not more than five or six are known to have regarded this power as a part of the general judicial power... [Moreover] a proposition to confer upon the federal judges revisory power over federal legislation was four times made in the Convention and defeated.[15]

But it does have the power, so how did it garner it? In effect, the Court gave it to itself in the famous *Marbury v. Madison* (1803) case. The substantive issue was a minor spat between two consecutive presidencies, but the consequences make it the most important case in American legal history. It involved William Marbury's commission as a justice of the peace. The commission was issued by President John Adams shortly before his term ended, but his secretary of State, John Marshall, failed to deliver it. The newly elected President Thomas Jefferson's secretary of state, James Madison, refused to deliver Marbury's commission, so Marbury applied directly to the Supreme Court for a writ of mandamus (a writ compelling public officials to perform their duty). The Supreme Court heard the case in 1803 and decided Marbury was entitled to his commission, but that the Court could not issue a writ of mandamus. Chief Justice John Marshall (the same person who, as Adams' secretary of state, failed to deliver Marbury's commission) wrote the opinion of the court, ruling that Marbury was entitled to his commission; a writ of mandamus was a proper legal remedy for enforcing Marbury's right, but the Court lacked the constitutional authority to issue it. The Judiciary Act of 1789 gave the Supreme Court original jurisdiction in such cases, but the Court ruled that this grant of authority was unconstitutional because Article III of the Constitution defined Supreme Court jurisdiction and that Congress could not expand it.

Prior to *Marbury*, the Supreme Court was the weakest branch of government. It was a crafty *coup d'état* in which the Court's weakness was advertised (we lack the power to issue the writ) and its strength asserted by ruling the Judiciary Act unconstitutional. If the Court had issued a writ of mandamus, it could not have forced Madison to honor it. The Supreme Court thus was faced with a serious challenge to its authority. Marshall's opinion saved the court's prestige and established the idea that the Supreme Court has the authority to review the constitutionality of congressional acts (and executive orders), although some have argued that Marshall's claim was more limited than most people think and that it was "entirely consistent with its recognizing a like power of the other branches of government to interpret the Constitution for themselves in deciding what they could and could not do in carrying out their constitutional functions."[16] After all, the only role explicitly mentioned as "defender and preserver" of the Constitution found in that document is the president's. This brings us an issue that divides Constitutional scholars and even the Justices themselves: How should the Constitution be interpreted?

Originalism or "Living Document"?

The battle lines regarding the proper role of the judiciary is drawn between originalists (or strict constructionists) and those who believe that the Constitution should be a "living document" to be contemporaneously and not historically interpreted. Originalism asserts that judges must not place their own interpretations on the Constitution, even if by adhering to this philosophy the consequences would be personally abhorrent. In deciding a case constructionists looks for "original intent" by perusing relevant material in an effort to discover the collective intention of the Framers. The goal of originalists is not to venerate the Founding Fathers long gone to their glory, but rather to restrain living judges from imposing their values on the whole country by interpreting in idiosyncratic ways what the Founders plainly said.

Richard Posner, Chief Justice of the U.S. Court of Appeals for the 7th Circuit, doesn't want judicial restraint because he views the Constitution and Bill of Rights as outdated and incapable of guiding modern society. He says that he sees no value spending any time at all studying the Constitution because: "Eighteenth-century guys, however smart, could not foresee the culture, technology, etc., of the 21st century. Which means that the original Constitution, the Bill of Rights, and the post-Civil War amendments (including the 14th), do not speak to us today."[17] In other words, the freedoms of religion, speech, assembly, and the press are outmoded concepts because they were articulated in the 18th century by white guys without smartphones! The world is indeed immensely more complicated today than when the immortal words of the Constitution and the Bill of Rights were penned, but their words still "speak to us" because they are timeless. Those documents were based on eternal principles and on a firm understanding of unchanging human nature and its demands.

Posner view is augmented by Barack Obama who, in a 2001 interview on Chicago radio station WBEZ-FM, revealed exactly what he tried to do as president: scrap the Constitution and spread the wealth. Obama bemoaned the fact that although the civil rights movement succeeded in gaining civil rights for all citizens, "The Supreme Court never ventured into the issues of redistribution of wealth, and of more basic issues such as political and economic justice in society." He wanted the Supreme Court "break free from the essential constraints that were placed by the founding fathers in the Constitution." He noted that the Constitution guarantees negative liberties, which says "what the Federal government can't do to you, but doesn't say what the Federal government or State government must do on your behalf."[18]

Obama obviously believes that government exists to mandate the level of wealth of its citizens to levels it considers acceptable, which is classical Marxist dogma. Both he and Posner see that the pesky Constitution sets inconvenient boundaries on government and guarantees the freedom to be left alone, which the modern Leviathan finds galling. Those who think like Obama and Posner see originalism as imprisoning us in eighteenth-century thinking and legal rigidity. They may have a point, but as Winston Churchill wrote in 1936: "It may well be that his very quality of rigidity, which is today thought to be so galling, has been a prime factor in founding the greatness of the United States. In the shelter of the Constitution, nature has been conquered, a mighty continent has been brought under the sway of man, and an economic entity established, unrivalled in the whole history of the globe."[19]

Supporters of a living Constitution may point out that the Supreme Court put its stamp of approval on slavery in *Scott v. Sandford* in 1857, and because originalists take the Constitution as they find it, they fear that such injustices could linger into perpetuity. Originalists find this absurd, and point out that justice issues are the proper domain of Congress, not the Supreme Court. Congress can amend the Constitution in ways that accord with contemporary views of morality, but until it does so, originalists argue, the justices are bound to find in the Constitution only that which is there. Chief Justice Taney put it this way in *Scott*: "If any of its [the Constitution's] provisions are deemed unjust, there is a mode described in the instrument itself by which it may be amended; but while it remains unaltered, it must be construed now as it was understood at the time of its adoption."[20] It was the executive branch's Emancipation Proclamation of 1863, legally cemented by the legislative branch's passage of the Thirteenth Amendment in 1865, that made slavery illegal, not a judicial ruling of unconstitutionality. When the demands of justice rise above the demands of the law, it is the legislature that should break the chains of law, not the judiciary.

Anger at the Court's vexatious verbal legerdemain is not limited to contemporary scholars. Even back in the early 1800s, Thomas Jefferson wrote of the Marshall Court: "The Constitution is a mere thing of wax in the hands of the judiciary, which they may twist and shape into any form they please." If the Constitution is a "living" document to be interpreted any way the Court's majority wants, why have a Constitution at all? If the Constitution is "living" in the sense that it can mean just about anything at all, then the old Constitution must be dead. We see its corpse being violated more than ever as the Supreme Court has taken on the role of judicial governance.

Take its ruling in *United States v. Windsor* in which the Court in a 5 to 4 decision declared a section of the Defense of Marriage Act (DOMA) restricting the definition of "marriage" and "spouse" to heterosexual unions to be unconstitutional. DOMA was passed by more than two-thirds of the House and more than three quarters of the Senate and signed into law by President Bill Clinton, but this was no concern to the five judges who believed they knew better. In his dissenting opinion, Justice Antonin Scalia made plain his distaste for the Court's usurpation of the proper role of Congress to make law and its violation of the principle of the separation of powers:

This case is about power in several respects. It is about the power of our people togovern themselves, and the power of this Court to pronounce the law. Today's opinionaggrandizes the latter, with the predictable consequence of diminishing the former. We have no power to decide this case. And even if we did, we have no power under the Constitution to invalidate this democratically adopted legislation. The Court's errors on both points spring forth from the same diseased root: an exalted conception of the role of this institution in America.

Depending on the issue and the ruling (whose ox is being gored), either liberals or conservatives may accuse the justices of judicial activism, and of course, both sides would be correct. I do not criticize legislating from the bench only when it offends conservative or religious sensibilities. I have written a book and articles criticizing judicial legislating when the Court was under the influence of hard-right laissez-faire and social Darwinist values in the early 20th century. During this period the Court repeatedly struck down legislation aimed at bettering the lives of the working classes. These decisions of the Court were soundly criticized at the time by progressives as judicial activism. If such activism was wrong then, it is wrong now.

My concern is that the only ox being gored when moral issues are before the Court belongs to Christians. Like Chancellor Kent, Justices send their clerks to get whatever legal justifications they can for the decision already made and dress it all up in legal hooey that can mean anything; only the ruling is clear—Christians lose again. This legal postmodernism does not want to give the plain words of the religious clauses of the First Amendment a "privileged reading" because, in this postmodernist world, words do not necessarily mean what they say and are "open to interpretation." This has placed important moral issues in the hands of a branch of government immune to public outrage and almost immune from repeal. In his first inaugural address, Abraham Lincoln warned us that the people no longer rule themselves if a majority of the unelected committee of nine can second-guess elected officials at all levels: "if the policy of the Government upon the vital questions affecting the whole people is to be irrevocably fixed by the decisions of the Supreme Court, the instant they are made in ordinary litigation between parties in personal actions, the people will have ceased to be their own rulers."[21]

Christian Rights Voted Down 5 to 4

The extent to which the Court has moved away from originalism may be gauged by the fact that up to 1940 fewer than 2 percent of its cases were resolved by 5-4 votes, but in the two most recent Courts, as of 2012, more than 20 percent have been decided this way.[22] Most of this 10-fold increase in 5 to 4 rulings have been the result of left-wing attacks on our Christian heritage. When the issue is a purely secular matter having limited implications beyond the issue in question, the Court tends to take on an originalist position and the vote is likely to be 9-0, or close to that. When the issue is a moral one impacting virtually everyone, the Court projects an Oracle of the Delphi-like image as the robed high priests issue (often separate) 5-4 decisions in the form of idiosyncratic interpretations of a relatively simple document. In doing so, they are stripping America of its Christian heritage and punishing Christians for daring to stand with God against Caesar when God and Caesar clash. The role of political ideology in these issues is apparent in the empirical analysis of Free Exercise and Establishment cases heard by the Supreme Court between 1996 and 2005 by professors Michael Heise and Gregory Sisk. Heise and Sisk found that Justices appointed by Democratic presidents rendered pro-religion votes only 30.1 percent of the time while Justices appointed by Republican presidents rendered pro-religion votes at almost double the rate (59%).[23]

The issue may be deeper than go beyond protesting the power of 5-4 opinions to one of examining the role of the swing voter in the Court. It was Sandra Day O'Connor for a long time, but on her retirement, it became Anthony Kennedy. It is truth without question that the Supreme Court is a highly politicized institution. The current Court has four solid liberals in Justices Breyer, Ginsberg, Sotomayor, and Kagan and four solid conservatives in Justices Roberts, Thomas, Alito, and Gorsuch. Gorsuch is the most recent justice, replacing the conservative icon, Antonin Scalia, in 2017. The votes of these Justices simply cancel each other out in cases involving moral issues and religious liberty, with conservative Justices generally seeking to protect it and liberal Justices generally trying to destroy it. If this is the case, the only opinion that really matters at present is that of Justice Kennedy. His single vote has more import than the 435 representatives and the 100 senators at the federal level combined, plus the thousands of state and local legislators. What a juristocracy boils down to is a dictatorship. In this nation of 320-plus million people, the only person whose opinion counts most of the time on moral issues that affect us all is that of the Court's swing voter.

If we must have a juristocracy sitting as a super-legislature with its self-proclaimed ability to divine the "correct" policy on all kinds of issues, we should ask why so many momentous Court decisions are based on 5-4 votes when other significant matters put to a vote elsewhere require more than a simple majority? It takes a supermajority of two-thirds of the Senate and House to amend the Constitution or to override a presidential veto of its legislation, but the Supreme Court needs only a 5-4 majority to override legislation. This is a clear indication of the kind of judicial supremacy that many of the Founding Fathers warned us about. Why should we not hold to the same supermajority principle when highly significant social and moral issues are before the Supreme Court?

Jeremy Waldron makes this point with reference to the Constitution of the State of Nebraska in which its Supreme Court consists of seven judges. The Nebraska Constitution states: "A majority of the members sitting shall have authority to pronounce a decision except in cases involving the constitutionality of an act of the Legislature. No legislative act shall be held unconstitutional except by the concurrence of five judges." Waldron goes on the say: "It seems like a good rule. So why is that not the decision-procedure on the Supreme Court of the United States?"[24] Amen to that.

Taking Back Full Legislative Power

If Congress does not like the practice of legislating from the bench, it should take its legislative powers back where the Constitution plainly put it. It could do this in a number of ways. One way would be to impose term limits for justices. Since the Constitution mandates life tenure (at a time when the life-span was about 50 years) for Supreme Court justices, this would probably require a Constitutional Amendment. This could perhaps be circumvented by retaining justices on the bench at lower levels; they would still be judges, but not judges with the final say. This is hardly a radical idea. Legal scholars Steven Calabresi and James Lindgren tell us that life tenure for Supreme Court Justices does not exist in any other democratic nation, and "it has also been rejected by 49 out of 50 U.S. states in setting up their state Supreme Courts. The life-tenured U.S. Supreme Court is thus an odd rarity among the world's high courts in continuing to retain its members for life."[25]

Term limits would assure that Justices would act more restrained in imposing their personal views—as they do among high court justices in other democracies—and perhaps goad them to act with a greater respect for the Constitution and the will of the people. According to a 2015 Reuters-Ipsos poll, there is widespread support for term limits, with two-thirds of Americans favoring 10-year term limit for Supreme Court justices. This issue is one sharing bipartisan support, with 66 percent of Democrats and 74 percent of Republicans supporting it. A paltry 17 percent of respondents supported life tenure.[26]

Another way would be to limit the Supreme Court to offer advisory opinions, as do many other national supreme courts. For instance, the United Kingdom Supreme Court may review a particular statute and issue a "declaration of incompatibility;" while it is taken seriously, it is not binding on the legislature. Such advisory opinions are anathema to the United States Supreme Court because it doesn't want to advise merely; it wants to rule. However, if this was to become the role of the Court, and a supermajority of two-thirds of the Court believed that a piece of legislation violates the Constitution, it can make that known to the legislative body that framed it through a "declaration of incompatibility" and ask it to consider the legislation further. This is the vision of separated powers that the Founders framed for the three branches of government. Each branch of government has a duty to show proper deference to another, but it is up to each to ascertain its own level of deference. After all, each branch has its own men and women learned in the Constitution, some with superior knowledge than possessed by many Supreme Court Justices. It is sheer hubris for the Justices to think that the wisdom of a bare 5-4 majority of them trumps the collective wisdom of these men and women.

It might prove instructive to heed the remarks of a British senior judge, Lord Bingham, on judicial governance. Noting that despite the recent establishment of an American style Supreme Court in Britain, Parliament continues to dominate: "The British people have not repelled the extraneous power of the papacy in spiritual matters and the pretensions of royal power in the temporal in order to subject themselves to the unchallengeable rulings of unelected judges."[27] This is a powerful sentence that should apply to the United States as well. More than 200 years earlier, Brutus (Robert Yates) anticipated Judge Bingham's concern about the power of an unelected judiciary. Brutus feared "the supreme court under this constitution would be exalted above all other power in the government, and subject to no control." He then compared the power of American high court judges to their English counterparts:

The judges in England are under the control of the legislature, for they are bound to determine according to the laws passed under them. But the judges under this [American] Constitution will control the legislature, for the supreme court are authorised in the last resort, to determine what is the extent of the powers of the Congress. They are to give the constitution an explanation, and there is no power above them to set aside their judgment. The framers of this constitution appear to have followed that of the British, in rendering the judges independent, by granting them their offices during good behavior, without following the constitution of England, in instituting a tribunal in which their errors may be corrected; and without adverting to this, that the judicial under this system have a power which is above the legislative, and which indeed transcends any power before given to a juridicial by any free government under heaven...When great and extraordinary powers are vested in any man, or body of men, which in their exercise, may operate to the oppression of the people, it is of high importance that powerful checks should be formed to prevent the abuse of it.[28]

However, the attack on Christianity is just as bad in Britain, which is also suffering from cultural degradation. Its university social science and humanities department are as infected as ours by the pernicious influence of the Frankfurt School's cultural Marxism. The words of Nola Leach of Britain's Christian Action Research and Education are all too familiar to American ears. Leach warns that Britain is:

> "sleepwalking into losing religious freedoms," thanks to a prevailing liberal culture that promotes a hierarchy of rights which demotes religion below all other considerations. "We now are heading towards a community where it's not just about live and let live – people are now saying, "you need to affirm my particular lifestyle and if that goes against your conscience, you have to do that". That's not equality; that's intolerance.[29]

Thus the British Parliament protects religious liberty no better than the U.S. Supreme Court, but at least the British public can throw the blighters out if it ever wakes from its sleepwalk.

Is Constitutional Amendment the Answer?

Assuming no action by the Congress to take back its legislative power, the only way we can hope to reestablish the republican democratic ethos the way the Framers intended it to be is to assure somehow that only Constitutional originalists be appointed to the Court. In a random telephone survey of 2,729 adult Americans from across the nation, 80 percent of Republicans and 42 percent of Democrats responded that appointing Justices who will interpret the Constitution as written rather than as they interpret it is an immediate priority.[30] If we were able to do this and the Court then handed down rulings abhorrent to contemporary standards of decency, as in the *Scott* case, then, as Justice Taney pointed out, the solution lies in the Constitution itself in the form of a Constitutional Amendment. It is in this sense that the Constitution is indeed "living" and flexible, but it would not be so flexible that it could be twisted by judicial whim into something entirely unrecognizable to its authors.

However, amending the Constitution is an arduous process requiring the assent of two-thirds of both Houses of Congress, but it should be when the aim is to overturn long-established laws and practices. If the various anti-Christian groups such as those mentioned in the previous chapter don't like an established law or practice, then convince your fellow Americans in the court of public opinion, not the anointed ones sitting in the marbled halls of Mount Parnassus. The amendment process has the benefit of being the *Constitutional* way of changing major tradition practice and laws rather than the u*nconstitutional* declarations of a bare majority of nine unelected lawyers.

Given the barriers to getting a Constitutional Amendment passed, Congress's power to overrule Supreme Court decisions has been exercised only four times in the history of the Republic; one in the 18th century, two in the 19th, and one in the 20th, although hundreds of amendments have been proposed. The first such case in which Congress used the amendment process to overrule the Supreme Court was *Chisholm v. Georgia* (1793) in which the Court ruled against of the state of Georgia's sovereign immunity claim, resulting in the Eleventh Amendment. The second is *Scott v. Sanford* (1856) in which the Court ruled that Congress had no power to prohibit slavery in the territories. This led to the passage of the Thirteenth Amendment in 1866 abolishing slavery. This Amendment legally cemented a fait accompli given that the slaves had already been freed by Lincoln's two Emancipation Proclamations. The third such case is *Pollock v. Farmers Loan and Trust Co.* (1895) in which the Court ruled that an income tax was unconstitutional. Congress proposed the Sixteenth Amendment in 1913 declaring that Congress has the power to lay and collect taxes. The final case is *Oregon v. Mitchell,* (1970) in which the Court ruled that Congress did not have the authority to set the voting age of people in state elections. This led to Twenty-Sixth Amendment in 1971 granting the right of any U. S. citizen 18 years of age or older to vote.

It is time to put the skids on the judicial governance that is eroding religious liberty in our country against the will of the great majority of Americans. Thomas Jefferson's words in the epigraph of this chapter are augmented by James Madison, who remarked in 1793 that judicial power over the legislature "can never be proper" and such was never intended by the Founders: "[A]s the courts are generally the last in making the decision [with respect to law], it results to them, by refusing or not refusing to execute a law, to stamp it with its final character. This makes the Judiciary department paramount in fact to the Legislature, which was never intended, and can never be proper."[31]

Sometimes we love Supreme Court decisions, and sometimes we hate them, but love them or hate them, it is still the ruling of a cabal of nine unaccountable super legislators. A ruling binding on all made by unaccountable individuals and which is almost immune to repeal fits the definition of despotism you will find in most dictionaries. Thomas Jefferson realized this long ago when he wrote in a letter to a Mr. Jarvis, in 1820: "To consider judges as the ultimate arbiters of all constitutional questions is a very dangerous doctrine indeed, and one which would place us under the despotism of an oligarchy."[32]

In more modern times, Justice Kennedy condemned the transgression of separation of powers, although he too often contributes to it. In his concurrence in *Clinton v. City of New York* (1998) he wrote: "Liberty is always at stake when one or more of the branches seek to transgress the separation of powers." The Supreme Court has all too often transgressed the separation of powers, and without knowing it, and has become the legal arm of the Frankfurt school's poisonous cultural Marxist agenda, striking down laws and practices that promote morality while imposing on us, laws and practices that most Americans find immoral. Many justices attended the same elite universities where the Frankfurters first set up shop in America, and at least some of its gristle rubbed off on the liberal wing of the Court. I am not asserting that any Justice is a committed cultural Marxist, but the Court is clearly if unwittingly, forwarding cultural Marxism's "long march through the institutions" agenda. In the next two chapters, we will examine the ways the imperial Court has interpreted the religious clauses of the First Amendment of late.

Endnotes

1. Quoted in Matthew, H. *Gladstone 1809-1898*, p. 276.
2. Pulliam, The quandary of judicial review, cited cases omitted).
3. Quoted in Dworkin, *Freedom's Law*, p. 342.
4. Peabody, Legislating from the Bench, p. 189.
5. Waldron, The core of the case, 1350.
6. Hamilton, A. (1788). The Judiciary Department. Federalist Papers No 78.
7. Yates, Anti- Federalist Paper No. 11.
8. Rodell 1955, p. 4.
9. Corbin and Walsh, p. 76.
10. Taylor, R., 1990, p. 42,
11. Corbin and Walsh, p. 77.
12. Sowell, Supreme Hypocrisy.
13. Quoted in Kaye, p. 22.
14. In Walsh and Hatch, Ideology, race, and the death penalty, p. 7.
15. Beard, C., The Supreme Court--Usurper or Grantee? p. 2.
16. George, R., Judicial Usurpation, p. 2.
17. Posner, The academy is out of its depth.
18. Obama's radio interview reposted by the American Thinker.
19. Churchill, W., What good's a Constitution? P. 743.
20. Walsh and Hemmens, p. 304.
21. Lincoln, A. Lincoln's first inaugural address.
22. Kuhn, D. The Incredible Polarization.
23. Heise and Sisk. Religion, schools, and judicial decision making.

24. Waldron, Five to four, p. 1697.
25. Calabresi and Lindgren, p. 38.
26. Hurley, Americans favor.
27. Cited in Grant, The rise of the juristocracy, p. 22.
28. Yates, The Power of the Judiciary.
29. Quoted in Edmunds, Britain is sleepwalking.
30. Miringoff and Carvallo, Religious liberty and the Supreme Court.
31. Madison, *Writings of James Madison*, p. 293
32. Jefferson, Thomas Jefferson on Judicial Tyranny.

Cases Cited

Chisholm v. Georgia, 2 U.S. 419 (1793).
Clinton v. City of New York, 524 U.S. 417 (1998).
Hurtado v. California, (110 U.S. 516 (1884).
Marbury v. Madison, 5, U.S. 137 (1803).
Oregon v. Mitchell, 400 U.S. 112 (1970).
Pollock v. Farmers' Loan & Trust Company, 157 U.S. 429 (1895).
Scott v. Sandford, 60 US 393 (1857).
United States v. Windsor, 570 U.S. __ (2013).

Chapter 5

Establishment Clause and Separation of Church and State

"We have believed that religious freedom cannot thrive in the absence of a vibrant religious community and that such a community cannot prosper when it is bound to the secular. And we have believed that these were the animating principles behind the adoption of the Establishment Clause."
Harry Blackmun, Justice of the United States Supreme Court

The Establishment Clause and its Meaning

Religion was so important to the Founding Fathers and to all Americans that they enshrined it in the very first words of the Bill of Rights as the "first freedom": "*Congress shall make no law respecting an establishment of religion, or prohibiting the free exercise thereof.*" The "no establishment" clause is a necessary foundation in the service of the "free exercise" clause because it protects the rights or those who may dissent from an established religion. The plain meaning of both clauses has been subjected to so much judicial sophistry over the last 70 years that left-wing secularists and atheists have come to believe that they mean not what they say, but rather that they proclaim an absolute and acrimonious divorce of church and state.

The Establishment Clause prohibits the United States Congress from creating a national church; the Church of the United States. After all, that is exactly what it says: "Congress shall make no law respecting an establishment of religion." This straightforward interpretation has evolved into a philosophy known as non-preferentialism. Non-preferentialism maintains that the Framers meant to forbid government policies and actions that prefer one religion over another; not to forbid policies that prefer religion over secularism. This view believes that government should give aid and comfort to religion, since it is the font of social morality if it does so in a non-preferential manner.

Non-preferentialism is closely allied with the accommodationist view that the purpose of the Establishment Clause is to protect the nation's religious pluralism. The new United States would privilege no one religion, and like-wise, it would dispense with theological support for the state. Adherents of this view believe that the government should accommodate religion when it performs the same functions that secular institutions do. That is, whenever government supports a secular institution such as public schools, charities, or hospitals it should support an analogous religious institution equally and allow them to function according to the tenets of their faith.

The non-preferential and accommodation views stand in stark contrast to strict separatism; that is, the belief that the Establishment Claus implies a ban on any government involvement in religious organizations whatsoever, even when the aid is based on neutral (non-preferential) criteria. This is the belief of secularists, atheists, and above all, cultural Marxists who want to obliterate religion completely from the public square and to create a thoroughly secular-ized society in which the political, civil, and social are one. Under this theory, the government is forbidden to approve anything religious, including our national motto "In God we Trust," legislative prayer, the invocation opening each session of the Supreme Court, and any number of other spoken and unspoken reminders that this country was founded on, and has prospered under, Christian principles.

Under the subtle but relentless push of radical leftists hostile to religion, this view has been prominent in state and national jurisprudence for some time. However, the historical evidence that the Framers intended strict separation of church and state is almost non-existent. In every state constitution in force after independence that mentioned "establishment," the term was used in conjunction with "preference," and never in terms of a strict separation.[1]

Why the Establishment Clause?

It was noted earlier that the American Revolution was a conservative one fought to uphold principles contained in the English Bill of Rights which they maintained the Parliament had violated. Unlike the French and Russian Revo-lutions, the Founders changed very little in terms of law and culture be-queathed to them by their British forefathers, and thus the American Revolu-tion was a conservative one designed to restore the old order of things. One thing the Founders radically changed, not only from the practices of the Brit-ish government but probably from every government that ever existed, was the non-establishment of a state religion. The Founding Fathers dedicated this new country to liberty, and the first liberty they intended to secure was religious liberty. Religious liberty could not be guaranteed if there is only one religion supported by the state in exchange for religious support of the state. In an 1814 letter to Horatio Spofford, Thomas Jefferson summed up the rela-tionship of church and state as it had long existed in Europe: "In every country and in every age, the priest has been hostile to liberty. He is always in alliance with the despot, abetting his abuses in return for protection to his own. It is error alone that needs the support of the government. Truth can stand by itself."

This kind of cozy relationship between priest and prince has been the norm ever since organized governments have existed in written history. The Code of Hammurabi dating back to around 1754 BC is one of the oldest written codes of law. King Hammurabi shrewdly buttressed the authority of the codes, and thus his own, with the approval of the gods. The prologue to the code reads: "Then Anu and Bel delighted the flesh of mankind by calling me, the renowned prince, the god-fearing Hammurabi, to establish justice in the earth, to destroy the base and the wicked, and to hold back the strong from oppressing the feeble: to shine like the Sun-god upon the black-haired men, and to illuminate the land."[2] The linking of the code to a deity was a piece of psychological gilding that was the template for the collusion of church and state in countries around the world.

The collision of church and state poses obvious problems for religious dissenters. There were religious dissenters in Europe ever since to rise of Christianity, such as Gnostics, Donatists, Lombards, and Cathars, but they kept wisely quiet most of the time. This changed rapidly when Martin Luther nailed his Ninety-Five Theses to the door of the Wittenberg Castle Church in 1515, setting the Protestant Reformation in motion. Luther's criticisms revolved around certain practices and dogmas of the Catholic Church, such as selling indulgences, purgatory, priestly confession, and the absolute authority of the Pope in religious matters. Luther translated the Bible into the vernacular and taught that it, not the Pope and his priests, was the only source of divinely revealed knowledge of salvation.

Luther's ideas found fertile soil coming as it did in the midst of the Renaissance, a cultural movement that profoundly affected intellectual life in Europe, and was aided by the mass production of Bibles made possible by Johannes Gutenberg's printing press. Luther's views met stout opposition from traditionalists, and Catholic and Protestant competition for state sponsorship led to numerous civil and interstate wars that devastated much of the continent. To end this religious strife, the various nations and principalities settled on the principle of *cuius regio, eius religio* ("Whose realm, his religion"). This meant that all individuals living in a given state must follow the religion of the state sovereign. This principle was embodied in the treaty known as the Peace of Augsburg in 1555 ending the religious wars (albeit, temporarily) and resulting in the legal division of Western Christian Europe into Protestant (Lutheran) and Catholic kingdoms.[3]

The Peace of Augsburg paid no heed to the issue of religious pluralism that was widespread among Protestants. The practice of any non-established religions was forbidden, and those who did were branded heretics and faced banishment, or worse if they did not repent. With the rise in popularity of Calvinism as a Protestant rival to Lutheranism came more conflict, including the Thirty Years War that engulfed much of Western Europe from 1618 to 1648. The war was sparked when Holy Roman Emperor, Ferdinand II of Bohemia, attempted to curtail the religious activities of his Protestant subjects, who appealed for aid to fellow Protestants in the empire. This war, or series of wars, ended with the Peace of Westphalia, which refers to the series of treaties that ended these religious wars. The Peace of Westphalia is seen by many historians as a profound turning point in the history of Western civilization by marking the beginning of the modern nation state. Among its many provisions was the abrogation of the Treaty of Augsburg's granting of sovereigns the right to control matters of religious faith in their territories. Ben Straumann views the treaty as a model for dealing with religious disagreements in a constitutional manner: "Clearly the treaties of Westphalia established a distinction between the public and the private, carving a sphere of purely private concern out of the public authority of the territorial ruler."[4]

The Peace of Westphalia meant that rulers no longer had the right to foist their religious convictions on their subjects; neither did they retain the power to interfere with their subject's religious will. The privileged status of established churches continued to exist, however, and people not in their fold continued to suffer discrimination, such as not being allowed to hold public office. Although this is an old European treaty, it arguably played a role in the deliberations that took place in Philadelphia in 1787. The Westphalian notion of sovereign states is one legal plank out of which the American Declaration of Independence was built, and the link between provisions for the free exercise of religion in the Treaty and the Religion Clauses of the American Constitution is evident. Two phrases appear in the Treaty of Munster, which is one of the two Westphalian treaties—the other being the Treaty of Osnabrück—that are remarkably like the religious clauses of the First Amendment in the American Bill of Rights. The first guarantees people "the free Exercise of their Religion" and the other describes "the Liberty of the Exercise of Religion."[5] America has lived up to the spirit of not foisting any religion upon its citizens, but government interference with "liberty of the exercise of religion" has been seriously eroded in an atmosphere in which one could take atheism as the evolving established religion of the United States.

Establishment as the Founders Meant It

To understand what is meant by an establishment of religion, I turn to Justice Joseph Story for the most authoritative view. Justice Story served on the Supreme Court for 34 years (from 1811 to 1845) and was acquainted with many of the men who penned the Constitution and the Bill of Rights. He had greater knowledge of the Constitution and wrote more books (12) and articles on the law, including his magisterial *Commentaries on the Constitution of the United States*, (three volumes) than all the current Supreme Court Justices combined. Justice Story first tells us the purpose of the Establishment Clause of the First Amendment:

> The real object of the First Amendment was, not to countenance, much less to advance Mahometanism, or Judaism, or infidelity, by prostrating Christianity; but to exclude all rivalry among Christian sects, and to prevent any national ecclesiastical establishment, which should give to a hierarchy the exclusive patronage of the national government. It thus cut off the means of religious persecution, (the vice and pest of former ages,) and of the subversion of the rights of conscience in matters of religion, which had been trampled upon almost from the days of the Apostles to the present age.[6]

Justice Story fervently believed that religion should be respected, accommodated, encouraged, and supported in a non-preferential manner. He would have been outraged by today's grotesquely distorted Establishment Clause jurisprudence that amounts to banning any support whatsoever for Christianity, and even denying Christians the liberty of exercising their faith in the public square. Story and his contemporaries saw the sole purpose of the Religious Clause was to deny the national government all power whatsoever to limit religious freedom Justice Story provides a hierarchy of three variations of the establishment from the weakest to the strongest:

> One, where a government affords aid to a particular religion, leaving all persons free to adopt any other; another, where it creates an ecclesiastical establishment for the propagation of the doctrines of a particular sect of that religion, leaving a like freedom to all others; and a third, where it creates such an establishment, and excludes all persons, not belonging to it, either wholly, or in part, from any participation in the public honours, trusts, emoluments, privileges, and immunities of the state.[7]

The first instance is a minimalist version in which support is given to a preferred religion but not to others, but there is no interference with the religious conscience of dissenters. In the second instance, the state officially establishes a particular set of doctrines but does not infringe the beliefs of dissenters. The third is the strong meaning of establishment in which all citizens must belong or suffer disabilities. This is "establishment;" saying voluntary prayers in schools and at football games, or Christian icons, in the public square is not even weak establishment in Story's hierarchy. However, all these things have been considered by a number of recent Supreme Court Justices to equate to the establishment.

An established religion is thus one that is legally recognized by the state as its official religion. This may mean that the state supports the established church financially and legally, perhaps even to the point of punishing dissenters. This is Story's strong form of religious establishment verging on theocracy. But a state established religion is not necessarily a theocracy in which rulers enjoy both secular and spiritual authority. In a theocracy, the marriage of religion and ruler is complete and absolute. State affairs and practices are assumed to be divinely guided, and the ruler may be cast as the deity's earthly representative, as in the notion contained in the concept of the "divine rights of kings."

An example of a modern theocracy is Saudi Arabia where the holy book of Islam, the *Qur'an*, serves as its constitution. The Saudis maintain religious courts governing all aspects of life and even has a special religious police force to monitor social compliance with sharia law. Non-Muslims living in Saudi Arabia cannot become citizens, and any Muslim converting to another religion, or anyone blaspheming Islam, may be put to death. Because the Qur'an was written in brutal times, and because it serves as a "God-given" constitution, current crimes and punishment in Saudi Arabia and in other Islamic states have maintained the same brutality to the present day. Punishments in Saudi Arabia include public beheading, amputations, stoning, and whipping, often for acts that are not even crimes in Western societies. Apostasy is punishable by death, as are many other offenses such as adultery, sorcery, murder, rape, witchcraft, homosexuality, and repeated drug abuse. Death by beheading is often followed by crucifixion so all may be witness to the consequences on non-conformity.[8]

As opposed to a theocracy, most modern states with established religions retain them mainly for traditional and ceremonial reasons—a weak kind of religious establishment that is weaker even than Story's minimalist definition. For instance, although the Church of England is the established religion of England, it is primarily like the monarch (who is officially the head of the Church of England), purely symbolic and ceremonial. It has no more power to influence the secular government than any other religion, nor does it receive supporting funds or special privileges from it. The establishment of the Church of England does not preclude the free worship of the multitude of religions that exist there, and all but the monarch can be of any religion or no religion at all. Britain is a secular society with an established religion just as it is a democratic society with a monarch.

It is not widely known that nine (some historians say eleven, depending on how strongly one defines establishment) of the thirteen American colonies had established religions at the time of the American Revolution. The Establishment Clause was written into the Constitution with the recognition that a plurality of denominations made an established national church politically unsupportable. Had the Founders established a national Church of the United States it would have endangered their efforts to forge national unity. If Congress had established the Episcopal Church, for instance, on the grounds that it constituted both the most numerous and influential denomination in the United States, it would have simultaneously disestablished churches in other states, such as the Congregational Church in Massachusetts and Connecticut, as well as angering members of the other denominations in the new nation. The Establishment Clause was thus a device for securing national unity and keeping religious passion out of American politics; in no way was it a declaration of hostility to religion or an excuse to interfere with the "free exercise thereof." Unfortunately, from the middle of the twentieth century onward, the Supreme Court has used it as if it this was exactly the intention. Some of these colonies collected taxes to support the established religion and even banished those not adhering to it. These colonies thus conformed to the strong variety of religious establishment, although most of them disestablished their religions within 25 years after the Revolution. Massachusetts was the last state to disestablish its religion, not doing so until 1834.[9]

The newly formed states were able to retain their established religions despite the Establishment Clause because the Constitution's Bill of Rights Amendments applied only to the federal government. Several states were reluctant to ratify the Constitution without clear-cut protections of individual rights, and the Amendments were specifically ratified to curtail federal encroachment on state and individual rights. The individual states retained all their sovereign powers except those specifically surrendered to the federal government, which are enumerated in Article I, Section 8 of the Constitution. The final Amendment of the Bill of Rights is the Tenth Amendment stating that: *The powers not delegated to the United States by the Constitution, nor prohibited by it to the States, are reserved to the States respectively, or to the people.* Since no powers involving religion were delegated to the United States, the Establishment Clause was not binding on the individual states.

This has changed over the years by the doctrine of incorporation that developed over time by various Supreme Court rulings relying on the authority of the Civil War Amendments, particularly the Fourteenth. Incorporation is a doctrine declaring that the restrictions and demands placed on the federal government by the Bill of Rights apply selectively or fully to the states. In essence, this means that states are now held to the same standards as the federal government with respect to incorporated constitutional rights. The Supreme Court has in piecemeal fashion applied the Bill of Rights to the states over many years and in many cases. The Establishment Clause of the First Amendment was not incorporated until 1947 in *Everson v. Board of Education* (discussed below), and in doing so has placed an interpretation of the clause that its authors would not recognize.

A number of scholars have claimed that Jesus sowed the seed of separation of the sacred and the secular when his enemies tried to maneuver him into answering the question of whether Jews should pay tribute to Rome: "Render therefore unto Caesar the things which are Caesar's; and unto God the things that are God's" (Matthew 22:20-22). This should not be interpreted as Jesus designating two entirely separate spheres to which people owe allegiance, or that he wanted a Godless state. Entirely separate spheres can lead to tragic choices if certain features of each sphere clash. If the sacred always prevails, we have a theocracy in which the state enforces religious dogma and punishes "heretics." If the secular always prevails, there is no religious liberty. The Founding Fathers saw too much of the former both at home and abroad and wanted no part of any established religion that the state could use to its advantage, just as the church could use the state to its advantage.

However, when political issues interact or clash with religious or moral considerations, some folks forget, or purposely ignore, the injunction to render onto God. These people view the secular sphere as absolute, and that the state is justified in making laws that govern even matters of religious conscience. They pour scorn on the idea that individual moral and religious conscience must always be sacrosanct and call Paul's response when ordered to stop preaching: 'We must obey God rather than any human authority' (Acts 5:29) superstitious bigotry. Because such people tend to be leftist worshipers of big government, they affirm that we owe taxes to Caesar but are blind to the fact that we owe everything to God. Nevertheless, there has been widespread interference in matters of religious conscience whereby religious believers have been coerced under the power of indictment into actions contrary to their beliefs. When people of good conscience have refused, many have paid huge financial and psychological costs. The Founding Fathers would have been appalled by this, for as James Madison said when arguing for a bill of rights to declare the freedom of religion: "There is not a shadow of right in the general government to intermeddle with religion. Its least interference with it would be a most flagrant usurpation."[10] Government grants itself the right to meddle with religion under the canopy of the Establishment Clause which, ironically, was meant to curtail exactly that.

Thomas Jefferson's "Wall of Separation"

The radical notion of a complete and sometimes hostile separation of church and state gained its first toe-hold in the 1947 case *Everson v. Board of Education*. This is the case in which the Supreme Court incorporated the Establishment Clause to the states and set the course for cases involving it from then on. As mentioned earlier, incorporation means that what once applied only to the federal government now applies to the states and opens the door to federal litigation against the states in religion-clause claims under the Fourteenth Amendment. *Everson* involved a New Jersey district school board using public funds to reimburse parents for bus fares to and from both public and parochial schools. In a 5 to 4 decision, the Supreme Court ruled that this did not violate the Establishment Clause. However, as was the case with *Marbury v. Madison*, the approach the Court took was of greater importance than its decision because:

> The *Everson* Court not only ascribed to the Establishment Clause separationist content, it imagined a past to confirm that interpretation. Both majority and dissent treated the history of the United States as if it were the history of Virginia. Despite dissimilarity of language, the Justices equated the Establishment Clause with Virginia's statute on religious freedom, thereby appropriating for the federal provision the separationist message and rhetoric of the state enactment. It was "sinful and tyrannical," wrote Jefferson, "to compel a man to furnish contributions of money for the propagation of opinions which he disbelieves."[11]

In the opinion of the Court majority, written by Justice Hugo Black, it relied on a novel interpretation of the Establishment Clause, stating that any government accommodation of religion is an unconstitutional establishment of religion:

> Neither a state nor the Federal Government can, openly or secretly, participate in the affairs of any religious organizations or groups and vice versa. In the words of Jefferson, the clause against establishment of religion by law was intended to erect 'a wall of separation between Church and State'...The First Amendment has erected a wall between

church and state. That wall must be kept high and impregnable. We
could not approve the slightest breach.

The words of Justice Black's opinion represent a radical change from a negative limit on federal power ("Congress shall make no law") to a positive federal
mandate to limit, nay, remove, religion from public life by erecting a wall to
close it in. Black's use of Jefferson's metaphor has turned the Establishment
Clause, once positively linked to the Free Exercise Clause as a protective, to a
weapon to attack it. It is if he magically found a contradiction between the
two Clauses, which should actually be read together like any other English
sentence. If they are properly read together as one, and if Black had read the
hundreds of historical statement of the men that went into crafting it (as opposed to jumping on an extra-Constitutional trope), he would never have
made a mistake. But given Black's animosity toward Christianity, it was no
mistake; he knew exactly what he was doing. Almost the entire historical case
for the strict separation of church and state notion rests with Jefferson's "wall
of separation" metaphor. The metaphor is clearly extra-constitutional since
Jefferson took no part in crafting the Bill of Rights, returning from his duties as
minister to France after it had been approved by Congress and sent it to the
states for ratification.[12]

Oddly, Black sided with the majority in stating that the school board's action *did not* violate the Establishment Claus because reimbursements were
made to parents of children of all faiths, and not to a religious institution. The
four dissenting Justices pointed out that Black's interpretation of the Establishment Clause ought logically to lead to the invalidation of the board's action. It is true that the board's actions should have been ruled unconstitutional if Black's contorted logic was to be the guide, but surely it is a giant leap
to say that a state helping parents to defray the costs of transporting children
of all faiths, or no faith, to school is tantamount to the United States, or at
least New Jersey, establishing an official religion. Thus, while the result in
Everson is consistent with the obvious meaning of the Establishment Clause,
Black's *reasoning*, with which four other justices seemed to concur, relies
upon an extra-constitutional "wall of separation" notion that became precedent in subsequent cases involving the Clause.

Justice Black was perhaps the Justice most hostile to religion that ever sat
on the Supreme Court. This may be explicable in terms of his background and
political views. Black was a New Deal Democrat, professional politician, and a
former member of the Ku Klux Klan and his white robes were always visible
beneath his judicial robes in religious cases. According to Black's biographer,
Howard Ball: Black "sympathized with the group's [the KKK's] economic,
nativist, and anti-Catholic beliefs."[13] Many issues involving aid to religious

institutions involved aid to parochial schools, which are overwhelmingly Roman Catholic. Perhaps Black had Catholics in mind when he contorted the plain meaning of the Establishment Clause to insist that it requires a "high and impregnable wall of separation" in which to imprison religion. But not only is Jefferson's "wall of separation" metaphor extra-constitutional, but the metaphor as currently interpreted is also inconsistent with Jefferson's actual practices and beliefs.

Jefferson's infamous metaphor is contained in a letter written in 1802 to the Danbury Baptist Association of Connecticut. The Danbury Baptists wrote complaining to President Jefferson about the infringement of their religious liberty by the Connecticut state legislature that supported the established Congregational Church. Citizens of Connecticut paid taxes to support the established church, and Congregationalists were privileged by state and local governments in a number of ways. In his response, Jefferson voiced sympathy for the Baptists in their opposition to the state's established religion and expressed support for the First Amendment's religious clauses. The full letter is reproduced below.

Gentlemen:

The affectionate sentiments of esteem and approbation which you are so good as to express towards me, on behalf of the Danbury Baptist association, give me the highest satisfaction. My duties dictate a faithful and zealous pursuit of the interests of my constituents, & in proportion as they are persuaded of my fidelity to those duties, the discharge of them becomes more and more pleasing.

Believing with you that religion is a matter which lies solely between Man & his God, that he owes account to none other for his faith or his worship, that the legitimate powers of government reach actions only, & not opinions, I contemplate with sovereign reverence that act of the whole American people which declared that their legislature should "make no law respecting an establishment of religion, or prohibiting the free exercise thereof," thus building a wall of separation between Church & State.

Adhering to this expression of the supreme will of the nation in behalf of the rights of conscience, I shall see with sincere satisfaction the progress of those sentiments which tend to restore to man all his natural rights, convinced he has no natural right in opposition to his social duties.

I reciprocate your kind prayers for the protection & blessing of the common father and creator of man and tender you for yourselves & your religious association, assurances of my high respect & esteem.[14]

The letter says absolutely nothing about limiting public religious expression; it only addressed state government interference with the public expression of faith, and is more sensibly read as "keep your hands off our churches and our religion." Jefferson was plainly not advancing the view that religion should be excluded from the public square. He did, after all, sign off in his capacity of President of the United States with the words: "I reciprocate your kind prayers for the protection & blessing of the common father and creator of man." What is more, during his two terms as President, he pursued policies and performed actions totally at odds with Black's "high and impregnable" wall notion. Jefferson approved the use of federal funds to build churches and to support Christian missionaries, so Jefferson was either a hypocrite for routinely violating his beliefs, or his use of the "wall of separation" metaphor has been grossly and purposely misinterpreted. Jefferson's wall was meant only to rip apart the cozy relationship that church and state had enjoyed in Europe which had caused such strife. The wall is supposed to protect religious believers from government interference, not to imprison them. Notice that Jefferson makes no promises to "see what I can do," because he could do nothing to interfere with Connecticut's laws. All he could do was to add his moral opinion should the Danbury Baptists wish to make his letter public. While stoutly opposing the established state churches that existed at the time, he recognized that he had to respect them. As David Barton sees it, the Danbury Baptists were concerned that a particular denomination was going to be recognized as an official national religion, and that Jefferson "calmed their fears by using the now infamous phrase to assure that the federal government would not establish any single denomination of Christianity as the national denomination."[15]

Jefferson's letter may also be read and interpreted in the context of his declaration in the Virginia Statute of Religious Freedom: "Almighty God hath created the mind free...." For Jefferson, the "wall of separation" exists to affirm natural rights, including those of faith and religious worship. The wall does not imprison the free exercise of religion; indeed, he affirms this free exercise of religion as a natural right. Jefferson simply affirmed in the Danbury Baptist letter the belief that the domination of one particular sect is inimical to religious freedom, and the only way to prevent this is a constitution forbidding the establishment of religion. This is the plain meaning behind the Establishment Clause. Neither does the metaphor mean that Jefferson was an enemy of religion. Professors Paul Butler and Alfred Scanlan highlight the high esteem in which Jefferson held religion: "Jefferson has written that religion was 'a supplement of law in the government of man,' and 'the alpha and omega of the moral law.'" [16] This hardly reveals a man who was hostile to religion. For Jefferson, the various denominations must stand on their own two feet; their survival and success depends on the force of their message and the faith and good example of their members, not on the coercion of the policeman's baton or the judge's gavel.

Although hundreds of individuals participated in some manner in the drafting of the Constitution and the Bill of Rights, James Madison was their main architect. Like Jefferson, Madison was deeply committed to religious liberty and to the notion that it was a necessary and valuable institution. In his *Memorial and Remonstrance against Religious Assessments* given before the General Assembly of the Commonwealth of Virginia, he said:

> Because we hold it for a fundamental and undeniable truth, "that Religion or the duty which we owe to our Creator and the manner of discharging it, can be directed only by reason and conviction, not by force or violence." The Religion then of everyman must be left to the conviction and conscience of every man, and it is the right of every man to exercise it as these may dictate. This right is in its nature an unalienable right...It is unalienable also because what is here a right towards men, is a duty towards the Creator... *This duty is precedent, both in order of time and in degree of obligation, to the claims of Civil Society.* Before any man can be considered as a member of Civil Society, he must be considered as a subject of the Governour of the Universe.

The Supreme Court and the Wall of Separation

Despite the countless statements favoring accommodation of religion and its importance to civil life made by the men who crafted the Constitution and the Bill of Rights, the Supreme Court has seen fit to focus on Jefferson's "wall of separation" metaphor and has used it to create a hostile interpretation of the religious clauses of First Amendment. The Court now reads the Establishment Clause as if Jefferson's figure of speech is written into it. Some Justices, however, have maintained the original plain meaning of the Establishment Clause. For instance, in *Zorach v. Clauson (1952)*, Justice William Douglas noted the growing hostility to religion in government and wrote: "But we find no constitutional requirement which makes it necessary for the government to be hostile to religion and to throw its weight against efforts to widen the effective scope of religious influence...We cannot read into the Bill of Rights such a philosophy of hostility to religion." Likewise, Justice Warren Burger in *Lynch v. Donnelly* (1984) wrote:

The concept of a 'wall' of separation between church and state is a useful metaphor but is not an accurate description of the practical aspects of the relationship that in fact exists. The Constitution does not require complete separation of church and state; it affirmatively mandates accommodation, not merely tolerance, of all religions, and forbids hostility toward any. Anything less would require the 'callous indifference' that was never intended by the Establishment Clause.

Chief Justice William Rehnquist perhaps voiced best how wrong Black's reading of Jefferson's metaphor was and how injurious to religious liberty it has proved to be. In his dissent in the *Wallace v. Jaffree* (1985) in which the Court used a strict separationist interpretation of the Establishment Clause to rule that silent prayer or "moment of meditation" in school was unconstitutional, Rehnquist wrote:

It is impossible to build sound constitutional doctrine upon a mistaken understanding of constitutional history, but unfortunately, the Establishment Clause has been expressly freighted with Jefferson's misleading metaphor for nearly 40 years...But the greatest injury of the "wall" notion is its mischievous diversion of judges from the actual intentions of the drafters of the Bill of Rights. The "crucible of litigation" is well adapted to adjudicating factual disputes on the basis of testimony presented in court, but no amount of repetition of historical errors in judicial opinions can make the errors true. The "wall of separation between church and State" is a metaphor based on bad history, a metaphor which has proved useless as a guide to judging. It should be frankly and explicitly abandoned.

Reinforcing the Wall: The Lemon Test

Rather than being "frankly and explicitly abandoned," the wall of separation was built higher and reinforced in *Lemon v. Kurtzman* (1971). In this case, the Supreme Court ruled unconstitutional a Pennsylvania act allowing the state to partially reimburse parochial schools for the salaries of teachers and a Rhode Island act that used state funds to supplement salaries at parochial elementary schools (primarily Catholic schools). This case established the so-called "Lemon test." The Lemon test lays out a three-pronged test detailing the requirements for state legislation concerning religion:

1. The statute must have a secular legislative purpose.
2. The principal or primary effect of the statute must not advance nor inhibit religious practice.

3. The statute must not result in an "excessive government entanglement" with religious affairs.

If any of these prongs are violated, the legislation is deemed unconstitutional under the Establishment Clause. While many Justices have opined that the Lemon test is a lemon, it remains a guideline for them. The bitterness can be tasted even in the ruling in the case that gave the test its name. In terms of the first prong; surely the legislative acts in question had a secular purpose: that of educating children while removing some of the financial burdens from the taxpayer, since the families of children who attend parochial schools bear most of the financial burden. Yes, it also had a religious purpose of adding spiritual and moral dimensions to the curriculum, and that assuredly serves a valuable secular purpose. I assume that all save cultural Marxists with their anti-Christian agenda agree with this.

As for the second prong, the acts ruled unconstitutional did advance religion in ways the Founders would have approved, but the Courts ruling just as surely inhibited religion by negatively impacting parochial school's ability to function. Catholic schools have been far more effective in educating disadvantaged minority students than public schools that have frequently failed them. Education scholars Anthony and Renee Setari have pointed out that the benefits of attending Catholic schools for minority children have been demonstrated repeatedly. They get better grades and demonstrate fewer behavioral problems. They add: "the closing of Catholic schools has impacted the educational outcomes of minority students and the overall social quality of the neighborhoods in which these schools were located."[17]

How is the closing of parochial schools serving any secular purpose except advancing the cause of cultural Marxism? It burdened the parents of children attending those schools because they must now pay higher tuition fees as well as support non-parochial schools with their taxes. The only way that can avoid this unfair double cost is to withdraw their children and place them in public schools, thus depriving their children of the moral compass they desired for them. The state discriminates against all religions because none can avail themselves of the public funding available to their sectarian counterparts. As legal scholar Arnold Loewy points out: "No serious scholar has ever contended that the Establishment Clause was intended to bespeak hostility towards religion. Yet that is exactly what happens in a regime that allows the State to pay a student's tuition or an English teacher's salary at a private non-religious school, but denies the same to students and teachers at a private religious school"[18] The third prong is addressed in the next chapter dealing with the Free Exercise Clause.

The Coercion Test

The Coercion test arose out of Justice Anthony Kennedy's accommodationist view expressed in *Allegheny County v. Greater Pittsburgh ACLU* (1989), in which the Supreme Court struck down the city of Pittsburgh's Christmas holiday display containing a crèche and a menorah. Kennedy proposed that the concept of "coercion" explains the limitations imposed on the states by the Establishment Clause. This test appears to be fully in accordance with the original and plain meaning of "establishment;" that is, forcing people to conform to a state-sanctioned religion. The coercion test proclaims that the government violates the Establishment Clause if it (1) provides direct aid to religion in a way that tends to establish a state church, or (2) coerces people to support or participate in religion against their will. In his dissenting opinion, Justice Kennedy gives us some comfort that there are always Justices on the Court who strive to protect our religious liberties, although Kennedy is not always as protective:

> Government policies of accommodation, acknowledgment, and support for religion are an accepted part of our political and cultural heritage. Rather than requiring the government to avoid any action that acknowledges or aids religion, the Establishment Clause permits government some latitude in recognizing and accommodating the central role religion plays in our society. Any approach less sensitive to our heritage would border on latent hostility toward religion, as it would require government in all its multifaceted roles to acknowledge only the secular, to the exclusion and so to the detriment of the religious.

Yet even this reasonable test has been used against the religious practice by a very broad interpretation of coercion. Coercion is typically defined as the use of force or intimidation to obtain compliance, but using the coercion test the various courts have ruled against school prayers at graduation, the singing of Christmas carols and the Pledge of Allegiance because these things have "offended" one or two delicate individuals.

In short, the Supreme Court has created a number of conflicting Establishment tests resulting in a confusing labyrinth that both contradicts the text of the Constitution and the cultural history of the United States. The Court appears to be operating from a "No one should be offended by public affirmations of religious faith" stance, and tends to rule accordingly. In this Republic of free citizens in which its legitimacy is supposed to depend on the opinions and aspirations of "we the people," every moral opinion and aspiration should have access to the public square. If the religion of our forefathers is somehow a blight on society rather than a blessing as the foundation of public morality, the people of each state (as outlined in the Tenth Amendment) should deliberate on it and fight it out at that level, as Thomas Jefferson said that that they should. The doctrines of republican democracy are violated when such matters are left to an elitist and unelected federal judiciary, many of whom have demonstrated hostility to Christianity, make those decisions for us by legal fiat. It is tragic that the Supreme Court cannot fathom, or will not heed, the considered opinions of the Founding Fathers. Robert Natelson, one of America's leading constitutional scholars, notes that the foundational values of America voiced by the Founding Fathers, converge on the basic principle that:

> Government should, directly or indirectly, foster religion. In this climate of public opinion, no Establishment Clause erecting a "wall of separation" between religion and state ever would have been adopted or even seriously proposed...For them, the relationship between good government and religion was interactive and symbiotic, rather than rigid and distant.[19]

But of course, the stalwart Christians who drafted the Constitution could not have imagined an America so debased as to have most of its important institutions—including the law—openly attacking the very values and practices that informed its drafting. Of course, the Constitution was written by rich white men, so perhaps we should scrap it and write a new one. We see such this idea being seriously suggested in left-wing articles, books, and blogs. This time we can leave Christian morality out of it altogether and infuse it with the values of the hard left. It is ironic that Thomas Jefferson, a champion of free speech and religious freedom who, because of his unfortunate "wall of separation" trope, has become a folk hero to those leftists who would deprive us of these precious rights. The new Constitution could be drafted by a committee of former Obama czars with a postmodernist professor, or two hired to actually put their ideas in real fuzzy writing so that it is entirely open to any and all interpretations. It would emphasize security over freedom, equality over equity, and a command economy over the free market—that much at least would be crystal clear. In short, it will be in all regards the opposite of the Constitution that built this nation, but one of which Georg Lukacs, Antonio Gramsci, and Barack Obama, would heartily approve.

Endnotes

1. Antieau, Downey, and Roberts: *Freedom from Federal Establishment.*
2. Edwards, *Hammurabi, King of Babylonia.* p. 23.
3. Straumann, The peace of Westphalia.
4. Ibid, p. 182.
5. Christenson, Liberty of Exercise of Religion, p. 726.
6. Story, *Commentaries on the Constitution of the United States.* p.728.
7. Ibid, p.725.
8. Hatch and Walsh, p. 318.
9. Kaminski, Religion and the Founding Fathers, p. 19.
10. Madison, The Founder's Constitution.
11. Jeffries and Ryan, A political history, p. 285.
12. Natelson The original meaning of the Establishment Clause.
13. Ball, Hugo L. *Black: Cold Steel Warrior,* p.16).
14. Jefferson, Jefferson's Letter to the Danbury Baptists.
15. Barton, The origin of the phrase 'Separation of Church and State.' p. 41.
16. Butler & Scanlan Wall of Separation, p. 290.
17. Setari & Setari, Trends in Catholic school, p 5.
18. Loewy, The positive reality and normative virtues, p. 539.
19. Nateldson, Original Meaning, p. 119.

Cases Cited

County of *Allegheny v. American Civil Liberties Union,* 492 U.S. 573 (1989)
Everson v. Board of Education, 330 U.S. 1 (1947)
Lemon v. Kurtzman, 403 U.S. 602 (1971)
Lynch v. Donnelly, 465 U.S. 668 (1984).
Wallace v. Jaffree, 472 U.S. 38 at 93 (1985).
Zorach v. Clauson, 343 U.S. 306 (*1952*).

Chapter 6

Religious Liberty:
The Free Exercise Clause

"The liberty enjoyed by the people of these states of worshiping Almighty God agreeably to their conscience, is not only among the choicest of their blessings, but also of their rights."
George Washington-first President of the United States

The Free Exercise Clause: Then and Now

The Free Exercise Clause of the First Amendment that forbids the United States Congress to pass any law prohibiting "the free exercise of religion" was the product of religious pluralism in America's colonies and states. It is yoked to the Establishment Clause for this very reason. Although the Establishment Clause refers to institutions (church and state) and the Free Exercise Clause refers to individuals, the two clauses depend on one another for their effectiveness in guaranteeing "essential rights and liberties." Unfortunately, the Supreme Court has been able to decouple the Clauses over time and has used the Establishment Clause for nearly 70 years to eviscerate the Free Exercise Clause. This decoupling has resulted in a much-written-about "tension" between the two clauses; a tension that those who wrote them would not recognize. Guided by the *Lemon* test and other extra-Constitutional inventions, the Court has shown a strong tendency to interpret the Free Exercise Clause such that any "entanglement" of state and religion of even the most negligible nature is a violation of the Establishment Clause. The situation is such at present that if individuals and institutions dare to take the Free Exercise Clause seriously and act upon its guarantees, their actions amount to an establishment of religion. The "entanglement" claim is effectively turned against free exercise claims as if the Free Exercise Clause is itself unconstitutional.

The incorporation of the religious clauses of the Fourteenth Amendment supplied the federal courts with inroads to monitor religious issues at the state level. The Free Exercise Clause restrains Congress from passing laws impinging on religious liberty and says nothing about the state, judicial, or executive branch impingement, thus the Fourteenth Amendment adds extra layers to the free exercise of religion. Although it does not specifically mention religious rights, what has come to be called the "liberty clause" encompasses all rights, including religious rights. The relevant section of the Fourteenth Amendment reads: "No state shall make or enforce and law which shall abridge the privileges and immunities of citizens of the United States; nor shall any State deprive any person of life, liberty, or property, without due process of law; nor deny and person within its jurisdiction the equal protection of the laws." Above all, the liberty clause was designed to protect liberties deemed fundamental, which are those rights enumerated in the First Amendment—freedom of religion, speech, association, press, and petition.

The Supreme Court incorporated the due process clause of the Fourteenth Amendment in *Cantwell v. Connecticut* (1940). The case involved Jehovah's Witnesses Newton Cantwell and his two sons going door-to-door handing out pamphlets in a largely Catholic neighborhood. One of the pamphlets contained a strong attack on the Catholic Church, which so incensed two citizens that they complained. The Cantwell's were arrested and charged with failure to obtain a required solicitors certificate and inciting a breach of the peace. The Cantwells responded that the government had no right to interfere with their free exercise of religion, and thus their rights had been violated. The Supreme Court agreed and stated that citizens had a right of free expression as well as freedom of belief. Justice Owen Roberts wrote in a unanimous opinion something that later Justices have ignored—people actually have the inalienable right to *act* on their faith:

> The constitutional inhibition of legislation on the subject of religion has a double aspect. On the one hand, it forestalls compulsion by law of the acceptance of any creed or the practice of any form of worship. Freedom of conscience and freedom to adhere to such religious organization or form of worship as the individual may choose cannot be restricted by law. On the other hand, it safeguards the free exercise of the chosen form of religion. Thus the Amendment embraces two concepts—freedom to believe and freedom to act.

However, by a slow but steady accretion of cases, the Court has managed to turn the religious clauses against each other by maintaining that acting on one's faith in some circumstances amounts to the religious establishment. These cases have provided Constitutional backing for removing religion from the public square. But as law professor Michael Paulsen states it: "The Establishment Clause of the First Amendment does not in any way authorize, and the Free Speech and Free Exercise Clauses do not permit, direct government discrimination against religion, religious persons, religious groups, or religious expression in government programs, policies, benefits, or forums. Ever."[1] But the government does exactly that.

Religious Free Exercise: Congress, Obama, and the ACLU

The United States Congress is at the forefront of defending America's religious heritage and has a more fundamental understanding of the Religious Clauses than the courts. Section 1 of U.S. Code § 6401, passed by Congress on October 27, 1998, reads:

> The right to freedom of religion undergirds the very origin and existence of the United States. Many of our Nation's founders fled religious persecution abroad, cherishing in their hearts and minds the ideal of religious freedom. They established in law, as a fundamental right and as a pillar of our Nation, the right to freedom of religion. From its birth to this day, the United States has prized this legacy of religious freedom and honored this heritage by standing for religious freedom and offering refuge to those suffering religious persecution.[2]

Unfortunately, these lofty phrases have become just words on paper as the courts have gutted their meaning by treating the Free Exercise Clause guarantees of religious conscience with no more significance than those given to secular systems of belief. This plundering of our religious rights was particularly brutal under the Obama administration. We have arrived at a time in our history when William Bennett has to ask "Have we come to the point where it is now considered a secular blasphemy to acknowledge the name of God at all?"[3]

Indeed we have reached that point. In June of 2016, retired Air Force Master Sergeant Oscar Rodriguez was manhandled by three airmen and removed from a colleague's retirement ceremony because during the flag folding part of the ceremony he used that three letter word: "God."[4] The video of his forceful removal went, as they say, viral on the Internet. Then there is the Department of Justice defunding a Young Marines chapter and a youth diversion program because its oath mentions God. A sheriff's youth diversion program with voluntary student-led prayers met the same fate.[4] Even worse, the Department of Veterans Affairs banned prayers at funeral services in Houston that contain the words "God" and "Jesus," regardless of the wishes of the bereaved families.[6] These families and friends were apparently unaware that the Obama administration's linguistic switch to "freedom of worship" from "free exercise of religion" stripped them of the right to use God's name in public. "Freedom of worship" is not the same as the "free exercise of religion" meaning in the Constitution. The former means simply that you can worship where and when you want, but leave the message behind in the church; the latter means that you are free to act on that message in the public square without fear of reprisal. The plain reading of the Free Exercise Clause embraces both the freedom to believe and freedom to act, as Justice Roberts maintained, but many modern Justices do not see this. The right to believe in God and his commands is enfeebled without a corresponding right to exercise it publically.

The erosion of religious liberty began very slowly and silently in 1947 with Justice Black's "wall of separation" in *Everson v. Board of Education,* so few people have noticed. The "slow but sure" strategy is exactly what cultural Marxism recommends as the one best suited to its aims. James Madison's warned us about such a strategy in his Speech in the Virginia *Ratifying Convention on Control of the Military* long before that hideous philosophy saw daylight: "There are more instances of the abridgement of the freedom of the people by gradual and silent encroachments of those in power than by violent and sudden usurpations."[7] The erosion back-peddled a few times, picked up speed after the sexual revolution of the 60s, and really emerged as a serious threat during the Obama administration. The Obama administration actively worked to intimidate religious believers in churches, charities, and small businesses with his mandates that they violate their consciences, making it "increasingly difficult for them to run a business or operate in the public square in accordance with their convictions."[8]

Despite Obama's hostility to religious freedom, he evokes the notion when it suits him. In one of his TV addresses, he characterized Donald Trump's plea to temporarily ban Muslims from entering the United States and Ted Cruz's plea to increase surveillance of Muslim neighborhoods, as "contrary to our character, our values, and to our history as a nation built around the idea of religious freedom." The implication was that Trump's and Cruz's pleas were motivated by Islamic animus. However, the pleas came in response to the 2015-2016 terrorist attacks in Paris and Brussels and in the context of plans to allow up to 100,000 Muslim refugees to enter the United States. Contrary to Obama's intimation, they were made on pragmatic safety grounds and not at all on religious grounds. We know with almost certainty that these refugees will be infiltrated by ISIS terrorists no matter how completely we think we have vetted them. Who doubts that ISIS would let such a golden opportunity go begging? Obama attacks religious freedom for Christians with his administration's policies, but he wanted to bring the threat of more Islamic terrorism to our shores in the name of religious freedom.

But the threat for the Obama administration is over, and Obama has left the stage to reflect on his legacy of dividing Americans by race, gender, ethnicity, and wealth. William Donohue reminds us that the threat long preceded him: "Removing religion from the womb of culture has become the practiced virtue of the ACLU [American Civil Liberties Union] over the past several decades."[9] He goes on to say that: "Separationist groups such as the ACLU, People for the American Way, and Americans United for Separation of Church and State are doing all they can to sweep religion's influence out of every nook and cranny of Americans' public life."[10] Donohue wrote this in 1985 when few perceived that the threat would become such that in today's morally degraded culture has led to a situation where: "the core of religious exercise gets no more protection than the practice of throwing rice at a church wedding." [11] This is music to the ears of cultural Marxists since we saw Gramsci's agenda in chapter 1 is to alter the American mind "so that it would become not merely a non-Christian mind but an anti-Christian mind." The ACLU is happy to advance this cause at every opportunity.

Ralph De Toledano, philosopher, journalist, prolific author, ex-socialist, and avid opponent of cultural Marxism wrote scathingly of the ACLU: "The ACLU has from its inception encouraged political and moral anarchy…it prefers that no one smarten up…about the aims and principles of its founder, Roger Baldwin, who wrote in 1935 that "Communism is the goal" In its early days, the ACLU was not shy about making known its agenda.[12]

The ACLU is not a communist organization, but it is definitely left-wing and no friend of Christianity. The ACLU has eagerly gone to the mat on religious freedom grounds defended peyote-smoking Native Americans, the right of turban-wearing Sikh men to join the army, Muslim prisoners to keep their beards, and the Santeria cult's right to slaughter animals ritualistically. When it comes to Christians declining involvement in private commercial activities on Christian grounds, religious freedom no longer applies. Perhaps ACLU is not anti-religious, just anti-Christian. I agree with the ACLU in the religious cases they have defended but find it strange that they are fine with defending drug-smoking, facial hair, turbans, and animal slaughter, but not with cases involving private voluntary commercial exchange that should be no business of the state. Rather than defending religious liberty, the ACLU has actually colluded with the state on numerous occasions to punish religious believers or to refuse to violate their religious beliefs. The leftist lawyers of the ACLU could care less that wanting to smoke dope, keep facial hair, or slaughter animals in the face of state objections is hardly in the same class as the state ruining the lives of conscientious Christians on behalf of other people who could have obtained such things as flowers, cakes, temporary accommodations, photographs, and birth control devices elsewhere with little or no trouble.

Interpreting the Free Exercise Clause

The Free Exercise Clause guarantees not just private beliefs; it explicitly says "exercise," which denotes that public actions not endangering the state or the public are protected. What good is the right to believe if it can't be publically expressed? As philosopher Roger Trigg says: "Totalitarian governments are no doubt quite satisfied for religious believers to think what they want as long as it is never 'manifested'...religion is public, not private, communal, not just individual, and a matter of action and not just propositional belief."[13] Obama's substitution of "freedom of worship" for "free exercise of religion" has made it possible to constrain religious expression in this sense by affording those who claim to be "offended" by Christians acknowledging God anywhere outside the confines of their churches or homes access to the courts to seek relief and, not incidentally, monetary compensation. Christians, however, cannot seek similar relief when offended by tax-supported public displays of shameful immorality and anti-Christian blasphemy such as Serrano's infamous *Piss Christ*. Whether one is religious or not, one should find this trend toward enfeebling religion frightening. If the culture has degraded so far as to allow the government to piecemeal strip us of what all the Founding Fathers, without exception, considered an inalienable right, it can strip us of all rights.

Despite assurances from the authors of the Religious Clauses that their words can be taken at face value, the Supreme Court examines them as if they were the ladies of Bletchley Park trying to decipher Germany's WW II Enigma code. The clauses mean exactly what they say and contain no cryptic meaning. Stephen Pepper notes that many provisions of the Bill of Rights contain buffering language that moderates their impact, and thus making them subject to different interpretations, such as the right to be free of "unreasonable" (what is "unreasonable?") searches, or that "excessive" (what is "excessive"?) bail or "cruel and unusual" punishment (what exactly does that mean?) be imposed. Compared to these rights, he points out that the Free Exercise Clause is "singularly absolute: 'Congress shall make no law...prohibiting the free exercise [of religion].'"[14] James Madison, the author of the religious clauses, considered religious liberty the bedrock of all liberty: "And he enshrined it in our Constitution, and so etched in our national consciousness, a principled and practical commitment to that liberty that has helped us to remain a free society ever since."[15] Take away this most fundamental of liberties or water it down to mean only freedom of private belief and worship, and we no longer have a free society.

We have seen how the Supreme Court has been chipping away at the Free Exercise Clause by using its radical relativistic interpretation of the Establishment Clause. Alexander Hamilton predicted as much in *Federalist Paper No. 78* where he warned that if there are no constraints on the judiciary, they will engage in judicial lawmaking of the sort that has been used to attack religious liberty. He wrote: "To avoid an arbitrary discretion in the courts, it is indispensable that they should be bound down by strict rules and precedents, which serve to define and point out their duty in every particular case that comes before them."

The practice of binding "by strict rules and precedents" is formally known as *stare decisis*. *Stare decisis* is Latin for "stand by things decided," and is the common law principle stating that courts should adhere to principles established by decisions in earlier cases. In his dissenting opinion in *Lynch v. Donnelly* (a 1984 case challenging the legality of Christmas decorations on city property) Justice Brennan commented that this long practice of common law has been purposely overlooked by the desire of the Court "to alter its analysis from Term to Term in order to suit its preferred results." Constitutional scholar Gerald Walpin notes that, "the majority in one [Supreme Court] decision proudly threw Establishment Clause stare decisis to the junk heap, by extolling the Court's lack of consistency as "sacrific[ing] clarity and predictability for flexibility—thereby admitting their failure to declare a rule of law that would—indeed, should—overcome personal views of individual Justices."[16] Few things better illustrate the Court's desire to eliminate God from the public square than the Court ignoring all pre-*Everson* precedent while paying strict attention to *Everson's* "wall of separation" precedent.

Precedent itself thus becomes problematic if it is not firmly grounded in Constitutional principles. When Constitutional principles and precedent are one and the same, all is right in the legal world. When they are not, we begin to find ourselves with a body of law that is nominally Constitutional but may bear little resemblance to the principles embedded in the document. In other words, once the Supreme Court hands down a ruling based on extra-Constitutional grounds, such as Jefferson's wall metaphor, those grounds magically become Constitutional. As a Constitutional law professor, Roger Pilon puts it: "It requires but a casual acquaintance with our constitutional history, however, to appreciate that many of today's constitutional precedents are derived from the Constitution by only the most strained reasoning."[17]

My intention is not to cast Supreme Court Justices as evil men and women purposely conspiring to strip us of our religious liberties. Many of them have been robust supporters of our rights, as the numerous 5-4 decisions attest. Some of them have been hostile to religion, as other Justices have pointed out, and with so many of them wedded to the idea that the Constitution should be a "living document," they are going with the flow of the times. As such, they are unwitting dupes of cultural Marxism's ever-tightening hand on the moral ambience of modern society. They are also slaves to their own aggrandizement as the sole interpreters of the document entrusted to them, and as "the priesthood that rules."

If judges cannot understand the plain words of the religious clauses, perhaps they should go to the source. In his first inaugural address in 1809, President James Madison stated exactly what they mean, to wit: "to avoid the *slightest interference* with the right of conscience or the functions of religion, so wisely exempted from civil jurisdiction." It is a mystery why the high priests of the Supreme Court cannot heed the plain words of the author of the clauses instead of twisting their meanings beyond his recognition as if they were postmodernist literature professors rather than judges.

We would still have freedom of religious exercise as Madison understood it if the Constitution was still read in "a sense most obvious to the common understanding at the time of its adoption," as Justice Oliver Wendell Holmes once said. Justices should be ruling according to what the Constitution *does* say, not what they believe that it *should* say. Furthermore, far from any hint of approval of government hostility to Christianity, Madison closed his inaugural address with these reverent words: "[W]e have all been encouraged to feel in the guardianship and guidance of that Almighty Being whose power regulates the destiny of nations, whose blessings have been so conspicuously dispensed to this rising Republic, and to whom we are bound to address our devout gratitude for the past, as well as our fervent supplications and best hopes for the future."

Free Exercise Clause and Compelling State Interest

James Madison believed that the state could interfere with religious exercise if, and only if, in performing such exercise the state would "be manifestly endangered." Mason's modifying language did not make it into the wording of Bill of Rights, but it signaled that the Free Exercise Clause would have limitations when there is a conflict between a person's interest in the free practice of religion and legitimate state interests involving safety and security. Thus, while the Framers consciously and deliberately chose to draft the Free Exercise Clause in absolute terms, Madison's thoughts on the matter have entered national jurisprudence.

Sincere religious belief cannot grant a person an excuse for criminal acts that unambiguously "manifestly endangers" the state. The 1993 bombing of the World Trade Center that killed six people and injured over a thousand is one such example. It was masterminded by Sheik Omar Abdel Rahman, who justified his actions at his sentencing hearing as his religious duty to wage war on the infidel. There can be no justification, religious or otherwise, for murder and mayhem. Nor can society allow the mass suicide/murder of 909 people of a sect led by Jim Jones. Jones' sect practiced what he called "Apostolic Socialism," which gave him the right to have multiple sexual encounters with both sexes and of all ages belonging to his "flock." The vast majority of free exercise/state interest conflicts are not, of course, as extreme as these.

Sometimes government passes a neutral laws that incidentally impinges on certain religious beliefs or practices. If an individual or group contests the law claiming that their beliefs or practices should be accommodated (afforded an exception from the law), the courts use one of three "standards of review" to assess the merits of the case: rational basis, heightened scrutiny, or strict scrutiny. If a court concludes that there is a fundamental liberty (the right to privacy, to vote, travel interest or suspect classification (race, religion, national origin) at stake, it will use the *strict scrutiny* test. To pass strict scrutiny, the law must be shown to further a "compelling governmental interest," and be "narrowly tailored" to achieve that interest. The heightened, or *intermediate scrutiny*, the standard is applied to so-called quasi-suspect groups (gender, age, the legitimacy of birth, and increasingly to sexual orientation). The least restrictive standard of review is the *rational basis test*. Under this test the courts assume a law to be Constitutional if it is rationally related to a legitimate government purpose even if it is not necessarily compelling.

The first Supreme Court case involving the Free Exercise Clause came almost 100 years after the ratification of the Bill of Rights in *Reynolds v. United States* (1878). George Reynolds was a member of the Church of Jesus Christ of Latter-Day Saints which at that time believed, circumstances permitting, that it was the duty of male members to practice polygamy, and if they did not they faced eternal damnation. After a long dissertation on the history of religious freedom in the United States, the Court noted that:

> Polygamy has always been odious among the northern and western nations of Europe, and, until the establishment of the Mormon Church, was almost exclusively a feature of the life of Asiatic and of African people. At common law, the second marriage was always void, and from the earliest history of England polygamy has been treated as an an offence against society...we think it may safely be said there has never been a time in any State of the Union when polygamy has not been an offence against society...polygamy leads to the patriarchal principle, and which, when applied to large communities, fetters the people in stationary despotism, while that principle cannot long exist in connection with monogamy.

The Court found no Biblical support for the practice of polygamy that would lend credence to Reynolds' claim. A number of characters in the Old Testament such as Solomon and David were polygamous, but there is a difference between the Bible describing ancient practices and affirming them. Although the Bible never explicitly condemns polygamy (except perhaps in the Ten Commandment's injunctions against adultery and coveting your neighbor's wife), every polygamist in the Bible was punished in some way, and there are numerous passages praising monogamy. It is illogical to claim as Reynolds did that failing to practice polygamy will lead to eternal damnation. After all, there are only so many women to go around, and if elite members of a congregation took a lion's share (Brigham Young, the Mormon leader, had 55 wives), this would be putting a lot of other members of the flock in danger of Hellfire. Not only is polygamy not given a seal of approval anywhere in the Bible, but the doctrine is also logically self-contradictory, as modern Mormons admit.

The Court further proclaimed that to recognize Reynolds' religious defense against criminal indictment would "permit every citizen to become a law unto himself," and that the state could regulate religiously conduct if it had a rational basis for doing so. Thus the so-called "rational basis test" became the standard for determining whether a law that impinged on a religious practice violated the Free Exercise Clause. Such a standard is easy for the state to satisfy. For almost a century thereafter the courts almost routinely rejected free exercise claims against generally applicable laws. The *Reynolds* Court gave examples of human sacrifice or the burning of widows on their husbands' funeral fires of idiosyncratic practices that the state definitely has an interest to prevent.

I think everyone would agree that there have to be some boundaries on religious liberty. Society cannot and should not allow any and all practices hiding under the umbrella of religious freedom. It cannot allow acts that jeopardize the health, safety, and lives of others in the name of religion, such as parents refusing a child life-saving medical procedures. If any and all practices were safe under religion's umbrella, there is nothing to stop me from founding a religion forbidding members to pay individual income taxes. I would soon have many converts despite the fact that it contravenes Jesus' command to "render onto Caesar."

An example involving the rational basis test is *Braunfeld v. Brown* (1961) in which the Court ruled that legislation designed promote some valid secular goal that did not directly interfere with religious practices was constitutionally sound. Abraham Braunfeld was an owner of clothing and home furnishing store in Philadelphia and an Orthodox Jew whose religion required him to observe the Sabbath, from sundown Friday to sundown Saturday. He compensated for this by opening his store on Sundays, which violated a newly 1959 enacted state law prohibiting non-essential forms of commerce on Sundays. The Court essentially ruled that while Braunfeld's free exercise of religion would have been violated if the state had required him to open on Saturday, it did not by requiring him to follow the state's "Blue Law" to close on Sunday. Although the requirement burdened his finances, it did not burden his religion. As a First Amendment fundamentalist, I disagree with the Court on this and believe that Braunfeld should have been accommodated. After all, was not requiring him to close his store on Sundays forcing him to silently affirm a Sabbath that was not his own?

In *Sherbert v Vener* (1963) the Supreme Court appeared to agree that the Constitution demands heightened scrutiny in Free Exercise claims and that there should be some degree of government accommodation of religious practices. In the Court's ruling, Justice William Brennan wrote that although previous Free Exercise claims had been rejected by the Court, the conduct that had been regulated "invariably posed some substantial threat to public safety, peace or order," Sherbert's did not. Adele Sherbert, a Seventh-day Adventist, was fired by her employer for refusing to work on Saturday, the Seventh-day Adventist Sabbath. She was unable to find other employment not requiring her to work on Saturday, so she filed for state unemployment benefits. The state of South Carolina refused her claim because she failed to accept available employment when offered. The state's decision was upheld by the South Carolina Supreme Court. In overturning that decision, the U.S. Supreme Court adopted the strict scrutiny standard of review requiring the state to demonstrate a compelling state interest to justify a generally applicable law burdening a religious practice. The Court further ruled that Sherbert's "conscientious objection to working on Saturday, as a fundamental right, was not "conduct within reach of state legislation."

In an earlier case, *West Virginia* State *Board of Education v. Barnette* (1943), the Court held that the Free Speech Clause protected students, who were Jehovah's Witnesses, from being coerced to salute the American flag and say the Pledge of Allegiance because "It requires the individual to communicate by word and sign his acceptance of the political ideas it thus bespeaks. Objection to this form of communication, when coerced, is an old one, well known to the framers of the Bill of Rights. It is also to be noted that the compulsory flag salute and pledge requires affirmation of belief and an attitude of mind." Being forced to affirm a belief one does not hold constitutes the meat of an argument I will make later when applied to wedding vendors.

Note that although the objection to saluting the flag was a religious objection, the Court decided the case on free speech claims to venture beyond the rational basis test.

Who then decides whether a given religious practice so "manifestly endangers" the state that is interfering with it becomes a state interest? It can be any government official testing the limits of their power until public opinion or the courts condemn or affirm their actions. One noteworthy example of how far down the road to Gomorrah we have traveled is the city of Houston's efforts to subpoena the sermons of five pastors in 2014. The state interest involved here were not sermons advocating mass insurrection or general mayhem, but something apparently more serious. The sermons actually urged congregants to exercise their free speech rights to speak out against a city ordinance allowing alleged transgender individuals to choose to use either a male or female bathroom. I wonder if a crazier issue has ever occupied legal beavers feeding at the public trough than this. The real scary thing is that Big Brother has so degraded the status of a religion that it has placed it below the status of an insane issue like who gets to do their business where. After all, if a person really is transgender, no one in the bathroom would know that "she' was born a "he," or vice-versa. On the other hand, no girl or woman wants to see Grizzly Adams in the next stall claiming that he identifies as a woman today. The city subsequently withdrew its subpoenas in the face of public outrage.

In *Employment Division v. Smith* (1990) the Court abandoned strict scrutiny and reached back to the rational basis test. The case involved drug counselors Alfred Smith and Galen Black; members of the Native American Church who were fired from their jobs at a drug rehabilitation clinic because they had taken sacramental peyote during a ceremony at their church. Because they had been fired for work-related misconduct, they were denied unemployment benefits on the basis of preserving the financial integrity of the workers' compensation fund. The Oregon Supreme Court ruled that the state's justification for withholding their benefits was outweighed by the burden imposed on the free exercise of religion. The state of Oregon appealed to the U.S. Supreme Court, which returned the case to the Oregon Supreme Court to decide if the sacramental use of illegal drugs violated the Oregon state drug law. The Oregon Supreme Court ruled concluded that it did but still maintained that the free expression of religion remained the paramount reason for ruling against the state.

The state again appealed to the U.S. Supreme Court with the new issue being: "Can a state deny unemployment benefits to workers fired for using illegal drugs for religious purposes, or does such state action violate the Free Exercise Clause? In a 6-3 decision, the Court ruled that Oregon could because Smith and Blacks' religious beliefs do not excuse them from compliance with an otherwise valid law. Writing for the majority, Justice Scalia noted that the free exercise exceptions to laws generally applicable should only be entertained if the religiously motivated conduct were conjoined with other constitutional protections, such as with free speech claims as in *West Virginia* State *Board of Education v. Barnette* and in *Cantwell*. We shall see, however, that subsequent free exercise claims conjoined with free speech and free association claims have been ignored by the Court.

The Religious Freedom Restoration Act

Congress was uncomfortable with the Court's *Smith* decision and responded by enacting the Religious Freedom Restoration Act (RFRA) of 1993. The RFRA requires the courts to apply strict scrutiny to all laws burdening religion. The RFRA reads in part: "Government may substantially burden a person's exercise of religion only if it demonstrates that application of the burden to the person (1) is in furtherance of a compelling governmental interest; and (2) is the least restrictive means of furthering that compelling governmental interest." The RFRA was passed by an almost unanimous vote in the House and Senate (only three senators voted against it). Upon signing the act into law, President Bill Clinton remarked:

> We all have a shared desire here to protect perhaps the most precious of all American liberties, religious freedom. Usually the signing of legislation by a President is a ministerial act, often a quiet ending to a turbulent legislative process. Today this event assumes a more majestic quality because of our ability together to affirm the historic role that people of faith have played in the history of this country and the constitutional protections those who profess and express their faith have always demanded and cherished.[18]

The drafters of the RFRA recognized that religiously neutral laws such as those at issue in *Employment Division v. Smith* can burden religion as much as laws that intend to do so, and thus the RFRA states that "Government shall not substantially burden a person's exercise of religion even if the burden results from a rule of general applicability." This is an important point I shall return to later as something an almost unanimous Congress deems just, but the courts do not. Despite the Congressional, Presidential, and public popularity and support of the RFRA, the Supreme Court in its arrogance struck it down as applied to state and local governments in *City of Boerne v. Flores*. This case involved the St. Peter's Catholic Church's efforts to obtain permits to expand the building since its congregation was outgrowing it. The city of Boerne, Texas, refused the church construction permits because construction would violate a zoning ordinance designating the area in which the church was located an historic district. The church contended in Federal Court that the denial was a violation of the RFRA, a contention with which the Fifth Circuit Court of Appeals agreed.

The Congress was given the authority under Section 5 of the Fourteenth Amendment to expand the definition of personal rights: "The Congress shall have power to enforce [the Amendment] by appropriate legislation, the provisions of this article." Congress's power to exercise this authority with regard to voting rights was upheld by the Supreme Court in the 1960s. The Church argued that if Congress can prohibit laws to prevent racial discrimination in voting it should be able to do the same to promote religious liberty. The Supreme Court's 6 - 3 decision, however, deemed that Congress had exceeded its authority in making the RFRA applicable to the states and found for the City of Boeme. In effect, the Court was saying that Congress had overstepped its authority in "forcing" the states to provide more protection of religious liberty than the First Amendment supposedly affords, and ruled that: "This is a considerable congressional intrusion into the States' traditional prerogatives and general authority to regulate for the health and welfare of their citizens." Holding such a popular act is "forcing" states to protect its people's religious liberty while at the same time the Court is continually forcing states to strip them of such liberty, once again reminds us of the Court's unconstitutional usurpation of legislative power and of its ability to make words mean one thing at one time and their opposite at another. Indeed, the states are often the defendants in cases in which the ACLU and sundry other groups complain about public displays of faith.

Justice O'Connor's dissent in *City of Boerne* points to how the Founders viewed religious liberty and is an opinion worth reading twice:

> The Religion Clauses of the Constitution represent a profound commitment to religious liberty. Our Nation's Founders conceived of a Republic receptive to voluntary religious expression, not of a secular society in which religious expression is tolerated only when it does not conflict with a generally applicable law...the Free Exercise Clause is properly understood as an affirmative guarantee of the right to participate in religious activities without impermissible governmental interference, even where a believer's conduct is in tension with a law of general application. Certainly, it is in no way anomalous to accord heightened protection to a right identified in the text of the First Amendment. For example, it has long been the Court's position that freedom of speech--a right enumerated only a few words after the right to free exercise--has special constitutional status. Given the centrality of freedom of speech and religion to the American concept of personal

liberty, it is altogether reasonable to conclude that both should be treated with the highest degree of respect.

Does Religious Liberty Deserve Special Treatment?

The Free Exercise Clause singles out religion as deserving of special protection not offered to secular systems of belief. One could argue that religion is singularly discriminated against rather than protected in our public schools since secular beliefs such as moral relativism and multiculturalism are aggressively promoted in them while religion is banned. But in theory, it is afforded special legal protection, which upsets the atheistic avant-garde which asks "What's so special about religion to warrant this heightened protection?" The short answer is that the Founding Fathers considered to so valuable to a moral society that they found its private and public practice to be crucial, and made that plain in the absolutist wording of the religious clauses. The long answer is contained in chapter two when I discussed the many benefits of Christianity for individuals and their societies.

However, the argument that there is nothing special about religion that warrants special protection requires addressing because that view has been seriously argued. For example, professor Micah Schwartzman wrote an article purporting to show that "religion cannot be distinguished from many other beliefs and practices as warranting special constitutional treatment. As a normative matter, religion is *not* special."[19] Given that premise, he maintains that the Religious Clauses "should be rejected as morally deficient"[20] or they should be reconciled by "expand[ing] the definition of religion to encompass secular doctrines."[21]

That the Religious Clauses should be called "morally deficient" and rejected or reduced to the level of secular beliefs would surely shock the great majority of Constitutional scholars who are aware that the Founding Fathers considered religious liberty to be the paramount liberty because it is the basis of a moral society. In the face of all the historical and sociological evidence, who can say that any secular belief system can function on such a basis? Democracy has produced relatively peaceful and well-ordered societies, but up until recently, its moral foundation was supplied by Christianity.

An organized religion is a belief system rooted in centuries of history and tradition that binds together a community of believers sharing a collective conscience. A religious conscience is of special significance to believers; it is at the center of their identities and self-understanding, and of the understanding of a transcendental reality beyond themselves. Religious people want to live a life connected to, and in accordance with, their transcendental truths and not be confronted with the tragic choice of allegiance to the state or to God. This alone makes it more special than secular systems that do not make intelligible claims about the human condition in terms of ultimate reality.

A conscience is not simply an individual matter of judgment. To the extent it is premised on the doctrine of a religious community, an attack on any individual's conscience is an attack on the collective conscience of that community. A conscience derived from a nonreligious source, however virtuous, does not possess the same compelling force. Violating the commands of God is taken far more seriously than violating the precepts of a secular faith. For the religious believer, the source of religious conscience is both prior and superior to the proscriptions and prescriptions of civil society and must take precedence as long as they cause no danger to the peace and safety of the state. This recalls James Madison's famous passage in *Memorial and Remonstrance*, and is worth citing again: "Before any man can be considered a member of Civil Society, he may be considered as a subject of the Governor of the Universe." The obligations individual believers owe to the Governor transcend those they owe to civil society, which is why cultural Marxists fear the religion and want to root it out.

Madison's passage suggests another reason that religion is special and deserves great respect and protection. Religion is a uniquely valuable check on government abuse of power because it recognizes a source of transcendental authority to which the state is subordinate. Natural God-given law has been evoked many times in history to limit the absolute power of the state. The best example of this is the ringing words of the Declaration of Independence: "We hold these truths to be self-evident, that all men are created equal; they are endowed by the Creator with certain inalienable rights." Inalienable rights are the foundation of our government and were the philosophical justification for American resistance to British rule. Conversely, anything that diminishes religion enhances Big Government to the delight of cultural Marxists. No other system of belief claims that its source of authority transcends that of the state. As professor Michael McConnell points out, the state relies on its citizen's voluntary compliance with the law, and thus the state has pragmatic reasons for deferring to principled religious values: "Since some persons, otherwise good and law-abiding citizens, will view religious claims as higher authority than civil law, it may be preferable [for the state] to accommodate them than to provoke confrontation and disobedience."[22]

The Atheist View

The attacks on Christianity that are rampant in our country today are driven by an atheistic worldview pushed up through the sewer cracks by cultural Marxists. Atheism has spread widely enough to allow for a significant proportion of Americans to remain silent when Christians are persecuted when they demand their First Amendment rights. An atheist worldview and anti-Christian persecution are mutually supportive because an increase in one leads inevitably to an increase in the other. The best way to defend against these attacks is to expose the emptiness of atheism.

In his book *Why Tolerate Religion?* Brian Leiter disparages religion as consisting of intrinsically "irrational" belief systems "unhinged from reason," which makes it hard to justify special respect, tolerance, or legal accommodation. He claims that religion is insulated from "reason and evidence" which he defines as "believing in something notwithstanding the evidence and reasons that fail to support it or even contradict it."[23] Atheists consider themselves "freethinkers" and, like Leiter, are of the opinion that God has been given his walking papers by reason and science, and use this assertion to push their idea ever forward that religious conscience deserves no special protection. But as shown in chapter two, as science has progressed it has resurrected a belief in God among many prominent scientists. Nobel Prize-winning physicist Max Planck is head and shoulders over Leiter in the brains department and can hardly be called irrational. In a lecture given in 1937, he remarked: "There can never be any real opposition between religion and science...Every serious and reflective person realizes that the religious element in his nature must be recognized and cultivated if all the powers of the human soul are to act together in perfect balance and harmony. And indeed it was not by accident that *the greatest thinkers of all ages were deeply religious souls.*"[24]

This fact is not well known among the general public, so there remains a widespread belief that scientists are mostly atheists, and lesser minds want to be in the same intellectual ballpark. However, a national study of 1,400 scientists found that only a piddling 9.8 percent described themselves as atheists. Of the remainder, 34.9 percent believed in God and held no doubts, 16.6 percent believed in God but had doubts, 19.2 percent believed in a higher power (deists), 4.4 percent believed 'some of the time," and 13.1 percent were agnostics.[25] While the rate of religious belief among PhDs is below that of the general American public, the rate is higher than the general public among MDs, with 76 percent of a national sample of physicians affirming their belief in God. Ninety percent of these physicians attend religious services at least occasionally as opposed to 81 percent of the general public.[26] With almost two-thirds of scientists and just over three-quarters of physicians reporting some degree of belief in a divine Creator, it is patently false that science and reason are on the side of atheism—science and reason are on the side of God.

Albert Einstein's view of atheism has led many prominent atheists to reconsider their prideful rejection of God: "The fanatical atheists are like slaves who are still feeling the weight of their chains which they have thrown off after hard struggle. They are creatures who – in their grudge against traditional religion as the 'opium of the masses' – cannot hear the music of the spheres."[27] British philosopher Antony Flew is one famous atheist who was led to reconsider his beliefs after reflecting on Einstein's "music of the spheres" and on the boggling complexity of DNA and the mystery of its origins. In 2004, Flew shocked the atheist world by announcing he had come to believe in God because he had been atheism's preeminent spokesman and had written many books and articles peddling it. When asked in an interview with Benjamin Wiker if he had "heard a voice" leading him to God, Flew replied that part of it was his growing understanding of Einstein's spheres and that the complexity of universe had to include Intelligence behind it. The other part was the even greater complexity of life itself, which he is convinced requires an Intelligent Source. While he used to believe that from a lifeless chemical soup could emerge the genetic code by chance, he came to view it that as an impossibility. He chides arch-atheist Richard Dawkins' argument that life can be attributed to a "lucky chance," and said, "If that's the best argument you have, then the game is over." He told Wiker that he did not reject atheism because he heard a voice, but rather "It was the evidence itself that led me to this conclusion."[28]

Anyone who has the time to examine with an open mind the same evidence that Flew did, must come to the same conclusion. Modern science has made it both easier and more difficult to believe in a divine Creator—easier for scientists; harder for laypersons. After the Copernican revolution, science's mechanistic view of the world pulled more and more scientists and other intellectuals into the atheistic fold, and others followed behind as their ideas entered public discourse. Contemporary science is far less mechanistic, and the sheer complexity of its fundamental phenomena has drawn more and more scientists back to the idea of a magnificent Intelligence behind it all. This whole circular process of belief-atheism-belief illustrates Francis Bacon's observation that: "A little philosophy inclineth man's mind to atheism, but depth in philosophy bringeth men's minds about to religion."[29] This "depth," however, makes it more difficult for less educated people to grasp the evidence about the nature of the universe today than it was in 1802 when William Paley offered his "watchmaker" argument for God's hand on creation. Appreciating Big Bang cosmology, the anthropic principle, and the boggling complexity of molecular biology requires a little more cognitive muscle. The general public is always two or three generations behind science in its basic grasp of the implications of scientific reality. Perhaps we shall again have religious liberty when Einstein's "music of the spheres" is heard by a critical mass of Americans.

Endnotes

1. Paulsen. Why the Supreme Court.
2. U.S. Congress, Title 22 - Foreign relations and intercourse, p.1.
3. Bennett, The de-valuing of America, p. 206.
4. Thomas, Air Force veteran removed.
5. Hammer, Feds establishing religion?
6. Fox News (2011). Houston veterans claim censorship.
7. Cited in Nowlan, *The American Presidents*, p.171.
8. Levin, The perils of religious liberty, p. 30.
9. Donohue, *The Politics of the American Civil Liberties Union*, p. 51.
10. Ibid, p. 62.
11. Laycock, The Supreme Court's assault, p. 108.
12. De Toledano. What the ACLU doesn't want you to know, p. 48.
13. Trigg Freedom of religion, p.118.
14. Pepper, Taking the Free Exercise Clause Seriously, p. 300.
15. Levin, The perils of religious liberty, p. 30.
16. Walpin, Five justices, p. 188.
17. Pilon, The long view, p. viii.
18. Clinton, *Public Papers of the Presidents*, p.2000.
19. Schwartzman, What if religion is not special? p. 1353.
20. Ibid, p. 1403.
21. Ibid, p. 1415.
22. McConnell, Accommodation of religion, p.16.
23. Leiter, *Why tolerate religion?* p. 39.
24. Planck, *Religion and natural science* p. 184; my emphasis.
25. Gross and Simmons, The religiosity of American college and university professors.
26. Easton, Survey on physicians' religious beliefs.
27. In Isaacson, Einstein, his life and universe, p. 390.
28. Wiker, How the world's most notorious atheist changed his mind.
29. Beckingham, Parallel passages in Bacon and Fuller, p. 450.

Cases cited

Braunfeld v. Brown, 366 U.S. 599 (1961).
Cantwell v. Connecticut, 310 U.S. 296 (1940).
City of Boerne v. Flores, 521 U.S. 507 (1997)
Employment Division, Department of Human Resources of Oregon v. Smith, 494 U.S. 872 (1990).
Lynch v. Donnelly, 465 U.S. 668 (1984).
Reynolds v. United States, 98 U.S. (8 Otto.) 145 (1878.

Sherbert v. Verner, 374 U.S. 398 (1963)
West Virginia State *Board of Education v. Barnette,* 319 U.S. 624 (*1943*). p. 633

Chapter 7

"Give me the Child:" The Spiritual Disarming of America's Schools

"God...should never have been expelled from America's schools...Without God there is no virtue because there is no prompting of the conscience. Without God there is a coarsening of the society. Without God democracy will not and cannot long endure."
Ronald Reagan, 40th President of the United States.

Moral Education

Although duplicitous Georg Lukacs and honest Abe Lincoln were poles apart in all matters of decency, morality, and political philosophy, they agreed on at least one thing: "The philosophy of the school room in one generation will be the philosophy of government in the next." Lincoln's words were intended to support the moral role of Christianity in public schools because of his belief that "The only assurance of our nation's safety is to lay our foundation in morality and religion."[1] If Lukacs had voiced similar intentions, he would have meant them to inculcate immorality, atheism, and worship of Big Government socialism. Schools are the great molders of children's minds. As the molders of young minds, one would think that all but committed cultural Marxists would desire and demand that moral lessons be "the philosophy of the school room." In pursuit of this goal, one would expect that *non-denominational* Christianity of the kind Thomas Jefferson counseled for the University of Virginia be included prominently in the curricula.

It was noted in chapter 2 that those who are anxious to ban God from our schools like to broadcast the falsehood that Jefferson founded the first university in the country free from traditional Christian teachings. They rest their case on the fact that he mandated that professors of ethics rather than professors of theology teach religion at the University of Virginia. He made this provision out of concern that theologians would teach their own narrow version of Christianity to the exclusion of others. This is not secularism; it is non-denominationalism. As Jefferson put it in his letter to the University's Board of Visitors [Regents]:

It was not, however, to be understood that instruction in religious opinions and duties was meant to be precluded by the public authorities as indifferent to the interests of society. On the contrary, the relations which exist between man and his Maker – and the duties resulting from those relations – are the most interesting and important to every human being and the most incumbent on his study and investigation.[2]

To grasp the importance of early moral training, we might remind ourselves of the proud Jesuit boast, "Give me the child for his first seven years, and I'll give you the man." Whatever the philosophy of the school room, presenting its content to children may be viewed as indoctrination. The term "indoctrination" has a negative connotation because we tend to apply it only when we disapprove of the content being transmitted, and prefer the term "socialization." Yet there is a difference. Indoctrination is typically inculcating a specific set of doctrines and principles to the exclusion of others, whereas socialization is a broader process by which children acquire a personal identity and learn the norms, values, behavior, and social skills valued in their society. The question we must ask ourselves is whether we want to inculcate the values and norms of compassion, morality, decency, hard work, and self-reliance, or do we want our children to become bongo-playing zombies animated with a hatred for the values that forged America and with a deep desire to be free of irksome responsibilities and to outsource their lives to big government.

The importance of teaching religion in school was deemed so important to the Founding Fathers that they made it a part of the Northwest Ordinance. The Northwest Ordinance was enacted in 1787 by the last Congress of the Confederation and is a document providing for the governance of the Northwest Territories, which would become the states of Ohio, Indiana, Illinois, Michigan, and Wisconsin. Among the acts of governance was one providing for the establishment of public schools. The document made plain what was to be the purpose of those schools in Article 3, Section 14: "Religion, morality, and knowledge, being necessary to good government and the happiness of mankind, schools and the means of education shall forever be encouraged."[3] The Ordinance's authors believed that schools were vital in the inculcation of necessary practical knowledge for the next generation of Americans to function as members of their society and, importantly, to function as moral members of their society. Toward that end, these wise men knew that religion must be an integral part of children's education, and two years after the Ordinance, many of the same men sitting in the first Congress under the new Constitution proposed the religious clauses of the First Amendment.

In our early republic, the Bible was used in schools as a text for instilling moral principles. The Bible was eventually replaced by other books such as Noah Webster's *Primer,* which was filled with moral Bible verses. Webster wrote in his *Advice to Children* that the purpose of education is to "enlighten the minds of youth in religious and moral principles and restrain some of the common vices of our country."[4] The Bible is virtually banned in schools today (teachers have been reprimanded and fired for having one on their desks), and Webster's *Primer* would likewise be laughed at and shunned for its moral content.

Liberals have rejected this wisdom of ages reflected in the Ordinance, believing that a completely secular education can foster morality. This kind of thinking plays directly into the cultural Marxist agenda, which is something Marxists have always relied on from their Western allies, calling them, in the words of Lenin, "useful idiots." Useful idiots do not have to have any particular commitment to Marxism to be its dupes. Rather, they are people who tend to be devotees of such philosophies as multiculturalism, moral relativism, and political correctness, and believe themselves to be free thinkers, all of which have the effect of leading them to reject God. That is their prerogative, and I would wish them well if they did not use their positions in schools and universities to infect young minds with this rubbish.

If you believe that spiritually disarming America's school children is of little consequence, you are directed by the 2000 *Congressional Record* where you will see the behavioral problems in schools before and after Justice Black's weighting of the Establishment Clause with Jefferson's "wall of separation" metaphor in *Everson.* The *Record* notes that:

> In 1940, public school teachers ranked the top seven disciplinary problems in public schools. They were talking out of turn, chewing gum, making noise, running in the hall, cutting in line, dress code violations and littering. In 1990, the problems had changed to drug and alcohol abuse, pregnancy, suicide, rape, robbery, and assault.[5]

Otherwise stated, disciplinary problems in our schools have gone from acts of youthful exuberance to immoral, destructive, and criminal behaviors. The permissive philosophies of radical individualism ("if it feels good, do it") and moral relativism ("nothing is inherently right or wrong") promoted by cultural Marxism have poisoned our educational system.

The Supreme Court has waged war on religion in its use of Justice Black's wholly erroneous view of the Establishment Clause to shut down religious freedom in our schools. The "wall of separation" trope and the "clauses in conflict" notion—neither of which can be gleaned from the Constitution and indeed are inconsistent with it—are the left's big guns.[6] Both clauses are negative restraints on the government, so they are pulling in the same direction, and thus there can be no "tension" between them. The negative in the Establishment Clause bars Congress from establishing an official state religion, and the Free Exercise Clause restrains Congress from inhibiting the "free exercise thereof." Both Clauses are restraints on government, not on religion. One only finds conflict in these Clauses if one is determined to do so, leading to the necessity of reading the Establishment Clause so broadly as to believe that any government involvement, even in the case of children praying in public school, amounts to "Congress" establishing a Church of the United States.

Even if there were a conflict between the Clauses, the Constitution contains no formula for deciding which should prevail. The Establishment Clause is surely the easiest clause to comply with because it can be violated by just one thing—establishing a state religion—whereas the Free Exercise Clause can violate in numerous ways. Thus if there is to be a hierarchy of Constitutional rights, the Free Exercise Clause should have priority. Historian Mark Noll, who specializes in the history of religion in America, emphatically declares that it was never the intention of the Founders to be hostile to the public expression of religion: "[T]he founders' desire for the separation of the institutions of church and state reflected a desire to respect not only religion but also the moral choice of citizens. It was not a provision to remove religion as such from public life. In the context of the times, it was more a device for purifying the religious impact on politics than removing it."[7]

Out with School Prayers: Engel v. Vitale (1962)

Everson opened opportunities for atheists to persuade the courts that anything remotely concerning Christianity should be banished from public schools. The first case to set this process in motion was *Engel v. Vitale*. At this time, school prayers were said in public schools across America. In New York State, the Board of Regents wrote a short prayer for recitation at the start of each school day which was published as part of their *Statement on Moral and Spiritual Training in the Schools*. As did our Founding Fathers, the Board of Regents viewed moral and spiritual training as part of a school's mandate and a tool for the development of moral character and good citizenship. The prayer was entirely voluntary, and any student objecting did not have to participate. The Board's prayer was purposely non-sectarian in order to defuse any question of preferentialism. The Board also took the decision as to the content of the daily prayer out of the hands of local communities for the same reason. This prayer was to be recited following the pledge of allegiance to the flag, and reads as follows: "Almighty God, we acknowledge our dependence upon Thee, and beg Thy blessings upon us, our teachers, and our country. Amen."

One would not expect significant opposition to such a minimalist prayer which is not even specifically Christian. After all, it makes reference to a monotheistic God as Creator of the universe to which Christians, Jews, and Muslims could pray for blessings for themselves, their teachers, and their country. But there was opposition from the parents of ten pupils in the New Hyde Park, New York school district, who brought suit in state court to stop the practice of the recitation of the prayer in school. The suit filed in the district court which ruled that the prayer was constitutionally permissible as long as it was voluntary, which it was. The lower court's ruling was upheld by the New York Court of Appeals. The parents appealed to the U.S. Supreme Court, joined by the ACLU and other groups wanting to purge Christianity from public life.

In a 6 -1 decision (two justices did not participate) The Supreme Court ruled the prayer an unconstitutional violation of the Establishment Clause. So once again the Court conflated "promotion of religion," which the Founding Fathers favored, with "establishment of religion," which they did not. The majority opinion was delivered by Justice Hugo Black. Much of Black's opinion was a rehashing of the history of the evils of established religion that he penned in *Everson* years earlier. Justice Black quotes a statement of James Madison made in *Memorial and Remonstrance against Religious Assessments* in support of his opinion:

> Who does not see that the same authority which can establish Christianity, in exclusion of all other Religions, may establish with the same ease any particular sect of Christians, in exclusion of all other Sects? That the same authority which can force a citizen to contribute three pence only of his property for the support of any one establishment may force him to conform to any other establishment in all cases whatsoever?

Is it not plain here that Madison is simply reiterating the Constitutional principle of non-official establishment of religion, and not a statement of hostility toward Christianity? After all, this is the same Madison who in the same document affirmed that freedom of religious thought and action was an unalienable right and that we owe a duty "to render the Creator such homage and such only as he believes to be acceptable to him. This duty is a precedent, both in order of time and in the degree of obligation, to the claims of Civil Society. Before any man can be considered as a member of Civil Society, he must be considered as a subject of the Governour of the Universe." Black's quoting of Madison in support of banning God from the public square is like quoting Ronald Reagan in support of outlawing capitalism.

The Court's opinion shows that it was oblivious to the fact that there is a universe of difference between an officially established religion and simple public homage to the Supreme Being in a way all religions can appreciate. Not once in his long opinion did Black engage the Regent's non-denominational argument, apparently believing that no prayer can be so. If neither sectarian nor non-sectarian prayers are Constitutional, our national religion must be secularism and confined to the values endorsed by the state. Secularism is a belief system that, while not being synonymous with atheism, posits that there (probably) is no God, and that religious belief systems must be rejected or ignored. If there is no higher power than the state, we must worship the state, as G. K. Chesterton warned (see chapter 2). The bending of our collective knees to the almighty state is the goal of all lovers of Big Government, particularly cultural Marxists.

The *Engel* Court obviously did not see the irony in opening each of its sessions with a similar non-sectarian prayer ("God save the United States and this Honorable Court") as "an establishing of religion," which it obviously is not, while striking down the New York invocation to God as establishing religion, which it just as obviously is not. In his dissenting opinion in *Engel*, Justice Potter Stewart made these common sense comments on the Court's majority ruling that school prayer amounted to the State of New York establishing an official religion:

> The Court does not hold, nor could it, that New York has interfered with the free exercise of anybody's religion. For the state courts have made clear that those who object to reciting the prayer must be entirely free of any compulsion to do so, including any "embarrassments and pressures." But the Court says that, in permitting school children to say this simple prayer, the New York authorities have established "an official religion." With all respect, I think the Court has misapplied a great constitutional principle. I cannot see how an "official religion" is established by letting those who want to say a prayer say it. On the contrary, I think that to deny the wish of these school children to join in reciting this prayer is to deny them the opportunity of sharing in the spiritual heritage of our Nation.

Maybe we should also shield students from *The Star Spangled Banner*, which contains some of the same sentiments found in the New York Regent's prayer. Part of the third verse of our national anthem reads: "Blest with victory and peace, may the heav'n-rescued land. Praise the Power that hath made and preserved us a nation! Then conquer we must, when our cause it is just, And this be our motto: 'In God is our trust.'" Given the similarity of sentiments, could not the twisted logic of *Engel* argue that *The Star Spangled Banner* establishes a religion, even though it, like the Regent's prayer, is strictly non-denominational?

If you think this far-fetched, *New York Post* columnist Gersh Kuntzman wrote a column calling for banning *God Bless America* at ball games, which he claims "is a song that offends everyone." He went on: "It's time for God to stop blessing America during the seventh-inning stretch...'God Bless America' should be sent permanently to the bench." Kuntzman claims that the song "is as divisive as American politics," and goes on to cite a poll that found "that 83.8% of people who described themselves as 'very liberal, dislike the song [no surprise there]" as did 88% of atheists" (birds of a feather). Not satisfied with that, he added "We atheists also hate having 'In God we Trust, on the currency and in the courtrooms of a country whose Constitution bars the 'establishment of religion'"[8] This is the same panty-waist who blamed the NRA for the mass shootings of an Islamic terrorist at a gay bar in Orlando, and who claimed his "frightening experience" firing an AR-15 semi-automatic rifle at a shooting range gave him temporary PTSD.

Out with the Bible: Abington Township School District v. Schempp (1963)

The next major school case heard by the Supreme Court involved the Bible reading in schools required by Pennsylvania and Maryland law was *Abington v. Schempp.* The Abington school district argued that its Bible reading served such secular purposes as: "The promotion of moral values, the contradiction to the materialistic trends of our times, the perpetuation of our institutions and the teaching of literature." The Schempp family filed a suit because although students could be excused from Bible readings if parents objected, they believed this measure that this was not sufficient to satisfy them.

Abington was actually consolidated with another case, *Murray v. Curlett* filed by the infamous Madalyn Murray O'Hair. O'Hair was the founder of the American Atheist group, and who unsuccessfully tried to defect to the Soviet Union because of its establishment of atheism. She objected to her sons being exposed to Bible readings in school.[9] The Court held that public schools engaging in officially sanctioned prayer or Bible reading to be unconstitutional under the Establishment Clause. The Court acknowledged that the Christian religion is closely identified with American history and government, but asserted that the Constitution requires that the government remain neutral in matters of religion. Although concurring with the majority 8-1 opinion, Justice Clark wrote the following:

"[W]e are a religious people whose institutions presuppose a Supreme Being." The fact that the Founding Fathers believed devotedly that there was a God and that the unalienable rights of man were rooted in Him is clearly evidenced in their writings, from the Mayflower Compact to the Constitution itself...Indeed, only last year, an official survey of the country indicated that 64% of our people have church membership, while less than 30% profess no religion whatever. It can be truly said, therefore, that today, as in the beginning, our national life reflects a religious people who, in the words of Madison, "are earnestly praying, as ...in duty bound, that the Supreme Lawgiver of the Universe ... guide them into every measure which may be worthy of his blessing."

By his concurrence with the majority, Justice Clark is saying that although the majority of Americans are religious, which he apparently approved of, and would like Christian moral precepts taught in public schools, their wishes must be sacrificed to the wishes of a small minority. The Court claims that it makes it rulings from a position of neutrality. This is pure fiction; no one makes ethical or moral dilemma without some commitment to a set of principles with which to interpret it and make a decision about it. The ruling in *Abington* was hardly a neutral stance, as Justice Potter Stewart argued in his dissent:

It might also be argued that parents who want their children exposed to religious influences can adequately fulfill that wish off school property and outside school time. With all its surface persuasiveness, however, this argument seriously misconceives the basic constitutional justification for permitting the exercises at issue in these cases. For a compulsory state educational system so structures a child's life that, if religious exercises are held to be an impermissible activity in schools, religion is placed at an artificial and state-created disadvantage. Viewed in this light, permission of such exercises for those who want them is necessary if the schools are truly to be neutral in the matter of religion. And a refusal to permit religious exercises thus is seen not as the realization of state neutrality, but rather as the establishment of a religion of secularism, or, at the least, as government support of the beliefs of those who think that religious exercises should be conducted only in private.

The *Abington* ruling was widely denounced by politicians and religious leaders, and there were calls to impeach Chief Justice Warren Burger. Some few school systems ignored the Court's ruling for some time, and other schools reacted by replacing the Bible readings with a period of silent meditation, but that was soon to fall afoul of the Court also.

Thou Shalt not Suffer The Ten Commandments: Stone v. Graham (1980)

In *Stone v. Graham,* the Supreme Court ruled unconstitutional a Kentucky statute that required the Ten Commandments to be posted on the walls of every classroom in the state. At the bottom of each copy of the Ten Commandments were the words: "The secular application of the Ten Commandments is clearly seen in its adoption as the fundamental legal code of Western Civilization and the Common Law of the United States." The Court applied the *Lemon* test in making its decisions that the Kentucky statute was unconstitutional because it had no secular purpose, and was "plainly religious in intent." The Commandments were merely posted on the wall and were not integrated into the curriculum, but the Court ruled that displaying could give students the impression that the state was promoting the beliefs they represent.

In a *per curiam* decision (a decision delivered in the name of the Court that does not identify specific judges), the Court ruled the posting of the Ten Commandments unconstitutional and said: "Posting of religious texts on the wall serves no such educational function. If the posted copies of the Ten Commandments are to have any effect at all, it will be to induce the schoolchildren to read, meditate upon, perhaps to venerate and obey, the Commandments." Is moral guidance no longer a "legitimate state interest"? Apparently not; let our schoolchildren rest content with meditating upon the *Walking Dead,* obscene rap lyrics, lust, greed, and envy while learning to place condoms on bananas in sex-ed class. No wonder American culture is descending into a moral morass. Heaven forbid that schoolchildren might actually read, meditate upon, venerate and obey, the Ten Commandments! It might corrupt them and turn them into decent God-fearing adults, which might undermine leftist hedonism and prevent children from becoming worshipers of Big Brother.

The preamble to the Constitution of Kentucky (other state constitutions have similar wording) identifies the "corrupting" rules that tell us not to kill, steal, lie, or covet our neighbor's goods or wife, and how they are intimately connected to our nation's history and culture:

> The Ten Commandments have profoundly influenced the formation of Western legal thought and the formation of our country. That influence is clearly seen in the Declaration of Independence, which declared that "We hold these truths to be self-evident, that all men are created equal, that they are endowed by their Creator with certain unalienable Rights,

that among these are Life, Liberty, and the pursuit of Happiness." The Ten Commandments provide the moral background of the Declaration of Independence and the foundation of our legal tradition.

In Justice Rehnquist's dissent he noted the Court's arrogance in overruling the Supreme Court of Kentucky (which ruled the display of the Commandments to be Constitutional) without hearing arguments, and how impractical and ridiculous it would be to try to shield school children from all religious influences:

> The fact is that, for good or for ill, nearly everything in our culture worth transmitting, everything which gives meaning to life is saturated with religious influences...One canhardly respect the system of education that would leave the student wholly ignorant of the currents of religious thought that move the world society for a part in which he is being prepared.

Thou Shalt not Meditate upon God: Wallace v. Jaffree (1985).

In *Wallace v. Jaffree*, the Supreme Court once again used the Establishment Clause to further render the Free Exercise Clause impotent. Before the Court was a 1981 Alabama Statute authorizing a one-minute period of silence in its public schools "for meditation or voluntary prayer." and a 1982 statute authorizing teachers to lead "willing students" in a state-written, prescribed prayer to "Almighty God...the Creator and Supreme Judge of the World." A federal district judge declared the statutes constitutional because they simply promote the view that religious observances should be accommodated in a non-coercive way, and that in no way does it "establish" religion. However, the Supreme Court disagreed and in a 6-3 decision ruled the statutes unconstitutional because the statutes violated "separation of church and state."

In Justice Warren Burger's dissent, he noted that "The notion that the Alabama statute is a step toward creating an established church borders on if it does not trespass into, the ridiculous. The statute does not remotely threaten religious liberty; it affirmatively furthers the values of religious freedom and tolerance that the Establishment Clause was designed to protect." Burger went on to point out the Court's hostility to religion: "To suggest that a moment-of-silence statute that includes the word "prayer" unconstitutionally endorses religion, while one that simply provides for a moment of silence does not, manifests not neutrality but hostility toward religion." Indeed, to say that children engaging in a one-minute silent prayer (or whatever else they may be meditating on) amounts to an establishment of religion is not only absurd, it amounts to judicial control over their thoughts and speech in violation of the Free Speech Clause of the First Amendment as well as the Free Exercise Clause. The Alabama statute simply provided schoolchildren with an opportunity to appreciate the Constitutional right to worship and believe (or not) as he or she deemed appropriate.

In Wallace, the Court once again read a conflict into the two religious clauses that simply is not there, as Justice Burger notes above. The Court has made the Free Exercise Clause subordinate to the Establishment Clause at every turn. By doing so, it implies that those who wrote the Clauses were crude and unlettered, unable to put together a sentence that was not self-contradictory. But it is the various Justices and their use of fallacious logic beginning with *Everson*, who are, at best, poor grammarians. The clauses are only in conflict if one believes that anything remotely religious in the public sphere amounts to the establishment, or if one conflates the terms "promotion" and "establishment" to mean the same thing. If one starts with those premises as axiomatic, then one can go about finding ways to support them (remember Judge Chancellor Kent's methodology?). They have to be pretty clever arguments buried in huge dissertations about the European experience with established religions because the clauses are so simply stated. The Establishment Clause simply says that Congress (that doesn't include little children praying) must not establish an official religion, and the Free Exercise Clause expressly forbids Congress from inhibiting its free exercise, anywhere. The very important point is that the free Exercise Clause says that Congress is forbidden to prohibit "the free exercise thereof." It does not say Congress must not prohibit the free exercise of religion "except in the public square."

In Justice William Rehnquist's biting dissent, he pointed out how alien the Court's ruling would have been to previous generations of Americans, especially the generation that wrote the Declaration of Independence, the Constitution, and the Bill of Rights:

> The Court strikes down the Alabama statute because the State wished to "characterize prayer as a favored practice." It would come as much of a shock to those who drafted the Bill of Rights as it will to a large number of thoughtful Americans today to learn that the Constitution, as construed by the majority, prohibits the Alabama Legislature from "endorsing" prayer. George Washington himself, at the request of the very Congress which passed the Bill of Rights, proclaimed a day of "public thanksgiving and prayer, to be observed by acknowledging with grateful hearts the many and signal favors of Almighty God." History must judge whether it was the Father of his Country in 1789, or a majority of the Court today, which has strayed from the meaning of the Establishment Clause.

If the State Alabama was behaving in an unconstitutional manner, then so was George Washington. So were all his contemporaries who wrote the document, and who endorsed prayer and promoted religion. Indeed, as far as the anointed ones on the Supreme Court are concerned, all individuals and institutions in America prior to the Court's mysterious epiphany in *Everson* were in violation of the Constitution. This is how far the Courts have taken us toward cultural Marxism's goal of not only making this nation not just non-Christian but anti-Christian. For instance, U.S. District Judge Samuel Kent once decreed that any student uttering the word "Jesus" at a school graduation would be arrested and locked up: "And make no mistake," Kent said, "the court is going to have a United States marshal in attendance at the graduation. If any student offends this court, that student will be summarily arrested and will face up to six months incarceration in the Galveston County Jail for contempt of court."[10] Locked up and charged for exercising the religious and free speech rights guaranteed in the First Amendment! This obnoxious bully was himself jailed for 33 months in 2009 for five counts of sexual assault on female employees (a fan of Marcuse's *Eros and Civilization* no doubt) and obstruction of justice.[11] Kent's bullying was made possible by the Supreme Court decision in *Lee v. Weisman.*

No Thanking God at Graduation: *Lee v. Weisman* (1992)

In its relentless battle against religious freedom, the Supreme Court delivered another devastating blow in its 5 - 4 decision in *Lee v.Weisman*. In this case, the Court interpreted the Establishment Clause so broadly that its boundaries could not be seen, but somewhere in that vast expanse, the Free Exercise Clause was buried. The case began with Robert E. Lee, the principal of Nathan Bishop Middle School in Providence, Rhode Island, invited a Jewish rabbi to deliver a non-sectarian prayer at the school's graduation ceremony in 1989. The parents of student Deborah Weisman objected and requested a temporary injunction barring the rabbi from saying the prayer. A district judge denied the Weismans' motion and the rabbi did deliver the benediction with the Weisman family in attendance. However, the Weismans' continued their objections and won a victory their appeal at the First Circuit Court of Appeals.

The school district then appealed to the Supreme Court. The school argued that not only was the prayer nonsectarian, but it was also doubly voluntary in that Deborah was free to remain seated during the prayer and she was free not to attend the ceremony. The majority opinion relied on the notion that Deborah was psychologically coerced into bearing the "burden" of having to listen to the rabbi's dedication and invocation. As Justice Kennedy put it in the majority opinion: "Attendance may not be required by official decree, yet it is apparent that a student is not free to absent herself from the graduation exercise in any real sense of the term 'voluntary,' for absence would require forfeiture of those intangible benefits which have motivated the student through youth and all her high school years." He further argued that even to stand when others do respectfully would mean that Deborah had been coerced into participation in, and granting approval of, something she presumably found offensive. Thus, millions of high school graduates across the nation cannot engage in what could be a moving spiritual experience because one student objected that she was coerced, and the Supreme Court bought it. We will see later that this "coerced to participate" reasoning does not apply to Christians being coerced on pain of financial ruin to accept and participate in practices they find highly objectionable.

In Justice Scalia's robust defense of religious freedom in his scathing dissent, he made some trenchant remarks. He noted that The Court has denied school graduation invocations on the grounds of "psychological coercion "when other institutions (such as Congress and the Court itself) are permitted them. Never one to mince words, he wrote mockingly that:

[I]interior decorating is a rock-hard science compared to psychology practiced by amateurs. A few citations of "[r]esearch in psychology" that have no particular bearing upon the precise issue here, cannot disguise the fact that the Court has gone beyond the realm where judges know what they are doing...The Court's notion that a student who simply sits in "respectful silence" during the invocation and benediction (when all others are standing) has somehow joined—or would somehow be perceived as having joined—in the prayers is nothing short of ludicrous....In holding that the Establishment Clause prohibits invocations and benedictions at public school graduation ceremonies, the Court...lays waste a tradition that is as old as public school graduation ceremonies themselves, and that is a component of an even more longstanding American tradition of nonsectarian prayer to God at public celebrations generally. As its instrument of destruction, the bulldozer of its social engineering, the Court invents a boundless, and boundlessly manipulable, test of psychological coercion.

No Prayers at Football Games: Santa Fe Independent School District. v. Doe (2000)

In *Santa Fe Independent School District v. Jane Doe*, the Supreme Court ruled that the practice of opening high school football games with a prayer is unconstitutional. The case was initiated in 1995 by parents who objected to the prayer. In response to the lawsuit, the school district changed its policy to permits only prayers initiated and led by students. A Federal Court of Appeals ruled that even the practice of student-initiated prayers of a non-denominational nature is unconstitutional. The Supreme Court agreed in a 6-3 decision.

We now have the weird notion that somehow a group of students initiating a prayer amounts to Congress establishing a religion. The complainants could not argue the notion that subtle coercion to participate was involved as in *Lee v. Weisman,* since attendance at a football game, is entirely voluntary. Where is the government coercion that the Court claimed to be present? Justice Stevens answers this for us:

> Undoubtedly, the games are not important to some students, and they voluntarily choose not to attend. For many others, however, the choice between whether to attend these games or to risk facing a personally offensive religious ritual is in no practical sense an easy one. The Constitution, moreover, demands that the school may not force this difficult choice upon these students.

Here we have the image of some poor snowflake facing the horrible "risk" of being exposed to a community-affirming prayer described by Stevens as an "offensive religious ritual," which says a lot about his hostility to religion. Students delivering their pregame message were surely surprised to find that the Court considered them bullying agents of the government, just as surely as school officials were surprised that they were "forcing" a "difficult choice" on students. The Court ruling inhibits the free speech as well as free exercise rights of students and tells Christian students that their beliefs and desires are subordinate to the beliefs and desires of a few malcontents. If the ruling did not have tragic consequences, it would be laughable.

Chief Justice Rehnquist delivered a strong dissent noting the hostility of other Justices to religion, America's heritage, and to the plain meaning of the Establishment Clause:

> The Court distorts existing precedent to conclude that the school district's student-message program is invalid on its face under the Establishment Clause. But even more disturbing than its holding is the tone of the Court's opinion; it bristles with hostility to all things religious in public life. Neither the holding nor the tone of the opinion is faithful to the meaning of the Establishment Clause, when it is recalled that George Washington himself, at the request of the very Congress which passed the Bill of Rights, proclaimed a day of "public thanksgiving and prayer, to be observed by acknowledging with grateful hearts the many and signal favors of Almighty God."

Christians Must let the Fox in the Chicken Coup or Burn the Coop

The inhibition of religion is not confined to K-12 schools. In *Christian Legal Society v. Martinez*, the Supreme Court ruled 5 - 4 against a First Amendment challenge by the Hastings chapter of the Christian Legal Society (CLS) to the policy of the University of California Hastings College of the Law governing the official recognition of student groups. Members of CLS were required to sign a "Statement of Faith" and to live in accordance with Christian beliefs and values and disqualified from membership anyone who engaged in "acts of sexual conduct outside of God's design for marriage between one man and one woman." Because of these prescriptions, the CLS was denied "registered student organization" (ROS) status. The CLS complained that it was the only group denied the right to participate in the life of the law school community on equal terms with other groups (60 in all) because of its faith-based nature, and that "To require a religious group like CLS to admit nonbelievers is a severe burden on its freedom of association." CLS also emphasized that it was the only group ever to be denied RSO status at Hastings.

Justice Alito wrote in his dissenting opinion, joined by Justices Roberts, Scalia, and Thomas, that the college's policy that required all student groups to accept all-comers was written *ex post facto* following the onset of litigation in 2004. He also noted that the bylaws of other ROSs at Hastings had provisions denying membership to students disagreeing with the views and objectives of the organization (surely the right to limit membership is essential to any group's identity and message), meaning that CLS was uniquely burdened. According to the dissenting Justices, the Court ruling turned a blind eye to three Constitutional rights of the CLS denied them by Hastings: (1) Freedom of religious expression (its bylaws were deemed unacceptable to Hastings, so it would not allow them to express this view); (2) freedom of speech (CLS was denied access to campus bulletin boards, facilities, and the school newspaper), and (3) freedom of association (unlike other ROSs, CLS was not permitted the freedom to choose with whom it wants to associate). It is as unlikely that an "unrepentant" homosexual would want to join the CLS as an African American is to want to join the KKK, a Jew the Nazi Party, or a cultural Marxist the American TEA Party Movement. It is more likely that Hastings' policy is just another pretext for banning Christianity from public life.

The most recent example anti-Christian attacks on higher education is California State Bill 1146 that would have allowed LGBT students to sue private religious universities for discrimination if they are disciplined for violating church teachings. These potential violations include engaging in homosexual activity and using restrooms, locker rooms and student housing that correspond with the gender with which they say they identify rather than with their biological sex. Due to opposition from Republican senators and from religious groups, in 2016 the California Senate amended that provision, but the bill still requires religious schools to prominently disclose the contents of the bill to students and for colleges to report to the state when students are expelled for violating moral codes. The sponsor of the bill, Democratic Senator Ricardo Lara, said that he will press forward to get the dropped provision reintroduced in 2017. The open goal of demagogues such as Lara is forced Christian colleges to accept the LGBT agenda and to surrender their belief systems or to shut down. Lara and company have found common ground with Georg Lukacs' educational goal for Hungary almost 100 years ago.

Christianity Exposing Itself

The Supreme Court has treated Christians displaying the symbols of their faith as akin to the stereotypical "dirty old man in a greasy raincoat" flashing in public. A case in point is *Roberts v. Madigan* from 1989 in which a federal court ruled it unconstitutional for a classroom library to contain books on Christianity, or for a teacher to be seen with a personal copy of the Bible at school. Kenneth Roberts, a fifth-grade teacher in Denver, had a Bible on his desk at school and read it during a 15-minute silent reading period in class. He was ordered by school principle to desist and to remove other Christian books from the library. Mr. Roberts filed suit claiming that Ms. Madigan's action inhibited religion by disparaging Christianity since other books in his classroom on Greek gods and American Indian religions were not banned. The Court noted that Mr. Roberts claimed that his "practice of reading his Bible during the class 15-minute silent reading period was a minimal, discreet exercise of the Free Exercise Clause of the First Amendment. As such, Principal Madigan and the School District unduly burdened Mr. Roberts' rights." Nevertheless, the Court ruled that Roberts' claim had no merit (and therefore neither did the Free Exercise Clause) and ruled against him. When Roberts appealed to the Supreme Court, in a 5-4 decision, the Justices let stand without comment the rulings of the lower court.

One of the latest examples of treating religious displays as corruption is that of a football coach and marine veteran Joe Kennedy. Kennedy lost his job at Bremerton High School in Washington State in 2015 because of the practice he has had since 2008 of kneeling and praying after games on the 50-yard line. When Kennedy filed suit, in *Kennedy v. Bremerton School District* (2017) a three-panel judge of the 9th Circuit Court of Appeals ruled that the district was justified with these words: "When Kennedy kneeled and prayed on the 50-yard line immediately after games while in view of students and parents, he spoke as a public employee, not as a private citizen, and his speech, therefore, was constitutionally unprotected." First Liberty President and CEO Kelly Shackelford said in a press release that, "Banning all coaches from praying individually in public just because they can be seen is wrong. This is not the America contemplated by our Constitution." In an interview on Fox News, Shackelford said, "It's almost like prayer is the new pornography."[12] Indeed, the Court of Appeals seems to be saying that Kennedy could engage in his "lewd" conduct in some secluded spot if you must, but don't corrupt others who might see you. As Shackelford says, this is not the Constitution envisioned by its authors, but it is the constitution that has been slowly mutilated by the Supreme Court with respect to religious liberty since 1947.

Justice O'Connor commented of the Court's increasing animosity to religion under its growing "strict separation" view of the Establishment Clause in *Board of Education of Kiryas Joel Village School District v. Grumet.* In this 1994 case, the Court ruled on the constitutionality of a school district in New York designed to coincide with the neighborhood boundaries of a religious community that practiced a strict form of Judaism. The association of state school boards filed a lawsuit claiming that the statute created a school district that limited access only to residents of Kiryas Joel, and the Court ruled the practice unconstitutional. The nuances of the case are less important than Justice O'Connor's penetrating remarks on the Court's growing animosity to religion:

> The Religion Clauses prohibit the government from favoring religion, but they provide no warrant for discriminating against religion...The Establishment Clause does not demand hostility to religion, religious ideas, religious people, or religious schools. It is the Court's insistence on disfavoring religion in *Aguilar* that led New York to favor it here. The court should, in a proper case, be prepared to reconsider *Aguilar,* in order to bring our Establishment Clause jurisprudence back to what I think is the proper track-government impartiality, not animosity, towards religion.

The *Aguilar* decision to which O'Connor refers is *Aguilar v. Felton* (1985), the case in which the Court held that public school teachers can offer remedial instruction to disadvantaged students who attend religious schools only if held off the premises of religious schools. Despite the fact that field supervisors monitored classroom activities for religious content (heaven forbid that children would be introduced to moral precepts), this ruling denied disadvantaged students attending religious schools the help they needed. Surely this is discriminatory, and as O'Connor indicated, "hostile to religion."

But O'Connor revealed that she is also uncomfortable with religion in some instances. In *Lynch v. Donnelly,* the issue involved the erection of a Christmas display in a park owned by a nonprofit organization in Pawtucket, Rhode Island, as part the observance of Christmas. The display contained decorations traditionally associated with Christmas, such as a Santa Claus, reindeer pulling Santa's sleigh, a Christmas tree, carolers, and many other things including one to which Daniel Donnelly objected—a nativity scene. In a minor victory for Christianity, the Court ruled that notwithstanding the religious significance of the crèche, the Establishment Clause had not been violated because the park was owned by a private group. Although Justice O'Connor ruled with the 5-4 majority, she made the point that allowing public displays of religious icons is endorsement, and "Endorsement sends a message to nonadherents that they are outsiders, not full members of the political community, and an accompanying message to adherents that they are insiders, favored members of the political community." In other words, O'Conner's message is that if an atheist or non-Christian is exposed to a crèche or across feels left out and offended, he or she should be protected from such feelings by law. The feelings of Christians offended by the removal of their symbols are, of course, of no consequence.

This is an argument that is beyond the pale of preposterous. As a Christian, I have been in synagogues, mosques, and temples and viewed Stars of David, crescent moons, and various non-Christian icons without ever feeling the least bit offended. During sojourns in Britain and France, I have also bluffed my way through *God Save the Queen* and *La Marseillaise* in the spirit of "When in Rome" and respect for my hosts. Is it not also the case that practicing Christians may feel that they are outsiders, not full members of the school community because they must shed their Christian faith at the school doors?

If someone feels left out and offended when they see something they are not a part of, that's entirely their problem, and they should seek treatment for their delicate psyches. There is no right not to be offended. As law professor Steven Smith put it writing about two women who objected to the prayer preceding town meetings in Greece, New York, complaining that "people don't realize how hard it is to be a minority faith": "You may, in fact, be an 'outsider' in the practical sense of holding a minority...view, but you have the same rights to speak, vote, run for office, be tried by a jury, etc., etc., as everybody else. In that decisive sense, you are an equal citizen; you have equal 'standing in the political community.'"[13]

Ken Klukowski, another law professor, made the same common sense point as Smith a bit more forcefully in response to the ACLU's successful effort to get a nativity scene removed from a Pittsburgh courthouse in *County of Allegheny v. ACLU*. He makes the point people see things protected by the First Amendment that may offend them every day, but you can't use that feeling of distaste to muzzle free expression. "If you don't like the nativity display, then don't look at it. So long as government agents are not compelling you to bow before it, pray to it, or put money in an offering box beside it, the Establishment Clause is not offended. [14]

The upshot of all this anti-Christian animosity, particularly as it relates to schools, has led "to a society that lacks a unifying or common narrative. When religion is exorcised from the public schools, we raise generation after generation of citizens with no clear sense concerning the foundations of moral values, ethical behavior, or interpersonal conduct. As a result, many Americans struggle with issues of worth and identity, lacking a clear sense of either self or community."[15] This is the tragedy wrought by an unaccountable legal priesthood that thinks it knows the Constitution better than its authors, and who, much to the delight of cultural Marxists, seem hell-bent on cleansing America of its Christian heritage.

Endnotes

1. Federer, *America's God and Country*, p. 392.
2. Jefferson, *The Writings of Thomas Jefferson* p. 415.
3. Yale Law School, Northwest Ordinance
4. Quoted in Sampson, *The Heart of Wisdom* p. 473.
5. Congressional Record, vol. 146, p. H8894.
6. Should anyone contest this, they may peruse the voluminous notes of the 90 men involved in crafting the First Amendment contained in the 1789 *Congressional Record*. Not once will they find the "separation" phrase or see any hint that any of these men remotely believed there to be a conflict between the two religious clauses.
7. Noll, *One Nation Under God*, p. 67.
8. Kuntzman, Major league baseball must permanently retire 'God Bless America.'
9. Ironically, one of O'Hair's sons, William J. Murray, became a Christian minister. He called his mother "an evil person," who was viciously rude and profanely vulgar spending her time viewing pornography and drinking and had statuettes of mating animals all over the house. She was certainly a powerful foot soldier for cultural Marxism. Both her sons were born illegitimately, which she seemed to be proud of. William characterized the O'Hair household as "dysfunctional, where God was denounced and Marxism taught." Madalyn, another son, and a granddaughter were kidnapped and murdered by fellow atheists (one of whom worked within her organization) in 1995.
10. McDowell and Hostetler. The new tolerance, p. 53.
11. Powel, Judge Kent reports to prison hospital in Massachusetts.
12. Shackelford, Court rules against Coach Kennedy.
13. Smith, *Town of Greece v. Galloway* symposium.

14. Klukowski, Symposium: Time to restore longstanding meaning.
15. Shrader, Thou shalt not, p. 5.

Cases Cited

Abington School District v. Schempp, 374 U.S. 203 (1963)
Aguilar v. Felton, 473 U.S. 402 (1985)
Board of Education of Kiryas Joel Village School District v. Grumet, 512 U.S. 687 (1994)
Christian Legal Society v. Martinez, 561 U.S. 661 (2011)
County of Allegheny v. ACLU, 492 U.S. 573 (1989)
Engel v. Vitale, 370 U.S. 421 (1962)
Lee v. Weisman, 505 U.S. 577 (1992)
Lynch v. Donnelly, 465 U.S. 668 (1984)
Roberts v. Madigan, 702 F. Supp. 1505 (D. Colo. 1989)
Santa Fe Independent School Dist. *v. Doe, 530 U.S. 290 (2000)*
Stone v. Graham, 449 U.S. 39 (1980)
Wallace v. Jaffree, 472 U.S. 38 (1985).

Chapter 8

The Impact of Same-Sex Marriage: Gay Rights v. Religious Liberty

"Many good and decent people oppose same-sex marriage as a tenet of faith, and their freedom to exercise religion is—unlike the right imagined by the majority [of the Court]—actually spelled out in the Constitution."
John Roberts, Chief Justice of the United States Supreme Court

Homosexuality: From Mental Illness to Protected Category

Religious freedom has been a given in the United States since its inception. Although these rights have been slowly eroded since the 1940s, in the first two decades of the twenty-first century, the erosion gathered speed as religious liberty has been pitted against gay rights. When these two contesting rights butt heads, it is almost a foregone conclusion that gay rights will prevail. The idea of granting special rights to homosexuals that trump religious liberty would have made the Founders apoplectic. Such a thought, however, would probably never have entered their minds because homosexuality was "The love that dare not speak its name."

Throughout history, homosexuals have been faced with the tragic choice of either denying their sexual identities or facing ostracism, prejudice, discrimination, and harsh legal penalties. It was just over three decades ago that the Supreme Court upheld Georgia's anti-sodomy statute in *Bowers v. Hardwick* (1986). The Court maintained that Georgia's statute served a legitimate state interest because it was related to "notions of morality." Justice Byron White, writing the majority opinion, stated that the Constitution does not confer "a fundamental right to engage in homosexual sodomy." Chief Justice Warren Burger's concurring opinion noted the "ancient roots" of prohibitions against homosexual sex, that its condemnation is firmly rooted in Judeo-Christian morality, and that it was a capital crime under Roman law. Burger cited William Blackstone's comments that homosexuality is an "infamous crime against nature...the very mention of which is a disgrace to human nature..." a crime not fit to be named."

While I find the Court's remarks in *Bowers* (even if quoting others) cruelly insulting, it is not because I sanctimoniously claim to love homosexuals but hate their sin, as in the cliché "Love the sinner but hate the sin." When we label a person a sinner, it is difficult to justify the claim that we love them, and it is hypocritical to claim that in any meaningful sense one *loves* any group of individuals outside their extended family. I don't love homosexuals, but I respect their humanity, dignity, and rights, and wish them no harm.

Neither do I condemn their private behavior as sin, although most Christians would not agree with me. The public behavior of some homosexuals participating in gay pride parades is truly vile and obnoxious, but their behavior in the privacy of their bedrooms is an expression of the sexual urges we all have, homosexual and heterosexual alike. Non-marital sex is considered a sin regardless of whether or not it is of a same- or opposite-sex nature, but who among us is so innocent of it that they feel entitled to cast the first stone? What I hate and condemn is the anti-Christian tactics of radical gay activists, not homosexuals per se. Cultural Marxists and gay activists see the fight against Christianity as total war, and nothing less than unconditional surrender is acceptable. As Rod Dreher notes: "Christians and other religious conservatives, who now understand that the left's culture warriors, having won the gay-rights conflict decisively, are determined to shoot the prisoners."[1]

Until 1973 the American Psychiatric Association (APA) listed homosexuality as a mental illness containing aspects of psychopathy, paranoia, and schizophrenia. Heavy criticism from the gay community led the APA to remove it from its list of mental illnesses and to characterize it as a "sexual preference," which is a phrase that implies choice. Choice suggests alternatives are possible, enabling family members and religious counselors to bombard homosexuals with moral exhortations and offers of therapy to help them to see that their choice was sinful. Up to and including the 1940s, many states had draconian strategies designed to "cure" people of their homosexuality. There are cases in which gay were subjected to electric shock treatment, aversion therapy, castration, and in rare instances, lobotomies were performed on gays and hysterectomies were performed on lesbians.[2]

The Prevalence of Homosexuality

Participants in gay pride parades love to chant "Ten percent is not enough, recruit, recruit, recruit!" The ten percent figure refers to claims that homosexuals constitute 10 percent of the human population. This figure is based on early studies by Alfred Kinsey, who used sampling methods that ensured the overrepresentation of homosexuals. Kinsey was a person who fit neatly into Herbert Marcuse's polymorphous perverse category. He lived in an "open" marriage with his wife, engaged in many deviant acts, tried to sanitize child sex abuse, and claimed that 95 percent of men engage in deviant sexual behavior such as incest and homosexual sodomy. In an effort to "normalize" his own lifestyle he had an interest in elevating the prevalence of deviant sexuality. In their book *Kinsey, sex and fraud: The indoctrination of a people,* Judith Reisman and Edward Eichel unmasked Kinsey's work as a massive hoax and laid bare his private life. They opened their book with these words: "No man in modern times has shaped public attitudes to, and perceptions of, human sexuality more than the late Alfred C. Kinsey. He advocated that all sexual behaviors considered deviant were normal while polemicizing that exclusive heterosexuality was abnormal and a product of cultural inhibitions and societal conditioning."

When assessing the prevalence of homosexuality, it is necessary to differentiate between same-sex attraction, homosexual behavior, and sexual identity. Studies often do not do this, and are done more to assess the health problems associated with homosexuality than to estimate its prevalence. However, there is ample evidence that a small but stable percentage of people regard themselves as unequivocally homosexual. An American study estimated the prevalence to be 2.1 percent of men and 1.5 percent of women.[4] A British survey found the prevalence of males who were gay to be 2.8 percent,[5] and a Dutch study found it to be 2.8 percent of men and 1.4 percent of women.[6] A large Canadian study of 289,767 students from British Columbia found that although only 1.5 of all boys identified as either bisexual, or mostly or completely homosexual, 3.5 percent of boys said they had had sex with a male in the previous year.[7] A 2012 Gallup poll of to more than 120,000 U.S. adults found that only 3.4 percent answered "yes" when asked if they identify as lesbian, gay, bisexual, or transgender (LBGT).[8]

No Exit: Homosexual Identity is not a Choice

In recognition of the growing scientific consensus that the roots of homosexuality are biological, the phrase *sexual orientation* has replaced sexual preference. The growing awareness of this fact led to the decriminalization of homosexual behavior in 2003 when the U. S. Supreme Court struck down Texas' anti-sodomy statute in *Lawrence v. Texas.* The Court ruled the statute unconstitutional because it discriminated against homosexuals since same-sex sodomy was legal but opposite-sex sodomy was not. The Court did a complete U-turn from *Bowers* in *Lawrence,* essentially saying that anti-sodomy laws served no state interest and were expressions of anti-gay animus. *Lawrence* freed homosexuals from state intrusion and allowed them leeway to define their own morality. This opened up the situation in which Christians who act on their faith are now the targets of state intrusion and who are given no leeway to define *their* morality. It is devout Christians who act in ways contrary to the LBGT agenda who are now faced with the tragic choice of either denying their religious identities or facing bigotry and legal sanctions.

Most homosexuals say that they have known from an early age that they were exclusively sexually attracted to members of the same sex.[9] In effect, this means that their sexual orientation is conforming to the way their brains, genes, and hormones bias them, despite social pressures to the contrary. As noted above, these pressures have included religious and family exhortations, psychotherapy, hysterectomy, lobotomy, imprisonment, and even the threat of death in some societies, to coerce them to change. Would anyone choose to be homosexual under those conditions? Homosexuals no more make a choice from equally likely alternatives to be homosexual than heterosexuals are to make a similar choice to be heterosexual. After all, did anyone in the throes of their awakening sexuality toss a coin or do the "Eenie meenie minie moe" thing to select the sex to which it should be directed?

The debate about the origins of homosexuality is often couched in either/or terms; either 100 percent biological or simply a choice influenced by developmental experiences or situational factors. Like many other things, the truth is never simple. After reviewing the genetic, epigenetic, neurobiology, and hormonal evidence, two prominent researchers concluded that: "The preponderance of evidence from sexual orientation research strongly suggests that human sexual orientation has biological underpinnings and that it is tightly regulated at the molecular level."[10] Thus, someone with an abiding unambiguous, and singular attraction to same-sex partners is probably closer to the "100 percent biological" end, while homosexual behavior displayed by those claiming heterosexual identity is probably attributable to situational factors.

Resistance to outside coercion to change is one thing, but the best evidence that a gay identity cannot be changed comes from people who have desperately tried to change of their own volition but could not. The nation's largest "ex-gay" Christian ministry founded in 1976, Exodus International, claimed that homosexuality could be cured by prayer and counseling, placing heavy emphasis on the adverse physical, mental, and spiritual consequences of a gay lifestyle. Exodus International was dissolved in 2013 after almost four decades of well-intentioned but fruitless effort. Alan Chambers, The president of Exodus International, spoke in a panel discussion at the annual conference of the Gay Christian Network saying that: "The majority of people that I have met, and I would say the majority meaning 99.9% of them have not experienced a change in their orientation or have gotten to a place where they could say that they could never be tempted or are not tempted in some way or experience some level of same-sex attraction."[11] Exodus International's four-decade crusade reveals that there are a number of gays who, for whatever reason, would like not to be, but who cannot change their biological "wiring" any more than a straight person can.

Same-Sex Marriage and its Implications

The *Lawrence* ruling was followed by the Supreme Court's ruling in *United States v. Winsor* (2013) invalidating a key section of the Defense of Marriage Act that restricted the terms "marriage" and "spouse" to opposite-sex couples. This ruling fermented a revolution that has turned the tables 180 degrees. Whereas it used to be a case of religious and legal authorities exhorting homosexuals to discard their identities, we now have gay activists and legal authorities demanding that Christians discard theirs when they clash with LGBT rights. This has occurred because *Winsor* appears to have elevated the level of scrutiny in gay rights cases. As previously noted, "level of scrutiny" is a vague legal concept that has been applied inconsistently, making it difficult to determine the current level of scrutiny in homosexual discrimination cases. Sexual orientation has not achieved "strict scrutiny" status along with religion, race, and national origin, but homosexuals have been transformed into a quasi-protected class and afforded heightened scrutiny, which sits between the strict scrutiny and rational basis standards of review. This new found protection has emboldened gay activists to embark on a crusade against Christian's religious rights. As noted above, religion falls into a protected class category which cannot be targeted for discrimination, but the government has no qualms about discriminating against religious believers when their actions oppose the demands of LGBT individuals.

Although *Winsor* merely settled a narrow claim for estate tax exemption under federal tax law, it set the terms for challenges to state bans on same-sex marriage. That is, while *Winsor* did not establish a Constitutional right for same-sex marriage, it was a clear indication that the Court was trending in favor of it. Indeed, it was only two years later when the Supreme Court ruled in a 5-4 decision in *Obergefell v. Hodges* (2015) that same-sex marriages are legal in every state. There were two issues before the Supreme Court in *Obergefell*: (1) Does the Fourteenth Amendment require a state to license a marriage between two people of the same sex? (2) Does the Fourteenth Amendment require a state to recognize a same-sex marriage when the marriage was lawfully licensed and performed in another state? Writing for the majority in *Obergefell*, Justice Kennedy concluded:

The Court, in this decision, holds same-sex couples may exercise the fundamental right to marry in all States. It follows that the Court also must hold—and it now does hold—that there is no lawful basis for a State to refuse to recognize a lawful same-sex marriage performed in another State on the ground of its same-sex character.

Scathing dissenting opinions by Justices Roberts, Scalia, Thomas, and Alito were mostly based on the Court once again undermining the democratic process. It was noted that of the 35 states that put the issue to the electorate, 32 opted to retain the traditional definition of marriage Of the other states allowing gay marriage before *Obergefell,* only eight states did so by legislative action; the others by judicial fiat. Justice Scalia called the decision "a naked claim [by the Court] to legislative—indeed, super-legislative—power; a claim fundamentally at odds with our system of government." Chief Justice Roberts invited anyone who wishes to celebrate the Court' decision to legalize same-sex marriage to do so: "But do not celebrate the Constitution. It had nothing to do with it." The other major concern addressed was religious liberty. In Justice Thomas' dissent he wrote:

In our society, marriage is not simply a governmental institution; it is a religious institution as well. Today's decision might change the former, but it cannot change the latter. It appears all but inevitable that the two will come into conflict, particularly as individuals and churches are on-fronted with demands to participate in and endorse civil marriages be-tween same-sex couples...[and this has] potentially ruinous conse-quences for religious liberty.

Justice Scalia took the ruling as an opportunity to attack again the Court's usurpation of the democratic legislative process and the dangers this poses:

Today's decree says that my Ruler, and the Ruler of 320 million Ameri-cans coast-to-coast, is a majority of the nine lawyers on the Supreme Court. The opinion in these cases is the furthest extension in fact—and the furthest extension one can even imagine—of the Court's claimed the power to create "liberties" that the Constitution and its Amend-ments neglect to mention. This practice of constitutional revision by an unelected committee of nine, always accompanied (as it is today) by extravagant praise of liberty, robs the People of the most important liberty they asserted in the Declaration of Independence and won in the Revolution of 1776: the freedom to govern themselves.

Justice Alito's comments are the most worrisome. First, he also points out that a bare majority of the Supreme Court has usurped legislative power and denied the people the right to have their say. Second, he chides the majority for their "discovery" of a new right unimaginable just a few decades ago and then forcing the rest of us to accept it. And third, he notes the chilling effect the decision will have on free speech and the bullying it will justify.

> Today's decision usurps the constitutional right of the people to decide whether to keep or alter the traditional understanding of marriage. The decision will also have other important consequences. It will be used to vilify Americans who are unwilling to assent to the new orthodoxy. In the course of its opinion, the majority compares traditional marriage laws to laws that denied equal treatment for African-Americans and women. The implications of this analogy will be exploited by those who are determined to stamp out every vestige of dissent...I assume that those who cling to old beliefs will be able to whisper their thoughts in the recesses of their homes, but if they repeat those views in public, they will risk being labeled as bigots and treated as such by governments, employers, and schools... If a bare majority of Justices can invent a new right and impose that right on the rest of the country, the only real limit on what future majorities will be able to do is their own sense of what those with political power and cultural influence are willing to tolerate.

The Gay Marriage Fight does not Mirror the Interracial Marriage Fight

Justice Alito notes in this passage that the moral claims evoked by the ban on interracial marriage in years past was cited in the majority opinion and jumped on to claim that the religious objection to same-sex marriage is animated by the same bigotry. This analogy has been the most effective of all morality-based arguments for same-sex marriage, although as Justice Thomas wrote in his dissent in *Obergefell* in which the plaintiffs made the spurious analogy: "Laws defining marriage as between one man and one woman do not share this sordid history. The traditional definition of marriage has prevailed in every society that has recognized marriage throughout history."

The interracial marriage issue was settled in, *Loving v. Virginia* (1967). The issue before the Court was the marriage of Richard Loving, a white man, and Mildred, a black woman, who had to leave Virginia to get married because of Virginia's anti-miscegenation law. Upon their return, they were arrested and sentenced to one-year imprisonment, which was suspended on the condition that they leave Virginia. In the Court's opinion striking down the Virginia law,

Chief Justice Earl Warren quoted the Loving's trial judge, Leon Bazile's rationale for the Virginia law and the Lovings' conviction: "Almighty God created the races white, black, yellow, Malay and red, and he placed them on separate continents. And, but for the interference with his arrangement, there would be no cause for such marriage. The fact that he separated the races shows that he did not intend for the races to mix." This is an argument made on religious grounds, but it is one man's claim that he can read the Almighty's mind as to why the different races are found on different continents, and not something explicitly found in the Bible.

Judge Bazile's reference to "separate continents" is based on Acts 17:26: "And he made from one man every nation of mankind to live on all the face of the earth, having determined allotted periods and the boundaries of their dwelling place." Deuteronomy 7:3 was also used to bolster anti-miscegenation laws: "Furthermore, you shall not intermarry with them; you shall not give your daughters to their sons, nor shall you take their daughters for your sons." But Deuteronomy 7:4 is clear that it was not race to which 7:3 was referring, but to marriage to people who worshiped other gods: "For they will turn your sons away from following Me to serve other gods; then the anger of the Lord will be kindled against you, and He will quickly destroy you." This is supported by Corinthians 6:14-15: "Do not be bound together with unbelievers; for what partnership have righteousness and lawlessness, or what fellowship has light with darkness?" It is clear that an anti-miscegenation case cannot be made on Biblical grounds.

While a Biblical rationale for opposing interracial marriage requires an eccentric interpretation, the rationale for opposing same-sex marriage is unambiguous and accepted by all three religions "of the Book." It is beyond question that all Biblical references to marriage beginning with Genesis see it as a lifetime commitment between a man and a woman. All references to homosexuality in the Bible condemn it (see for instance, Leviticus 20:13, Romans 1:26-27 and First Corinthians 6:9). Unlike the beliefs of those who were opposed to interracial marriage, those who refuse to recognize same-sex marriages make their stand on solid religious ground. However, I am of the opinion, shared by many theologians, that much of the harshness of the Old Covenant's Mosaic laws have been abrogated, and that Christians now live under the New Covenant of Christ's love for all.

Unlike the same-sex marriage issue, religion played a supporting role in the fight against anti-miscegenation laws. In *Perez v. Sharpe* (1948), Perez challenged California's interracial marriage ban, and the California Supreme Court agreed, becoming the first court to strike down an interracial marriage ban, and did so in light of *religious* arguments. As Fay Botham notes that these arguments arose from Catholic doctrine that "has no law forbidding "the intermarriage of a nonwhite person and a white person"…that the Church "respects the requirements of the State for the marriage of its citizens as long as they are in keeping with the dignity and Divine purpose of marriage."[12]

Arguments were also made by a number of religious groups in *Loving* that bans on interracial and religion-based justifications for them, distorted the understanding of both religion and marriage. These groups became involved, according to Susan Gold, "because of their commitment 'to end racial discrimination and prejudice' and because of the 'serious issues of personal liberty' raised by the Lovings' ordeal."[13] Both the Court majority in *Obergefell* and gay activists are seriously in error in conflating real religious objections to same-sex with concocted religious objections to interracial marriage.

In short, the issues of interracial and same-sex marriage are fundamentally different in at least two ways. First, after the legalization of interracial marriage, no dissenters were forced to participate in or facilitate one on pain of ruinous civil penalties and possibly jail, but religious dissenters who operate wedding-related businesses are forced to affirm same-sex marriage or face those penalties. Second, unlike the distortions and idiosyncratic interpretations of Biblical passages used to oppose interracial marriage, Old Testament opposition to homosexuality is unambiguous and not easily subjected to any alternative interpretation. I am not in agreement with these Old Testament teachings since I am convinced that homosexuality is just as biologically based as heterosexuality, but my opinion is irrelevant. The relevance lies in the beliefs of those being burdened because they adhere to them. Because these people adhere to Old Testament views, it does not mean that they hate homosexuals, or they are bigots who wish to harm them. With Douglas Laycock, I know of: "no American religious group that teaches discrimination against gays as such…. The religious liberty issue with respect to gays and lesbians is about directly facilitating the marriage, as with wedding services and marital counseling."[14]

Consequences of the Homosexual Victory

The fears expressed by the dissenters in *Obergefell* were already a reality years before. Religious believers have increasingly become the new pariahs targeted for state intrusion designed to deny them leeway to define their moral convictions the way homosexuals can now define theirs. The intolerance, intimidation, and legal threats once aimed at homosexuals are now aimed at people with religious beliefs that marriage is only to be between men and women, and who act on those beliefs. Religious dissenters know that same-sex marriage is now the law of the land, and they simply want to be left alone to live their lives in accordance with their beliefs. But the moral beliefs of religious believers are summarily dismissed by LGBT activists as bigotry. Such intolerant attacks are becoming commonplace according to Andrew Koppleman: "A standard—but unfair—rhetorical move within the gay rights movement is to treat all its adversaries as mindless bigots" and that "it is a move that is increasingly successful."[15]

Koppleman gauges the extent of this success by the number of court cases in which the cause of LGBT rights has triumphed over the cause of religious liberty. An example of a successful attack (in the sense that it has public exposure that has gone unanswered) it that of National Gay Rights Lobby's Steve Endean: "Religion-based bigotry is not synonymous with bigotry. It is a uniquely vile form of bigotry as the prejudice, hostility, and discrimination behind the words are given a moral stamp of approval."[16] Gay activists do not want to contest religious beliefs in the give and take of the public forum. When it comes to LGBT issues, it's "We talk, you listen!" Their contempt and desire for the destruction of moral views was reported by David Penkof in the *Seattle Post-Intelligencer* who wrote that gay Democratic Washington state Sen. Ed Murray and a spokesperson for a Michigan gay-rights group called the Triangle Foundation, "have both told me that people who continue to act as if marriage is a union between a man and a woman should face being fined, fired and even jailed until they relent." [17]

A state senator (albeit, a Democrat) saying that someone should be fined, fired and jailed for exercising the rights of free speech and religious expression would have poleaxed any of the Founding Fathers. Yet the courts routinely rule in favor of the latter over the former and finding new rights and ignoring old ones. This is an affront to both the Constitution and to our Christian heritage. As Douglas Laycock put it: "If the Court feels free to enforce the *unenumerated* rights it likes and to strip all independent meaning from the *enumerated* rights it does not like, it's hard to see how the existence of a written Constitution affects its decisions."[18]

Some people see LGBT rights versus religious liberty as a clash between two Constitutional rights. This is wrong. What we have is a clash between rights enumerated in the Constitution and *statutory* rights. The legislation is not lawful per se until it passes Constitutional muster; that is, it must be viewed by the courts as consistent with the United States Constitution and with the constitution of the state making the law. It has always been black letter law that legislation may not limit the rights of individuals contained in the Constitution under which it was written. The relevant enumerated rights of Christians (and all Americans) that Laycock says are being stripped when gay rights are at issue are free to exercise of religion, free speech (including freedom fromf compelled speech), and freedom of association, all guaranteed by the First Amendment. The statutory rights clashing with Constitutional rights are those contained in such legislation as public accommodation laws. There is nothing wrong and everything right in providing rights not included in the Constitution. After all, that is why the Bill of Rights was added to it in the first place. However, such newly minted rights should not be granted preference at the expense of the ancient and natural rights enumerated in the Constitution.

Homosexuality in the Schoolroom

It is said that nature abhors a vacuum, and where there is one the void will be promptly filled. With God, prayer, and morality banished from the classroom, the vacuum is being filled with curricula designed to stamp out "hegemonic heterosexuality" by the affirmation and even the promotion of homosexuality This void is most rapidly filling in Canada, but America is not far behind. A 2011 editorial in a Vancouver gay and lesbian magazine noted that "The gay rights movement is shifting norms in Canada. And with that comes a message to those who won't evolve: your outdated morals are no longer acceptable, and we will teach your kids the new norms."[19] In public schools across Canada, and increasingly in the United States, this agenda is in full swing, and parents have no say in the matter. Gay activists have allied with radical feminists and atheists to attack and destroy all forms of traditional institutions, particularly religion. They want freedom for themselves and should have it, but in their "take no prisoners" attitude they want to take away the freedom of Christians by forcing them to acquiesce to their agenda and to sit quietly while their children are indoctrinated into affirming practices their parents find aberrant.

If it is the case that homosexuality is as biologically ordained as heterosexuality, why should anyone be worried about the promotion of homosexuality schools or elsewhere. If gays can't become straight, then straights can't become gay. But there is a big difference between sexual orientation (an abiding singular attraction to one sex or the other) and sexual behavior. Sexual orientation may be a biological given, but sexual behavior is a conscious choice. The active promotion of the gay agenda in schools sends clear signals to youth that electing to engage in homosexual behavior is acceptable, or even laudable.

The American College of Pediatricians (ACP) informs us that it is not uncommon for a certain percentage of children and adolescents to have same-sex attractions, but also that almost all of this group "will ultimately adopt a heterosexual orientation if not otherwise encouraged."[20] The acceptance of homosexuality as simply an alternate lifestyle and its active promotion in schools and in the print and electronic media may lead more young people to become "otherwise encouraged" into experimenting with homosexuality. If troubled and unpopular young people with feelings of negative self-worth and armed with pro-gay indoctrination happens to fall in with a gay activist group, they can be led to identify with the gay lifestyle. They may finally feel welcome and valued, even if only as a desirable sex partner, which carries heavy health risks. As the ACP put it: "The homosexual lifestyle, especially for males, carries grave health risks," and add: "For many youths, homosexual attraction develops due to negative or traumatic experiences, such as sexual abuse. These students need therapy for the trauma, not affirmation of a 'gay identity.'" [21]

Revealing such evidence often leads to charges of "homophobia." This is schoolyard name-calling that attempts to shut down rational discussion of the issue by shifting the focus from the issue and onto those who disagree with the approved view, while at the same time claiming the moral high ground. Hatred and bigotry are other terms aimed at people who reveal unwanted evidence. For instance, the ACP has been designated as yet another of its ever-expanding hate groups by the Southern Poverty Law Center (SPLC) for making the above statements aimed at protecting young lives but is anti-gay bigotry according to the SPLC[22]. Yet the affirmation and promotion charged by the ACP is exactly what is happening in our schools. Scot Livery cites the *Homosexual Manifesto*, by Michael Swift, which first appeared in the *Gay Community News* in 1987. The manifesto began with a quite disgusting paragraph: We shall sodomize your sons... We shall seduce them... wherever men are with men together. Your sons shall become our minions and do our bidding. They will be recast in our image."[23]

The *Manifesto* continues as if written by Karl Marx himself: "The family unit-spawning ground of lies, betrayals, mediocrity, hypocrisy, and violence-- will be abolished. The family unit, which only dampens imagination and curbs free will, must be eliminated...All churches who condemn us will be closed. Our only gods are handsome young men." [24]

Swift characterized his *Manifesto* essay as "an outré, madness, a tragic, cruel fantasy, an eruption of inner rage, on how the oppressed desperately dream of being the oppressor," but many a truth played out, in reality, is hidden in jest. After all, he also wrote that "Dreams when striven for CAN become a reality." Judge for yourself how far Swift dreams have becomes a reality.

The slow and subtle tactics employed by gay activists are torn from the pages of cultural Marxism and Fabianism. In order to advance the homosexual agenda, it is necessary to get the schools and universities talking about it in a supportive way to desensitize the public. Homosexual sexual imagery should be downplayed and gay rights promulgated as an abstract question of social justice. Gay activists Marshall Kirk and Erastes Pill reveal their stealthy agenda in their *The overhauling of straight America*. The first step is to cast homosexuals as victims in need of protection. They want to launch a media campaign to promote this image of gays-as-victims to both generate sympathy and to reduce "the mainstream's sense of threat, which lower its guard, and which enhance the plausibility of victimization. First, let the camel get his nose inside the tent--only later his unsightly derriere."[25]

We noted in chapter one that President Obama's "safe schools" czar, Kevin Jennings, is America's own Georg Lukacs, dedicated to promoting homosexuality in K-12 schools. In a true Fabian "wolf in sheep's clothing" fashion, it is being sold to the public in the name of safe schools, anti-bullying, and anti-discrimination—who could be against that? In a 2005 publication called *From Teasing to Torment: School climate in America*, the Gay, Lesbian, and Straight Education Network (GLSEN), founded by Jennings, tells us that 90 percent of the LGBT youth surveyed have experienced at least verbal harassment at school, although more for "the way they look or their body size" (39%) than their sexual orientation (33%).[26] Kids being what they are, I do not doubt this, but a larger government survey found almost as much teasing and bullying of various sorts of all school children, so why single out sexual orientation for special protection buttressed with pro-homosexual propaganda?[27] Why don't fat kids get a special agenda normalizing and promoting obesity; after all "body size" gets more teasing that homosexuality according to the GLSEN report. One reason is that largely on the basis of *From Teasing to Torment*, GLSEN received close to $1.5 million in government grants to promote its agenda in schools.[28] A million and a half dollars to promote homosexuality from the U.S. government that considers it a grievous secular sin to grant even a single dollar to promote Christian morality in our schools.

Much of the content of the GLSEN agenda is revealed in a Family Research Council document called *Homosexuality in your child's school*.[29] Among the many practices listed are the promotion of "gender neutral" bathrooms, exhorting students to attend gay pride parades, cross-dressing days, and a seminar "for youth only," on "fisting" (placing the fist in the anus of another male). Among the books GLSEN recommends for the curricula is *Rainbow Boys*, in which a teen has homosexual sex, graphically detailed, with an adult male contacted via the Internet, and *Queer 13* describing a 13-year-old boy's sexual encounter with an adult male in a bathroom. Such books have replaced religious and other works teaching morality, and are couched in approving terms implying this is just a normal part of growing up. If this all sounds just too sick to be true, check out the full list of recommended books for the educational curriculum on GLSEN's website at http://www.glsen.org/educate/resources/curriculum.

Unlike the case of parents who objected to schools prayers when they were the norm, there is no opt-out choice for parents who object to pro-homosexual indoctrination. One parent, David Parker, was arrested by the

Lexington, Massachusetts, police and jailed for "trespassing" at his son's elementary school during a meeting with the school principal over his objections to homosexual materials in the curriculum, but was repeatedly told that his was not possible. He refused to leave the meeting until his objection was resolved, which resulted in his arrest. Parker spent the night in jail and was told by his arraignment judge that if he set foot on any school property again, he would be arrested again for trespassing. Our neighbors to the north are worse. According to Lee Duigon, A *Lifesite News* headline says it all: "Toronto schools will not 'condone' exemptions from pro-homosexual classes." In the article, Chris Bolton, chairman of the Toronto District School Board, said that the board has "a policy of forbidding exemptions from the board's radical pro-homosexual curriculum, insisting ... that any attempts by parents 'would not be condoned' in their schools." The curriculum "specifically states that parents cannot remove their children from the classes for religious reasons."[30]

Canada also has a Constitution, the preamble of which states that "Canada is founded upon principles that recognize the supremacy of God." The Canadian Constitution also contains guarantees of "freedom of conscience and religion," but as in the United States, these guarantees apparently mean nothing when they run afoul of the LGBT agenda. When parents are denied the right to monitor the moral education of their children, it is plain that we are on our way to full-blown cultural Marxism, as socialist Norman Thomas happily predicted in 1944 (see chapter 1), "without knowing how it happened."

Health Risks of the Homosexual Lifestyle

Apart from the tyranny of running roughshod over parental and religious rights, there are other reasons to be worried about the promotion of the homosexual agenda in our schools. Medical professionals concerned with disease control have a behavioral category called "Men who have sex with men" (MSM). A 2015 Center for Disease Control and Prevention (CDCP) report noted that MSM accounted for 72 percent of new HIV infections among all persons aged 13 to 24. MSM are about 60 times more likely to contract HIV than other men and 54 times more likely than women. The report also noted that in 2013 MSM accounted for 81 percent of the estimated HIV diagnoses among all males aged 13 years and older, and 65 percent among all persons receiving an HIV diagnosis. Of MSM diagnosed with full-blown AIDS among all adults and adolescents in the United States, 40 percent were blacks/African Americans; 32 percent were whites, and 23 percent were Hispanics/Latinos. The large overrepresentation of blacks in the MSM population (6% of U.S. male population; 40% of AIDS cases) is the reason that black females (7% of the U.S. female population) accounted for 68 percent of heterosexual women newly diagnosed with HIV in 2010.[31] The SPLC has not yet designated the

CDCP as a hate group for publishing these "anti-gay" statistics, but stay tuned.

AIDS, along with other risk factors, leads to homosexuals having a significantly shorter average lifespan than heterosexuals. A major review of suicide studies by the Suicide Resource Prevention Center (SRPC) found that school-age homosexuals attempt suicide at least five times more often than heterosexual youths of the same age.[32] Of course, not all suicide attempts are the result of a genuine desire to end one's life, but it is indicative of some serious mental health issues. However, homosexuality per se is probably not causally related to psychological maladjustment; that is, the psychological disturbances we observe in homosexuals are not inherent in homosexuality but rather both by how they perceive others in society as viewing them and because of the typical homosexual lifestyle. Whatever the case may be, homosexuals have a much lower age of death than heterosexuals.

A 1994 American study examined 6,737 obituaries from 18 homosexual journals over 13 years during the years of the AIDS epidemic and was compared with an equal number of obituaries obtained from a variety of local newspapers. The obituaries from the local newspapers revealed that the median age at death of married men was 75 and for married women, it was 79, which mirrored national averages (unmarried and divorced heterosexuals died significantly earlier--men at 57 and women at 71—marriage is good for you). For gay men who died of AIDS, the median age at death was 39, for those dying of other causes the median age at death was 42 and 44 for lesbians. The study noted that gays and lesbians had a highly elevated risk compared heterosexuals of dying from murder, suicides, drug overdose, accidents, and a variety of diseases other than AIDS-related diseases.[33] These researchers are not saying that the median age of death of gays and lesbians is somewhere in the 40s, as some have interpreted these findings to mean. They are simply saying that among these almost 7,000 gays and lesbians who did die and were featured in obituaries, they died dramatically younger than heterosexual men and women during the same period.

A Canadian study of deaths among gay and bisexual men from 1987 to 1992 found that life expectancy at age 20 for gay and bisexual men ranged from 34 to 46.3 years compared to 54.3 years at age 20 for all men. Under the assumption that gay and bisexual men comprised three percent of the population, the researchers estimated that the probability of living to age 65 for them was 32 percent as opposed to 78 percent for all men. The research team also noted that: "we estimate that nearly half of gay and bisexual men currently aged 20 years will not reach their 65th birthday." [34]

Married same-sex couples fare a little better. A 2009 Danish study of 4,914 men and 3,419 women in a same-sex marriage found the excess death rate for was 33 percent for men and 34 percent for women compared with the death rate of Danish opposite-sex married men and women. They estimated that only 1 to 6 percent of Denmark's homosexual population was married, and did not give death rates for unmarried gays and lesbians. They did note, however, that married homosexuals have fewer exposures to the factors, especially promiscuity, that put unmarried homosexuals at elevated risk of death. The Danish study noted that with the advent of new treatments for HIV/AIDS, people with that horrible disease are living longer than previously and that AIDS deaths among gays who are married dropped precipitously with treatment availability.[35]

However, treatment for HIV-positive people and people with full-blown AIDS is inordinately expensive. The CDCP estimates that the lifetime cost of treatment was $379,000 in 2010 ($419,000 in 2016 dollars), so the burden has shifted from an emotional one suffered by the loved ones of gays lost to AIDS to a massive financial one suffered by the taxpayers. The report notes that almost 30 percent of those living with the HIV are uninsured.[36] With over one million people being treated in the United States for HIV/AIDS in 2010, the financial burden forced on the taxpayer by a small segment of society engaging in behaviors that are avoidable is enormous.

I do not want to paint all homosexuals with the same brush; there is more than one "homosexual lifestyle." As is the case with all group generalizations, gays tend to be defined by the worst of their members; that is, by the aggressive "in your face; queer and proud" gay who boasts of his promiscuous life and curses Christian morality. There are gays who live in monogamous relationships, and even gays not in a relationship who shun the promiscuous lifestyle, either from fear of the negative consequences or personal morality. There are even gays and lesbians who condemn the practices of their more radical brothers and sisters for religious or libertarian reasons. We should leave homosexuals alone to live their lives, but should resist with all our might the nauseating "recruit, recruit, recruit!" indoctrination taking hold, both surreptitiously and overtly, in our schools.

Endnotes

1. Dreher, Traditional Christians under siege 2015, p. 32.
2. Painter, The sensibilities of our Forefathers.
3. Reisman and Eichel, *Kinsey, sex and fraud*, p.2.
4. Gilman et al., Risk of psychiatric disorders.
5. Mercer et al., Increasing prevalence of male homosexual partnerships.

6.   Sandfort et al., Same-sex sexual behavior and psychiatric disorders.
7.   Saewyc et al., Not yet equal.
8.   Gate and Newport, Special report: 3.4% of U.S. adults identify as LGBT.
9.   Ryan, Helping families support their lesbian, gay.
10. Ngun, and Vilain, The biological basis of human sexual orientation. p. 178.
11. Throckmorton, Alan Chambers.
12. Botham, *Almighty God created the races*, p. 310.
13. Gold, *Loving v. Virginia*, p.72.
14. Cited in Anderson, *Marriage, reason, and religious liberty*, p. 8.
15. Koppleman, Theorists, get over yourselves. p. 939.
16. Cited in Laycock, Religious liberty and the culture wars, p. 870.
17. Benkof, Why California gays shouldn't celebrate.
18. Laycock, The Supreme Court's Assault, 112, my emphasis.
19. Cited in Duigon, The push is on!
20. American College of Pediatricians, What you should know.
21. Ibid.
22. Lenz, American College of Pediatricians defames gays and lesbians.
23. Lively, *Redeeming the Rainbow*, p. 202.
24. Ibid, p. 203.
25. Ibid, pp. 208-210.
26. Harris Interactive, Inc. and Gay, Lesbian & Straight Education Network.
27. Lipson, *Hostile hallways.*
28. Heyer, Public school LGBT programs.
29. Sprig, *Homosexuality in your child's school.*
30. Duigon, The push is on!
31. Center for Disease and Prevention. HIV Cost-effectiveness.
32. Suicide Resource Prevention Center. Suicide prevention for lesbian, gay, bisexual, and transgender youth.
33. Cameron, Playfair, and Wellum. The longevity of homosexuals.
34. Hogg et al., Modelling the impact of HIV disease, p. 675.
35. Frisch and Brønnum-Hansen. Mortality among men and women in same-sex marriage.
36. Center for Disease and Prevention. HIV Cost-effectiveness.

Chapter 9

Executive Branch Attacks on Religious Institutions and Businesses

"The conscientious scruples of all men should be treat-
ed with great delicacy and tenderness: and it is my
wish and desire that the laws may always be exten-
sively accommodated to them, as a due regard for the
protection and essential interests of the nation may
justify and permit."
George Washington, first President of the United
States.

The Nature of Catholic Charities

The Catholic Church has escaped Supreme Court attacks on school prayers, Bibles, and religious icons in its schools, and activist exhortations to promote homosexuality, because Catholic schools are private, not public, schools. On the other hand, the Catholic Church is almost uniquely burdened by executive branch infringements on religious liberty by its mandates regarding adoption of children by same-sex couples, abortion, and contraception. Many other denominations may agree with the Catholic stance on one or more of these issues, but the Catholic Church is especially burdened because the many hospitals, schools and universities sitting under its umbrella employ thousands of people, many of whom are not Catholic. Because Catholic institutions perform the same functions as secular institutions, they are subject to the same laws. The Church has been fine with this since colonial times, but since abortion and homosexual behavior have become legal, it has been told that it must violate its religious principles. Catholicism has a long and noble history of benevolence to people in need as an expression of its faith, but the tyranny of political correctness is hell-bent on driving the Church out of the charity business or bankrupting it if it does not genuflect to the LGBT agenda.

The abortion issue has been a thorn in the side of the Catholic Church since abortion was legalized in 1973, and the adoption by same-sex couples issue since Massachusetts became the first state to legalize same-sex marriage in 2003 (by judicial fiat; not a legislative act). These changes in the law have pitted Catholic Charities USA (CCUSA) against the wishes of gays and lesbians to adopt children, and against those seeking an abortion or contraceptive devices.

Both the rights of homosexuals to adopt, and the pregnant women to have an abortion, are rights that were hardly contemplated when the Ursuline Sisters and the Jesuits established the first hospitals, almshouses, orphanages, and other forms of first social welfare in North America in the 1600s.[1] Despite centuries of charitable work among the needy, CCUSA is vilified by homosexuals and feminists as hateful and bigoted because it will not provide the services they demand. But it is not really about services they can obtain elsewhere, it is about poking their fingers in the Church's eye by enlisting the law to force a tragic choice on it; serve us or serve no one. Contrary to Washington's wish and desire expressed in the epigraph, the Church's conscientious scruples have not only not been "extensively accommodated," they have been extensively vilified and scattered to the winds.

Most Catholic charities were administered at the dioceses level until the mass immigration of the late 1800s stretched their resources to the limit. This moved the Church toward an institutional approach to its charitable work by eventually placing all Catholic welfare agencies and hospitals under a single umbrella. The ongoing process of centralized administration eventually led to the founding of the National Conference of Catholic Charities in 1910, which in 1986 changed its name to Catholic Charities USA. [2] CCUSA is the largest private provider of welfare services of all types (food, housing, medical attention, counseling, disaster relief, and many other services) in the nation. Local branches of CCUSA serve millions of people nationwide each year regardless of their religious, social, or economic background. CCUSA also gladly serves homosexuals in matters that do not conflict with religious doctrine.

This is where the conflict begins. The Catholic Church avows that its faith and its service to others are unbreakably coupled. While Protestant based welfare agencies believe that their services are an expression of their faith, none are as adamant about it as Catholicism. Charles Degeneffe quotes an early *Catholic Charities Review* article stating that: "A Catholic specialized service agency is not just a social agency. It is an official charitable agency of the Church. Our social services, therefore, are not just a label auspices. They are an expression of an article of faith." [3] If the law demands that a Catholic charity provide a service at odds with an article of its faith, it is in effect demanding that it violate its faith—which it will not do.

It was not long ago that the very idea that the government demand that the Church must violate its principles in accordance with state law would be met with cries of outrage. From the very beginning of the United States, churches have been left strictly alone to conduct their affairs as they see fit. When the United States acquired the Catholic Louisiana Territory in 1803, the Ursuline Sisters wanted assurances from President Jefferson that the Protestant United States would allow them to continue their charitable work in accordance with their faith. Jefferson replied that: "The principles of the constitution and government of the United States are a guarantee to you that it will be preserved for you, sacred and inviolate, and that your institution will be permitted to govern itself according to its own voluntary rules, without interference from the civil authority."[4]

Contrast Jefferson's attitude toward the Ursuline Sisters with that of the Obama administration's persecution of the Little Sisters of the Poor. The Little Sisters of the Poor was founded in 1839, and their spiritual calling is defined by their mission statement contained on their website: "Our MISSION is to offer the neediest elderly of every race and religion a home where they will be welcomed as Christ, cared for as family and accompanied with dignity until God calls them to himself." The Obama administration required them to provide all employees with all forms of contraception in their insurance plans or face huge daily fines, which would have effectively shut down this immensely valuable mission. Five of the 12 federal district judges in the Tenth Court of Appeals dissented from the majority opinion in *Little Sisters of the Poor v. Burwell* (2015) favoring the government with these words: "All the plaintiffs in this case sincerely believe that they will be violating God's law if they execute the documents required by the government. And the penalty for refusal to execute the documents may be in the millions of dollars. How can it be any clearer that the law substantially burdens the plaintiffs' free exercise of religion?" The United States Supreme Court vacated the ruling and sent it back to the Court of Appeals. The case was still pending at the time of writing, but perhaps the Trump administration will put an end to such unconscionable government interference in matters of religious conscience, making a rehearing superfluous.

Same-Sex Adoption and the Catholic Church

However, the ascendancy of Donald Trump to the presidency is no guarantee of religious liberty as long as the courts maintain their hostility to it. Presidents Ronald Reagan, George H. W. Bush, Bill Clinton, and George W. Bush all made fine statements in support of religious freedom, but the courts continued their relentless efforts to banish religion from public life. We continue in an age in which situations sometimes arise for individuals, institutions, and societies in which tragic choices must be made. The most difficult of conflicts containing the possibility of ending in a tragic choice are those involving ideological or moral rights issues in which both sides have just claims. The

Catholic Church in Boston had to make a tragic choice when faced with conflicting demands from its faith and from the state over the issue of same-sex
adoption. When thus confronted, in 2006 Catholic Charities of Boston announced it would cease offering adoption services altogether. The Bishop of
the Archdiocese of Boston wrote: "Sadly, we have come to a moment when
Catholic Charities in the Archdiocese of Boston must withdraw from the work
of adoptions, in order to exercise the religious freedom that was the prompting for having begun adoptions many years ago."[5]

Catholic Charities is the largest and oldest private organization ministering
to abandoned or orphaned children in need of adoption. It placed far more
Boston area children—many of them difficult to place, such as children with
physical or mental health problems, older or unruly children, or the offspring
of mixed races—than any other adoption agency in Massachusetts.[6] Other
Catholic Charities across the nation such as those in Illinois and Washington,
DC, have also either stopped providing adoption services or have scaled back
their services in the face of the loss of public funds. What Massachusetts did,
in effect, was to sabotage its own social welfare interests by demolishing its
most effective partner in placing its most difficult cases. The burden here has
been placed on children who may no longer be adopted by anyone, although
children have been transferred to (now overburdened) secular state agencies.
Unlike current politicians, Thomas Jefferson realized the value to society of
the work of the Catholic Church in his letter to the Ursuline Sisters in which
he even offered them patronage: "It's [the Ursuline services] furtherance of
the wholesome purposes of society, by training up it's (sic) younger members
in the way they should go, cannot fail to ensure it the patronage of the government it is under."[7]

The anti-discrimination argument is that when religious organizations work
for the welfare of children and provide other services to the needy and at the
same time accept taxpayer money to do so, there attaches an obligation is to
treat all comers equally. This argument discounts considerations of the freedom of the Catholic Church to conduct its operations in accordance with its
faith, thus resulting in the loss of a valuable social service not easily replaced.
The courts have placed the equality rights of same-sex couples above the
religious rights of the Church. Because the Church refused to bend its knee to
the affirmation of the rights of same-sex couples as the state says it must, its
decision to cease adoption services altogether has received scathing respons-
es from gay activists. For example, Jamie McGonnigal writes: "Over and over
again, the Catholic dioceses have made the conscious decision to abandon
orphans and foster children rather than place them in loving, forever homes,
based on nothing in their actual belief system...It is indeed heartbreaking to

see those who claim 'Christian' beliefs act so hatefully by leaving thousands of children with nothing to fall back on." [8]

McGonnigal employs typical left-wing tactics of labeling any position other than its own as hate. He purposely ignores the fact that for religions that do not accept the legitimacy of same-sex marriage to comply with state demands that they do means that they must violate religious doctrine, or as McGonnigal dismissively put it, "their actual belief system." The Church has fulfilled its faith-based practice of caring with love as an integral part of their religious mission; what, if anything, has the LGBT community done for children? It is the hatred of homosexual activists for Christianity that forced the Church to close shop. LGBT activists chose to approach the Church for same-sex adoption knowing full well that it could not acquiesce, and by doing so advancing their cause of vilifying it. The Church "abandoned" these children with great reluctance, and only because the state says it must unless it abandons its faith.

Catholic objections to same-sex marriage are principled and fundamental. Marriage in the Catholic Church is more than a ceremony; it is a sacrament binding man and woman together. Canon 1055 §1 of the *Catechism of the Catholic Church* on matrimony states: "The matrimonial covenant, by which a man and a woman establish between themselves a partnership of the whole of life and which is ordered by its nature to the good of the spouses and the procreation and education of offspring, has been raised by Christ the Lord to the dignity of a sacrament between the baptized."[9] The Church does not condemn homosexual feelings since a person cannot help what he or she feels; it condemns acting on those feelings. Of course, if one's feelings are for one's own sex, not acting on them leaves a person with a life of celibacy shorn of intimacy. While I do not agree with the Churches position on this, it is the Church's position that matters for the Church, not mine or anyone else's.

It is plain that the Church deems marriage to be in accordance with both divine and natural law and to be between a man and a woman "ordered by nature" for "procreation." It cannot countenance same-sex marriage without violating the very core of its doctrine. To demand that it does so is an especially egregious violation of the First Amendment's Free Exercise Clause. The law, to its shame, has done nothing to protect religious freedom in its refusal to accommodate religious beliefs in this regard while doing its best to demand acquiescence with politically correct orthodoxy from everyone and every institution.

Cardinal Raymond Burke spoke out against the increasing hostility to Christianity on the part of President Obama and his administration in an interview with Polish writer Izabella Parowicz. He writes about how unimaginable the current war on Christianity would have been just a few short years ago and how "we the people" have let this happen in the context of a culture sufficiently debased that so very many have lost all respect for America's founding principles. He notes former President Obama's hostility toward Christianity and Western civilization in general, and how he wanted to restrict the freedom of religion to freedom of worship within the confines of a church or home. He notes that the public is only half aware that such things that were unimaginable to earlier generations of Americans, and hopes that when the public, "realize what is happening, will insist on electing leaders who respect the truth of the moral law as it is respected in the founding principles of our nation."[10] Perhaps it was partly the "irredeemable deplorable" realizing this that put Donald Trump into the White House.

It is a pity that the men and women of the Obama administration did not value freedom as Justice Robert Jackson did in the 1943 case, *West Virginia State Board of Education v. Barnette*. Jackson wrote: "Those who begin coercive elimination of dissent soon find themselves exterminating dissenters. Compulsory unification of opinion achieves only the unanimity of the graveyard." Jackson went on to write one of the most quoted sentences in Supreme Court history: "If there is any fixed star in our constitutional constellation, it is that no official, high or petty, can prescribe what shall be orthodox in politics, nationalism, religion, or other matters of opinion, or force citizens to confess by word or act their faith therein."

Religious organizations, motivated by religious principles, do so much good in society for the needy, but they require leeway to do so in accordance with those same religious principles. To require them to violate these principles puts a burden on those whom they serve to the benefit of no one and is manifestly a danger to everyone. The battle over contending rights, values, and identities, while resulting in a symbolic victory for LGBT rights, has led to a consequence for needy children that neither side should find palatable. LGBT activist who celebrates such a victory are the heartless ones, for they are well aware that the Church simply cannot violate its faith. They went ahead to test the waters until they made their point, and at the expense of poor children. They behaved like a betrayed paramour who kills his former lover under the principle of "If I can't have her; no one will."

Discrimination: Reasonable and Unreasonable

Equality is the rubric under which demands for non-discriminatory treatment are made by same-sex couples seeking to adopt. There has always been a tension on many fronts between those who favor equality over freedom and those who place freedom over equality. America is a land forged by people who believed in the latter but is being replaced by people who demand the former. The refusal to cater to same-sex couples wishing to adopt is without doubt discrimination, but it is also the freedom to act according to the dictates of conscience. It is the freedom to refuse to endorse practices that violate centuries-old beliefs and practices. The problem is that "discrimination" has become a trigger word in the mind of the American public conjuring up pictures of Bull Conner and lynch mobs in the old South. They see the word denoting unjust or prejudicial treatment of certain categories of people based on arbitrary and unreasonable grounds, and never on reasonable grounds. The Catholic Church (or other churches being bullied into conformity such as the Salvation Army) does not discriminate in same-sex adoption cases on arbitrary and hateful grounds. These churches provide numerous services for homosexuals, but not services that violate church teachings, a reason that is hardly arbitrary.

The Constitutional basis for filing discrimination suits against those who refuse to serve all comers equally is the equal protection clause of the Fourteenth Amendment stipulating that no state may deny any person in its jurisdiction "the equal protection of the law." The courts have heretofore interpreted the anti-discrimination intent of this clause as being limited only to intentional discrimination that is arbitrary or unreasonable, but not to discrimination that aimed at avoiding the endorsement of a cause repugnant to the discriminator(s) even though there is discrimination "in fact." According to Deborah Dewart: "What the Equal Protection Clause clearly forbids is irrational, arbitrary or unreasonable discrimination. Discrimination is not 'arbitrary' where its purpose is to avoid endorsing a cause." [11] Dewart's reasoning is that because the Catholic and other churches consider homosexual behavior a sin and not a civil right, discrimination against same-sex couples who wish to be availed of its adoption services is entirely reasonable because *not* to discriminate would be to endorse what they consider a sin.

The Supreme Court distinguished between reasonable and unreasonable discrimination in *Hurley v. Irish American Gay, Lesbian, and Bisexual Group of Boston (1995)*. The Court unanimously ruled that private organizations were permitted to exclude a group if it represented a cause contrary to the values or message the organization wants to convey. The case involved the South Boston Allied War Veterans Council, organizers of the annual St. Patrick's Day Parade refusing the Irish American Gay, Lesbian, and Bisexual Group of Boston a place in it. In the unanimous opinion, Justice Souter wrote that to require private citizens to include a group advancing a message that the organizers do not wish to convey in order to make private speech conform with the public accommodation requirements of Massachusetts "violate[s] the fundamental First Amendment rule that a speaker has the autonomy to choose the content of his own message and, conversely, to decide what not to say." Putting it plainly, the free speech-based ruling stated that it the government lacks the constitutional power to mandate the speech of private individuals when they do not agree with the message other groups want to express.

While *Hurley* was decided on free speech grounds, it could have also been similarly decided on the First Amendment's Free Association clause, as was *Boy Scouts of America* et al. *v. Dale* (2000). This case involved the Boy Scouts revoking James Dale's membership after he announced that he was gay. In that 5-4 decision, Chief Justice Rehnquist, delivering the opinion of the Court, noted that the Boy Scouts is devoted to instilling its system of moral values in young people that are inconsistent with homosexual conduct. He added:

> It also asserted that the right to engage in free association activities is protected by the First Amendment. This right is crucial in preventing the majority from imposing its views on groups that would rather express other, perhaps unpopular, ideas. Forcing a group to accept certain members may impair the ability of the group to express those views, and only those views, that it intends to express...freedom of association ... plainly presupposes a freedom not to associate.

There are fewer and fewer champions of Constitutional freedom such as Rehnquist being appointed to the Supreme Court and other federal courts, especially those appointed during Obama's tenure. Thus courts are increasingly telling individuals, organizations, and businesses that they must labor for, associate with, and endorse messages, they find repugnant in the name of non-discrimination regardless of their religious beliefs. Being told that you cannot say "No" to promoting, participating in, or laboring for something that one finds morally objectionable makes one a slave without choices.

Law professor David Bernstein has something astute to say about discrimination, people who take easy offense, and the tension between equality and liberty. He feels that we are becoming a nation of snowflakes melting when we are "offended" by an ever-increasing number of acts, and seek legal remedies for our pain. We have, according to Bernstein, become a society so obsessed with equality that we are feeding the Leviathan that will crush us: "A society that undercuts civil liberties in pursuit of the "equality" offered by a statutory right to be free from all slights will ultimately end up with neither equality nor civil liberties..."[12]

What Professor Bernstein is basically saying is that if providing ingress to Big Brother government to further intrude on everyone's life by censoring speech and demanding conformity with the orthodoxy does not scare you, it should. It should scare you whatever your politics or sexual orientation because while the intrusion may favor you today, it may not be tomorrow. Those who believe that by crushing the precious the rights of religious dissenters do so in the name of protecting LGBT rights should heed the words of Ayn Rand: "The smallest minority on earth is the individual. Those who deny individual rights cannot claim to be defenders of minorities."[13] The rights of all must be protected, but not at the expense of more fundamental rights hard-won by previous generations who considered them inalienable. LGBT rights can be protected without stomping on the rights of Christians. No one says that same-sex couples are not entitled to adopt; only that they are not entitled to adopt from institutions that object to their lifestyle on religious grounds. Faith-based adoption agencies should be accommodated by opt-out provisions in the spirit of living and let live if we want to preserve liberty.

Abortion, Abortifacients, Contraception, and Obamacare

Few issues more strongly divide modern America and raise more hackles than the abortion issue, and no other single moral issue has engaged the courts to the extent that abortion has. Analogies such as comparing abortion to the Holocaust on one side and characterizing its prohibition as slavery on the other abound at the zealous extremes of the debate. Such hyperbole makes it difficult to offer a definition without causing offense to one side or the other, but let me try to offer a definition of abortion here that is as value neutral as I can make it: Abortion is the intentional termination of a pregnancy by the removal or expulsion of an embryo/fetus from the uterus resulting in its death. Some individuals view this "termination" as simply a medical procedure analogous to removing a tumor, while others see it as the murder of an unborn child.

As long as women have become pregnant without the support of a committed mate (and sometimes when they do), they have sought an abortion. Attitudes regarding abortion have fluctuated across the centuries, with the first laws regulating abortion found in the Code of Hammurabi, and providing fines for causing "miscarriage." The penalties for those who performed abortions were more severe than for those seeking them. This is illustrated by the case of Eleanor Beare in England, who was indicted in 1732 for "destroying the Foetus in the Womb of Grace Belfort, by putting an iron instrument up into her body, and thereby causing her to miscarry" (*Rex v. Beare*, 1732). The Crown prosecutor opened his case stating:

> Gentlemen...the Misdemeanor for which the Prisoner stands indicted, is of a most shocking Nature; to destroy the Fruit in the Womb carries something in it so contrary to the natural Tenderness of the Female Sex, that I am amazed however any Woman should arrive at such a degree of Impiety and Cruelty, as to attempt it in such a manner as the

Prisoner has done, it has really something so shocking in it, that I cannot well display the Nature of the Crime to you: It is cruel and barbarous to the last degree.[14]

At the instigation of religious leaders and the American Medical Association, by the turn of the twentieth century every state prohibited abortion at any stage of pregnancy except where a woman's life was at risk.[15] Enforcement of the law was slack, however, and various estimates put the number of illegal abortions performed at around 1 million per year in the 1960s.[16] Many of these illegal abortions were performed by shady or reformist physicians, but most were performed in dangerous and unsanitary conditions by any individual claiming expertise in such matters. Because of the conditions under which they were performed, it was estimated that 5,000 women died each year from illegal abortions.[17] Publicity surrounding deaths caused by abortion created a growing opposition to abortion laws, and the stage was set to challenge abortion laws in the Supreme Court on privacy grounds.

By 1973 seventeen states had amended their abortion laws to allow abortion under certain conditions (rape, incest, health risks, and so on), but most still had restrictive laws. In *Roe v. Wade* (1973) the U.S. Supreme Court gave women the right to unlimited access to abortion in the first trimester, allowed the states to regulate abortion in the second trimester, and permitted states to prohibit it in the third trimester unless the life or health of the mother was at risk. In the case of *Doe v. Bolton* (1973), argued on the same day as *Roe,* in invalidating Georgia's abortion laws the Supreme Court ruled that a woman may obtain an abortion after *viability* (the point at which the fetus is able to survive outside the womb) only if it was necessary to protect her health.

The age of viability is ever changing with the invention of more life-supporting technology. Whatever the age of viability may be at any time, it does not matter to the Catholic Church (and other denominations also) because, for it, a new and unique individual is created as soon as sperm meets egg to form a zygote. The argument is that zygote contains all the genetic information that is present in the embryo, the fetus, the baby, and the adult man or woman. As such, the zygote is as deserving of its life as any person at any other seamless stage of development. This is not just a theological position. In their Amicus Curiae Brief filed on behalf of the Little Sister of the Poor, The Association of American Physicians & Surgeons wrote:

It is undisputed as a matter of science that a new, distinct human organism comes into existence during the process of fertilization – at the moment of sperm-egg fusion – and before implantation of the already-developing embryo into the uterine wall. Many drugs and devices labeled by the U.S. Food and Drug Administration as "emergency contraception," however, have post-fertilization (i.e., life-ending) mechanisms of action which destroy the life of a human organism. In other words, these drugs and devices can work after a new human organism is created (at fertilization). Such "contraceptive" methods may prevent implantation and therefore "pregnancy," as defined by Respondents and their amici, but by preventing implantation these drugs and devices end the life of a unique human being.[18]

Yes, you guessed it; for daring to try to protect the unborn, the Association of American Physicians and Surgeons has been designated yet another hate group by the Southern Poverty Law Center.

The theological position of the Catholic Church's position is plainly stated. Pope John Paul declared that the Church position "is unchanged and unchangeable," adding, "I declare that direct abortion, that is, abortion willed as an end or as a means, always constitutes a grave moral disorder, since it is the deliberate killing of an innocent human being. This doctrine is based upon the natural law and upon the written word of God."[19]

You don't have to agree with this position, but you should respect it. If someone requires an abortion, the procedure is legally available, she does not have to burden the Catholic Church with litigation because a Catholic hospital, or Catholic physician or nurse, will not provide one. Because devout Catholics view abortion as murder, requiring them to assist in one is akin to requiring them to be a party to a conspiracy to commit murder. Note that many other Christian denominations, as well as Judaism and Islam, share the Catholic view, but because Catholicism is the largest denomination in the United States it gets to bear the brunt of litigation.

The Health and Human Services Mandate in Obamacare

David Barton lists no less than 93 acts of well-documented hostility toward people and institutions of Judeo/Christian faith on the part of Barrack Obama and his administration in his article "America's most Biblically-hostile U.S. President."[20] These things range from relatively mild insults about white Americans "clinging to their religion and their guns," to major policy decisions that rock the foundations of our free society. The most egregious of these acts of hostility pertinent to this chapter is Obama's Health and Human Services (HHS) mandate under the Affordable Care Act (Obamacare). The mandate requires employers to provide employee health plans that include coverage for contraceptive services, including sterilization and abortifacients (the products The Association of American Physicians & Surgeons called "post-fertilization life-ending"). The HHS mandate issue is not just an issue of contraception or the Catholic Church's interests; it is a clear violation of Constitutional rights and religious freedom. Obama boasted before a pro-choice crowd in St. Louis that his mandate forces religious employers to pay for contraception, sterilization, and abortifacients. He adopted his Mussolini-like pose and said to the cheering crowd, "Darn tootin!"

Imagine Washington, Jefferson, or Madison (or any decent person) actually boasting of forcing anyone or any institution to act in ways contrary to conscience. Note what James Madison had to say about the value of protecting conscience above all: "To guard a man's house as his castle, to pay public and enforce private debts with the most exact faith, can give no title to invade a man's conscience, which is more sacred than his castle, or to withhold from it that debt of protection for which the public faith is pledged by the very nature and original conditions of the social pact." [21]

Obama's former HHS Secretary, Kathleen Sebelius, made remarks similar to Obama's at a Pro-Choice America fundraiser, where she admitted that the Obama administration is "at war" with America's religious conscience. Sebelius told the cheering crowd that "we are in a war" with religious dissenters who will be forced to choose between violating their religion or financial ruin. [22] The HHS mandate provides an exemption for religious employers who object to practices contrary to their moral teachings, but the "exemption" it is drawn so narrowly that it does not cover the vast majority of faith-based service organizations. Religious employers are exempt only if their sole purpose is to teach and instill their religious doctrine, and both hire *and serve* people of their own faith exclusively. They must also qualify as a religious order or church as defined by the tax code. It has been pointed out that, "Most religious institutions providing health, educational or charitable services to others have no protection. Rev. Larry Snyder notes that even Jesus and His disciples would not qualify for the exemption in that case because they were committed to serving those of other faiths."[23]

In the final analysis, the so-called "accommodation" still forces religious institutions to provide employees with health plans covering free services that violate their religious convictions or face crippling fines should they refuse. If I'm a woman who believes I might have gotten pregnant as a result of last night's fling, I might want to take an abortifacient to end it. To do so, I would sacrifice a Starbucks or two to buy them myself rather than appeal to the powerful hand of the state to try to try to make the Catholic Church violate its faith. But then, I don't have the hostility to the religious foundations of morality that these uber-liberal activists have, or to the very notion of morality itself. Make no mistake; these folks actually boast that they oppose morality as "the other of liberalism."[24]

Apparently, Obama believes that providing contraceptives constitutes a compelling state interest such that the state would be "manifestly endangered" were they not provided free of charge by their employers since such interest is supposed to be the only Constitutionally valid reason for religious conscience to take a back seat. Of course, this does not even pass the laugh test. The estimated employer cost of providing contraceptive coverage in 2010 was about $26 (or $29.74 in 2016 dollars) annually per enrolled female.[25] Providing such coverage is cost effective for employers as it may actually save money because of the medical costs associated with unintended pregnancies, so they certainly do not refuse on economic grounds. Surely women employed by companies and organizations that object to contraception can buy their own contraception rather than demand that their employers violate their religious consciences.

Ironically, much of this situation arose out of attempts by the Bush administration to protect religious liberty. In the last month of his presidency, George W. Bush was growing more concerned about increasing government interference with health care workers' religious rights and issued HHS regulations in 2008 to protect that right. To no one's surprise, in 2011 to Obama administration rescinded Bush's regulations and substituted its own. In theory, the Obama regulations provide some limited protections, but they are written in unclear language that is open to "interpretation." Under the Obama's HHS mandate, a healthcare worker who suffered a violation of conscience could not file a suit in a court of law; only the HHS itself can enforce whatever remains of laws protecting conscience.[26] Because Obama only appointed fellow cultural Marxist types to administer federal agencies, complaints of conscience violation forwarded to the HHS fell on hostile ears. I use the past tense because we do not yet know how the HHS will behave under the Trump administration.

This hostility resulted in Representatives John Fleming (R-LA) and Vicky Hartzler (R-MO) introducing the Conscience Protection Act of 2016. This is a noble thing, as are the federal and state RFRAs, but they would not be needed if the court's still respected and applied the Constitutional protection of religion in the First Amendment. In support of Fleming and Hartzler's efforts, the United States Conference of Catholic Bishops sent a letter to them outlining how Obama's HHS responds to religious freedom violation complaints. The Bishops wrote that the HHS: "despite repeated questions and objections from Congress—has allowed valid complaints to languish, sometimes for years, without resolution."[27]

Hillary Clinton pressed for strong enforcement of Obama's HHS mandate in her 2015 *Women* in the *World* speech. She said that: "All the laws we've passed don't count for much if they're not enforced. Rights have to exist in practice, not just on paper. Laws have to be backed up with resources and political will, and deep-seated cultural codes, *religious beliefs*, and structural biases have to be changed." Clinton couched her speech in terms of women's rights around the world, but made no mention of the barbaric genital mutilation and semi-slavery of women in many Muslim countries, but rather she specifically targeted Hobby Lobby (see below) for its refusal to supply abortifacients to its employees in their insurance packages: "America moves forward when all women are guaranteed the right to make their own health care choices, not when those choices are taken away by an employer like Hobby Lobby."[28] In other words, if Hillary doesn't like your religious beliefs you must change them. If she had been elected president in 2016, she would have used the powerful arm of the law to either make you do so or suffer the consequences. Thank God the "irredeemable deplorables" provided Donald Trump an opportunity to drain the liberal swamp that was sucking all morality from American life; thus denying Hillary the opportunity to try to make people change their religious beliefs.

Cardinal Francis George spelled out the possible repercussions of the Health and Human Services (HHS) mandate for the Church if it remains the law of the land. He also notes the huge changes that have taken place recently with regard to the government failing to respect the religious freedoms that have been respected and revered since colonial times. Cardinal George is essentially outlining the results of the cultural Marxist agenda, whether or not it is acknowledged as such by the leftists who are implementing it. The cardinal wrote about what will happen if the HHS regulations are not rescinded, saying that there are four very unpalatable choices for service providers: (1) Break their connection to the church and it her moral and social teachings. (2) Pay huge fines for not providing insurance policies that cover drugs and practices abhorrent to the Church. (3) Sell the institution. (4) Close down. Cardinal George remarked that "The Church would love to have the separation between church and state we thought we enjoyed just a few months ago, when we were free to run Catholic institutions in conformity with the demands of the Catholic faith, when the government couldn't tell us which of our ministries are Catholic and which not, when the law protected rather than crushed conscience."[29]

State bullying on the abortion issue continues unabated, and there is no guessing which side of the abortion debate it favors. In 2016, the United States Court of Appeals for the Ninth Circuit in *National Institute of Family and Life Advocates* et al. *v. Harris* et al. upheld a California law requiring pro-life pregnancy centers refer clients to abortion clinics. Because these pro-life centers are staffed by Christians, we have yet another judicial ruling demanding that they surrender their faith. Of course, there is no counter law require abortion clinics to refer clients to a pro-life pregnancy center. This is just another example of hypocrisy, double-standards, and anti-Christian bias increasingly displayed by the courts and legislative bodies in this country in the modern age.

One Small Victory: *Burwell v. Hobby Lobby Stores, Inc.* (2014)

The Hobby Lobby case to which Hillary Clinton referred to earlier is *Burwell v. Hobby Lobby Stores, Inc.* (2014) which was a small victory for religious dissenters. In this case, the Supreme Court ruled that Hobby Lobby, a chain of retail arts and crafts stores owned by Daniel and Barbara Green, does not have to provide contraceptive methods to its employees that violate their Christian beliefs. These contraceptives included abortifacients that *end* pregnancies rather than *prevent* them. The Court held that "closely held" corporation owners have religious rights under the Religious Freedom Restoration Act (RFRA) of 1993. "Closely held" corporations are businesses in which more than 50 percent of the value of its stock is directly or indirectly owned by five or fewer individuals. The Court ruled the HHS claim that Hobby Lobby has to provide abortifacients does not hold because the government has found "least-restrictive-means" that it has used for religious and non-profit organizations but did not offer to closely held corporations. By "least restrictive means" the Court means that there are other ways of accessing the contraceptives in question that are less restrictive of religious liberty than the HHS mandate. These include government provision of contraceptives, tax credits, or other financial support for those who want them. Although Burwell was saturated with Constitutional issues, the Court relied on the federal RFRA rather that the Free Exercise Clause of the First Amendment, which is another indication that it finds the Clause irrelevant today.

In an interview with the *Bay Area News* Senator Ted Cruz characterized the decision as a repudiation of the Obama Administration's ongoing onslaught against people of faith being forced to comply with an unconstitutional mandates, and further noted that, "The right to religious liberty, as enshrined in the First Amendment, remains under an incredible assault by this [Obama] Administration on a variety of fronts.[30]

As noted above, the "least restrictive means" test is a standard used by the courts to determine the validity of legislation that restricts a fundamental liberty in some way. If it does, and if it reflects a compelling state interest, the government must use the least restrictive measures to achieve its goal. A case (one among many) that illustrates that the least restrictive means test does not typically apply to Christians is a case decided by the California Supreme Court in 2008 in *North Coast Women's Care Medical Group vs. Superior Court* (2008). The suit was brought by a lesbian named Guadalupe Benitez seeking artificial insemination at the North Coast Women's Care Medical Group. Two physicians at the clinic refused to perform the treatment on the grounds that such treatment to an unmarried woman violated their Christian beliefs, although Benitez claimed that they refused because she was a lesbian. Benitez was referred to an outside physician, who performed the procedure.

In responding to the suit, the North Coast physicians asserted that to force them to perform an artificial insemination violated both their free speech and free exercise of religion. The court disagreed, ruling that the asserted rights do not exempt them from laws prohibiting discriminating based on sexual orientation and that the state has a compelling interest in ensuring equal access to medical treatment. Somehow the court failed to understand that artificial insemination is a voluntary elective procedure and not a medical emergency, or that it is not a "treatment" for a condition threatening one's health under any usual definition of the term. The referral to another physician surely satisfied the least restrictive means test, but this was not good enough for Benitez, who wanted her pound of flesh. She eventually settled the suit for an undisclosed sum of money.

In effect, the Court was telling the North Coast physicians that they should have labored on Benitez's behalf despite their conscientious objections which, of course, is involuntary servitude. Big Government has thoroughly discarded our nation's deepest principles in the name of a forced equality. It repeatedly shows a callous indifference to the rights of Christians. Every time it violates Christian rights it both weakens the influence of religion and enhances its own power by weakening the influence of intermediary institutions. Leftists have always been acutely aware of this principle, but the Founding Fathers were clear that freedom of conscience is not to be subordinate to the government. As Thomas Jefferson put it: "Our rulers can have authority over such natural rights only as we have submitted to them. The rights of conscience we never submitted, we could not submit. We are answerable for them to our God." [31] Jefferson also stated that "no provision in our Constitution ought to be dearer to man than that which protects the rights of conscience against the enterprises of civil authority. It has not left the religion of its citizens under the power of its public functionaries, were it possible that any of these should consider a conquest over the consciences of men either attainable or applicable to any desirable purpose."[32] But in our morally degraded society, freedom is not as valued as equality, and even forced labor is acceptable if it means treating LGBT individuals exactly the way we treat everyone on all matters and in all venues regardless of principled objections. That is called "involuntary servitude," which is forbidden by the Thirteenth Amendment and is a concept explored in the next chapter.

Endnotes

1. Denegeffe, What is Catholic about Catholic charities?
2. Ibid.
3. Ibid, p. 378.
4. Jefferson. From Thomas Jefferson to Ursuline Nuns.
5. Rutledge. Caught in the crossfire, p. 297.
6. Ibid.
7. Jefferson. From Thomas Jefferson to Ursuline Nuns.
8. McGonnigal. Catholic Charities abandons thousands.
9. Catechism of the Catholic Church. Matrimony.
10. Burk. Cardinal Burke on faith, the right to life, and the family.
11. Dewart. On Writ of Certiorari to the United States Court of Appeals, p. 8.
12. Bernstein. Defending the First Amendment, pp. 14-15.
13. Cited in Miniter, *Saving the Bill of Rights*, p. 278.
14. Cited in Walsh and Hemmens, p.274.
15. Garrow. *Liberty and sexuality.*
16. Rosenberg. *The hollow hope.*
17. Stuntz. Self-defeating crimes.
18. The Association of American Physicians & Surgeons. Amicus Brief.
19. Catholic Answers. Abortion.
20. Barton. America's most Biblically-hostile U.S. President.
21. Cited in Sheehan. *James Madison and the spirit of republican self-government, p. 153.*
22. Cited in Olson, Cardinal George criticizes Sebelius' declaration of "war on citizens."
23. Cited in Dolan, Wall Street Journal op ed on religious freedom.
24. Brown, Pornography and feminism.
25. Glied, The cost of covering contraceptives.
26. Goodrich, The health care and conscience debate.
27. United States Conference of Catholic Bishops, Letter,
28. Brennan, .Hillary's infamous women in the world talk.
29. George, What are you going to give up this Lent?
30. Cruz, cited in Bay Area News.
31. Jefferson, Notes on the State of Virginia.
32. Jefferson, From Thomas Jefferson to Richard Douglas.

Cases Cited

Boy Scouts of America et al. *v. Dale*, 530 U.S. 640 (2000).

Burwell v. Hobby Lobby, 573 U.S. ___ (2014)

Doe v. Bolton, 410 U.S. 179 (1973),

Hurley v. Irish American Gay, Lesbian, and Bisexual Group of Boston, 515 U.S. 557 (1995).

Little Sisters of the Poor v. Burwell, No. 13-1540 (10th Cir. 2015)

National Institute of Family and Life Advocates et al. *v. Harris* et al. (3:15-cv-02277).

North Coast Women's Care Medical Group vs. Superior Court (44 Cal. 4th 1145) (2008).

Rex V. Beare, 1 Ld. Ray. 414, 464. c Dana v.

Roe v. Wade, 410 U.S. 113 (1973).

Chapter 10

State Administrative Law and Christian Wedding Vendors

> *"If any earthly institution or custom conflicts with God's will, it is your Christian duty to oppose it. You must never allow the transitory, evanescent demands of man-made institutions to take precedence over the eternal demands of the Almighty God."*
> Martin Luther King, civil rights activist

You *Will* Bake me a Cake, you Bigot!

Suppose I am invited to a colleague's marriage but decline because I know that he was involved in a long-term sexual relationship with the woman when he and she were married to others, and that violates my religious beliefs. A liberal may think me something of a prude, but I'm confident that he or she would defend my right to refuse to attend. Suppose further that I'm a baker who refused to condone their actions by baking them a wedding cake decorated with a covert message referring to their previous liaisons they could chuckle about. Any sane person would say I have the absolute right not to place my seal of approval on something that offends my religious conscience by agreeing to bake the cake.

What if my colleague was gay and I have a conscientious objection to condoning same-sex marriage. Ah, that's different. Liberals would call me a bigot for refusing to bake him a cake and believe that the state should force me to. In both cases, I am discriminating on the basis of religious conscience. In the first instance where adultery is involved it is acceptable to liberals, but in the second in which homosexuality is involved it is not. The state insists that we must all go beyond tolerating same-sex marriage to actually endorsing it. I personally do not have a problem with two gays or lesbians wanting to make a commitment to one another; love is love regardless of sexual orientation. It is not the desire for commitment among homosexuals that is a problem for religious liberty; it is radical LGBT individuals hell-bent on vindictively destroying the lives of anyone who does not endorse their agenda in word and deed and who runs off to Big Brother to make them do so. In a free society, any business agreement requires willing participants; forced participation is tantamount to state-sponsored slavery.

It is one thing for the government to take on the Catholic Church—a mighty institution that has survived for centuries—but it is quite another for it to try to bully individuals running small businesses into submission. An egregious example of the state's denial of religious freedom, and of its comfort with forced labor, is the case of the devoutly religious Colorado baker, Jack Phillips, owner of Masterpiece Cakeshop. In 2012, Phillips refused to bake a same-sex wedding cake for Charles Craig and David Mullins and was charged with violating Colorado's anti-discrimination laws. According to a gloating ACLU website: "The [Colorado Civil Rights] Commission also ordered Masterpiece Cakeshop to change its company policies, provide 'comprehensive staff training' regarding public accommodations discrimination, and provide quarterly reports for the next two years regarding steps it has taken to come into compliance and whether it has turned away any prospective customers."[1]

In a court case appealing the commission's decision, the judge upheld the commission's ruling and Phillips was actually *ordered* by the court to bake same-sex wedding cakes if asked to do so. Under a Colorado law, he could jailed for contempt of court if he refuses. The judge cited Colorado state law prohibiting businesses from refusing service based on race, sex, marital status or sexual orientation. In doing so, the judge blurred the line drawn between serving and participating. The plaintiffs did not deny that Phillips told them: "I'll make you birthday cakes, shower cakes, sell you cookies and brownies, I just don't make cakes for same-sex weddings."[2] The distinction between serving cakes for secular purposes and participating in a ceremony that Christians (as well as almost any religion one can name) believe is repugnant to God is presumably plain to everyone except the court. Baking a cake celebrating same-sex marriage is tantamount to endorsing it, but the court essentially told Phillips that he has no right to follow his faith and must embrace the concept of same-sex marriage.

Phillips' attorney, Nicolle Martin, called the ruling Orwellian and "offensive to everything America stands for. They are turning people of faith into religious refugees....Is this the society that we want to live in – where people of faith are driven out of business?" The requirement of Phillips to submit he and his staff to "sensitivity training" to mold their thoughts in politically correct directions smacks of totalitarianism, and his forced submission of reports to the state is essentially "designed to demonstrate that he doesn't exercise his belief system anymore – that he has divested himself of his beliefs."[4]

Phillips appealed the ruling to the Colorado Supreme Court, which refused to hear the case. Ria Tabacco Mar, staff attorney for the ACLU's LGBT Project, gloated over the Court's decision, saying. "We all have a right to our personal beliefs, but we do not have a right to impose those beliefs on others and harm them."[5] Who is imposing their personal beliefs and harming whom? Phillips was going about his life baking cakes and not imposing anything on anyone. It was Craig and Mullins who came to him demanding that he violate his faith by helping them to celebrate their wedding; this is the very definition of "imposing." If Phillips does not have the right to impose his beliefs on Craig and Mullins, which he did not, they should not have the right to impose their beliefs on Mr. Phillips, which they did. The state imposing a set of beliefs on Phillips that he finds repugnant and then actually ordering him to perform an act that affirms those beliefs is the very essence of tyranny. The pretense of state neutrality to religion is laid bare in these cases discussed in this chapter, for the state could hardly be less neutral to religion than when it places one private citizen at the disposal of another.

Thomas Jefferson wrote in his *Bill for Establishing Religious Freedom* "That to compel a man to furnish contributions of money for the propagation of opinions which he disbelieves and abhors, is sinful and tyrannical." Jefferson referring to taxation to support a religion to which a person does not belong, but it is just as relevantly applied to the government serving as a conduit for compulsory servitude by forcing people to support the propagation of opinions they abhor. James Madison referred to religious conscience as the "most sacred of property," but religious individuals are being forced to use that property, and the property that constitutes their livelihood, to service a practice that violates everything their consciences hold dear. As Jefferson said, this is indeed tyranny of the most egregious sort that few ever expected to see in the USA.

Involuntary Servitude

Being told you cannot say "No" is involuntary servitude. As Deborah Dewart put it: "A requirement to actively perform personal services imposes a direct and crushing burden—a critical component in some cases. Courts decline to specifically enforce personal service contracts because enforcement might constitute involuntary servitude…Thirteenth Amendment concerns lurk just beneath the surface."[6] The Thirteenth Amendment legally ended slavery and involuntary servitude in the United States in 1865, but the latter is making a comeback with the advent of same-sex marriage. The relevant part of the Thirteenth Amendment reads: "Neither slavery nor involuntary servitude, except as a punishment for a crime, whereof the party shall have been duly convicted, shall exist in the United States, or any place subject to its jurisdiction." What does the law "as written" have to say about involuntary servitude today? Courts have the authority to require a person to perform affirmative acts a person has a legal duty to perform, but this only applies to civic duties such as serving on juries, paying income tax, and selective service registration. It is pointed out that: "It has generally been held that this power does not extend to *compelling the performance of labor or personal services*, even in cases where the obligated party has been paid in advance."[7] Apparently, this does not apply to the likes of Jack Phillips or other devout Christians in the wedding business.

The United States Congress has defined involuntary servitude quite plainly in U.S. Code § 7102, with section B being particularly relevant to wedding vendor cases:

> The term "involuntary servitude" includes a condition of servitude induced by means of—(A) any scheme, plan, or pattern intended to cause a person to believe that, if the person did not enter into or continue in such condition, that person or another person would suffer serious harm or physical restraint; or (B) the abuse or threatened abuse of the legal process. The term abuse or threatened abuse of the legal process means the use or threatened use of law or legal process, whether administrative, civil, or criminal, in any manner or for any purpose for which the law was not designed, in order to exert pressure on another person to cause that person to take some action or refrain from taking some action.[8]

Supreme Court rulings have said essentially the same thing. Mr. Justice Holmes in *Bailey v. State of Alabama* (1911) noted that "involuntary servitude" has a broader meaning than slavery, adding: "The plain intention was to abolish slavery of whatever name and form and all its badges and incidents; to render impossible any state of bondage; to make labor free, by prohibiting that control by which the personal service of one man is disposed of or coerced for another's benefit which is the essence of involuntary servitude." Justice Holmes' use of the terms "badges and incidents" is apropos here. An "incident" is something that occurs as a casual result of something else, and the clearest incident of slavery is the compulsory service of one person on behalf of another. A "badge" of slavery harkens back to some locations in the Old South where slaves sometimes wore copper badges to identify them as being available to be hired by others on behalf of their masters. Being identified as a wedding vendor *and* a devout Christian is arguably a badge of slavery leading to incidents of involuntary servitude.

In the more recent case of *United States v. Kozminski* (1988), the Supreme Court defined involuntary servitude as a compulsory condition:

in which a person lacks liberty especially to determine one's course of action or way of life"…[it] "necessarily means a condition…in which the victim is forced to work [for the benefit of another] by the use or threat of physical restraint or physical injury, or by the use or threat of *coercion through law or the legal process*…we find that in every case in which this Court has found a condition of involuntary servitude, the victim had no available choice but *to work or be subject to legal sanction.* (my emphases).

The constitutional law thus explicitly forbids what state civil "rights" commissions across the country are attempting to do; that is, to force Christian wedding providers to provide their services to facilitate same-sex weddings, even if it is repugnant to their religion. Thus, not only do these petty officials violate the Free Exercise Clause, they violate the intent of the Thirteenth Amendment. Furthermore, they violate the Free Speech Clause of the First Amendment.

Defense to State Intrusion Based on Free Speech Claims

When the Catholic Church was faced with state mandates to accommodate same-sex adoption, it reluctantly closed shop and served no one, but small business people catering to the public cannot abandon their livelihood and find another line of work when the state sends its bullies around. Businesses with connections to wedding services, such as photographers, florists, and bakers have been the particular targets of legal actions for refusing their services to facilitate same-sex weddings. There are numerous such cases pitting gay rights against religious freedom, and in every case, gay rights have trumped religious freedom. Because the Supreme Court continues to treat the first freedom as "What freedom?," some defendants in gay rights v. religious freedom cases have not relied on the Free Exercise Clause but rather on the Free Speech Clause of the First Amendment. They have done this because the religious expression is conduct, and the courts have treated a conduct as speech when it conveys a message.

The classic case on this issue is *Spence v. Washington* (1977). Harold Spence hung an American flag with a peace symbol upside down and festooned with peace symbols to protest the Vietnam War for which he was arrested, charged, and convicted. Upon overturning Spence's conviction, the Supreme Court promulgated a simple test for determining if the conduct is expressive and triggers First Amendment protection: (1) Conduct is expressive if a person intended to express a particularized message, and (2) that message is understood by the audience. Spence was using the flag to express ideas which all those who viewed would understand.

This standard was reinforced in *Texas v Johnson* (1988) when Gregory Johnson was convicted of desecrating the American flag by burning it at a Republican National Convention to protest Republican policies. In a 5-4 decision, the Supreme Court overturned Johnson's conviction and concluded that his action was "sufficiently imbued with elements of communication to implicate the First Amendment." In other words, some conduct is protected speech under the First Amendment as symbolic speech. It was rendered protective by Johnson's communicating something he considered important by burning the flag, and his conveyance of this particular message, unpopular though it may have been, is protected by the Freedom of Speech Clause.

The Free Speech Clause is interpreted as both the right to speak freely and the right to refrain from speaking at all. Being forced to speak, verbally or symbolically in the form of conduct, is compelled speech. Compelled conduct triggers a free speech claim if the person being compelled is forced to convey a message with which he or she disagrees. *Wooley v. Maynard* (1977) was a case in which George Maynard, a Jehovah's Witness, viewed the New Hampshire motto, "Live Free or Die" he was required to display on his vehicle license plate repugnant to his moral, religious, and political beliefs. The Supreme Court ruled that the statute ineffective required individuals to "use their private property as a 'mobile billboard' for the State's ideological message." The Court held that the State's interests in requiring the motto did not outweigh free speech principles under the First Amendment, including "the right of individuals to hold a point of view different from the majority and to refuse to foster an idea they find morally objectionable." The Court also held that the requiring them to do so was compelled speech and that the State may not "'invad[e] the sphere of intellect and spirit which it is the purpose of the First Amendment to our Constitution to reserve from all official control.'"

Elane Photography

An early example of the reliance on free speech claims in religious freedom cases is a 2006 New Mexico case in which Elaine Huguenin, co-owner of Elane Photography, refused to photograph the same-sex wedding of Vanessa Willock and Misti Collinsworth on religious grounds. Willock and Collinsworth hired another photographer but filed a complaint against Elane Photography. Legal counsel for Elane claimed that "Photographers, writers, singers, actors, painters and others who create First Amendment-protected speech must have the right to decide which commissions to take and which to reject."[9] The New Mexico Human Rights Commission disagreed and found Elane Photography guilty of discrimination in violation of the state's public accommodation law; a law of general applicability. Recall that the federal RFRA states that: "Government shall not substantially burden a person's exercise of religion even if the burden results from a rule of general applicability." Also, recall that the Supreme Court ruled the RFRA did not apply to the states. Thus the Commission was able to rule that the state provides businesses a license to sell goods and services to the general public, and nothing grants them a license to reject customers based on race, religion or sexual orientation. The issue in *Elane Photography v. Willock* (2012) was identical to the issues is Spence, Johnson, and Wooley; to wit: "Whether applying a state public-accommodations statute to require a photographer to create expressive images and picture books conveying messages that conflict with her religious beliefs violates the First Amendment's ban on compelled speech."

The decision of the New Mexico Human Rights Commission was upheld by the New Mexico Court of Appeals in 2012. Justice Richard Bosson concurred with the majority opinion, but he was not comfortable with it In his written opinion Bosson stated: "The Huguenins are not trying to prohibit anyone from marrying. They only want to be left alone to conduct their photography business in a manner consistent with their moral convictions....they are compelled by law to compromise the very religious beliefs that inspire their lives. Though the rule of law requires it, the result is sobering." The Huguenins were ordered to pay court costs and $6,637.94 in attorneys' fees to Willock and Collinsworth. Thus the New Mexico State Supreme Court not only punished Huguenin for exercising her rights of free exercise of religion, speech, and association, it added insult to injury by forcing her to pay Willock and Collinsworth's attorney's fees. In 2014, the United States Supreme Court denied Elane Photography's petition for certiorari, letting the New Mexico ruling stand, and by doing so put its seal of approval on involuntary servitude and on the abridgement of freedom of religion and speech which it had defended in the previously discussed non-religious cases.

Elaine Huguenin was not just prohibited from expressing a religious position with which the state of New Mexico disagreed; she was also compelled to affirm the state's position as her own. This is not only unconstitutional under *Wooley,* but also under *Agency for International Development v. Alliance for Open Society International, Inc.* (AOSI). The question in this 2013 case was whether a requirement that non-governmental organizations should have an explicit anti-prostitution policy in order to receive federal funding. In the 6-2 majority opinion (Justice Kagan did not take part), Chief Justice Roberts wrote: "It requires them [AOSI] to pledge allegiance to the Government's policy of eradicating prostitution." Was not Elane Photography required to "pledge allegiance" to the LGBT agenda? The First and Thirteenth Amendment rights of devout Christians are sacrificed on the altar of anti-discrimination laws. Apparently, Americans can hold any position, pro or con, on any imaginable issue with repercussions—with the exception of same-sex marriage.

Betty and Richard Odgaard

The vindictive and pecuniary interests of gay couples who purposely seek services from those who they know will refuse them on religious grounds is illustrated by Lee Stafford and Jared Elders. These two hustlers asked Betty and Richard Odgaard a Mennonite couple, to host their wedding. The Odgaards ran an art gallery, bistro, flower, and gift shop, and hosted weddings in in a former church sanctuary. When the Odgaards refused to host their wedding on religious grounds, Stafford and Elders filed suit with the Iowa Civil Rights Commission. When word got out, the Odgaards received e-mails containing death threats and hateful messages saying such things as they were "finished" and "doomed." and referring to them as "mother f***er racist sons of bitches from hell," and saying "F**k you, f**k your God, f**k your religion." These are examples of the kind of hateful bigots the state puts before decent Christians who just want to live their lives in accordance with their faith.

The Iowa Civil Rights Commission tried to force the Odgaards into performing the wedding despite Stafford and Elders admitting, contrary to their previously sworn statements that they had been married months before asking the Odgaards to host it. This is a clear indication of targeting to destroy. Betty Odgaard noted that "We hire and serve gays and lesbians... and we respect that good people disagree with our religious conviction against hosting a ceremony that violates our faith. We simply ask that the government not force us to abandon our faith or punish us for it."[10] Nevertheless, faced with state bullying and years of crippling legal fees, they settled the suit by paying $5,000 to the couple and agreed to stop hosting all weddings. Without the income generated by hosting a wedding, the Odgaards were forced to close their life's work rather than violate their faith. Stafford and Elders pocketed their lucre and, with state collusion, destroyed the livelihood of an elderly Christian couple.

Barronelle Stutzman

Barronelle Stutzman, a 72-year-old grandmother, and owner of Arlene's Flowers, is another victim of the Gay Gestapo; this time betrayed by someone she considered a friend. In 2013, Stutzman declined to provide flowers for same-sex marriage for long-term customer and friend, Robert Ingersoll, because her personal involvement in the celebration of same-sex marriage would amount to a denunciation of her faith. Ingersoll, Washington State, and the ACLU filed discrimination lawsuits against Arlene's Flowers and Stutzman personally, which means that any assets she has beyond the flower shop (other property, personal savings, etc.) could be taken from her. In February 2015, a court ruled that both the state and Ingersoll may collect damages and attorneys' fees from Stutzman personally and from her business. This ruling means that Stutzman may lose her business, her home, and her savings. The judge also told her that she must either agree to decorate same-sex weddings or stop doing weddings altogether. She decided to refuse all weddings while awaiting her appeal bore the Washington State Supreme Court. The Washington State Supreme Court upheld her conviction, holding that the government can indeed force citizens to participate and endorse acts they believe to be immoral. Stutzman's attorney, Kristen Waggoner, commented on the unmistakable message contained in the ruling: "the government will bring about your personal and professional ruin if you don't help celebrate same-sex marriage. Laws that are supposed to prohibit discrimination" are being used "to force [religious dissented] to conform and to silence and punish them if they don't violate their religious beliefs on marriage."[11]

Washington's Attorney General, Bob Ferguson, offered to settle the suit for $2,001 if Stutzman would agree to cater same-sex weddings or not to cater to weddings at all. Stutzman replied that it is clear that Ferguson does not understand or appreciate her religious objections, and that she is no longer free to act on her beliefs. Ferguson did not understand that while Stutzman obviously did not relish losing her business and personal savings, the issue was not about money, but about religious freedom, which the Washington State Constitution guarantees, but obviously just on paper. She also noted that she had employed and served members of the LGBT community, but that she could not work in the furtherance of a homosexual wedding. Her full letter is a heart rendering appeal to be allowed to practice her faith and not to have her livelihood taken away for doing so. [12] Who would have thought that such a letter would have been written in the United States of America?

Stutzman appealed to the Washington Supreme Court (*Washington v. Arlenes Flowers, 2017)* which rejected her claim that her work is an "inherently expressive" act. In the court's unanimous decision, it wrote: "Certainly, she argues that she intends to communicate a message through her floral arrangements. But the major contest is over whether Stutzman's intended communications actually communicated something to the public at large—whether her conduct was 'inherently expressive.' And her actions in creating floral arrangements for wedding ceremonies do not satisfy this standard." This is a strange comment since all wedding floral arrangements express a message that the public "at large" understands. Stutzman's refusal expressed her faith in what she sees as God's word, which members of the public perceive. The court ruling made plain the mainstream status of the Free Exercise

Clause among the judiciary these days, stating that "the only fundamental right implicated in this case is the right to religious free exercise."

The use of the adverb "only" here is an insult to the Constitution, its Framers, and to America itself. The court dismissed the free exercise right as of "lesser importance" than a free speech claim, even though the Framers placed the former in front of the latter. It also stated that Stutzman's free exercise claim must be "balanced" with the state statute. The Washington Supreme Court placed its thumb on the scale in favor of a mere statute, and it left the pan containing the Constitution's "first liberty" swinging impotently in the fog of 59 page of legal whitewash. The case has been appealed to the United States Supreme Court. It remains to be seen if the Court will hear it or let the ruling stand and ruin the health and finances of this elderly Christian woman.

Aaron and Melissa Klein

In 2013, Aaron and Melissa Klein, owners of Sweet Cakes by Melissa, refused to bake a wedding cake for the lesbian wedding of Rachel Cryer and Laurel Bowman, stating that it would violate their religious consciences. The Klein's, parents of five children, believed their decision was protected by their right to practice their religion as they see fit. The Oregon Bureau of Labor and Industries saw it differently and found that they had violated Oregon's anti-discrimination laws. The Kleins received many hate-filled e-mails and phone calls they have shared a number of these e-mails with TV interviewers, one reading "You stupid bible thumping, hypocritical bitch. I hope your kids get really, really, sick and you go out of business." Wedding vendors became so harassed by gay rights groups that they were forced to stop doing business with Sweet Cakes by Melissa, which had to close its doors. Aaron took a job as a garbage man making about half the income they previously had.

In July 2015, the commissioner of the Bureau of Labor and Industries, Brad Avakian, ordered the Kleins to pay damages to the lesbian couple of $135,000 for "emotional, mental and physical suffering." The Kleins initially refused to pay, but the state came after them with a vengeance, garnishing what assets they could, until they finally paid. This case is to be heard by the Oregon Court of Appeals, but few doubt the outcome. Tyler Smith, the Klein's lawyer, complained about the government's abuse of power "And that being completely ignored by the state agency, when they're prosecuting based on a statutory classification that this is now a protected status under a statute, when the Kleins have clearly protected constitutional rights that should supersede that and be more protected than a statutory right."[13]

History and Constitutional law are firmly in Smith's corner. Alexander Hamilton noted in *Federalist Paper No. 78*: "Whenever a particular statute contravenes the Constitution, it will be the duty of the judicial tribunals to adhere to the latter and disregard the former." [14] Justice Kennedy expressed the identical position in the 1989 Texas flag burning case—*Texas v. Johnson*: "For we are presented with a clear and simple statute [the Texas "breach of the peace" statute"] to be judged against a pure command of the Constitution [freedom of symbolic speech]." Hamilton and Kennedy were simply stating that the United States Constitution sits above and governs all statutory law beneath it, and if a statute conflicts with it, the Constitution prevails. The use of anti-discrimination statutes to persecute Christian businesses clearly contravenes the Constitution. These state statutes of recent origin have triumphed over rights of religious expression, free speech, and to be free of involuntary servitude. Such violations of Constitutional rights in furtherance of statutory requirements are unheard of except in same-sex marriage cases.

Memories Pizza

The Case of Memories Pizza shows that the gay Gestapo will target a person's livelihood for even expressing opposition to same-sex marriage. Sixty-one-year-old Kevin O'Connor and his daughter Crystal own Memories Pizza in Walkerton, Indiana. O'Connor and his family were forced into hiding and the store to temporarily shut down their store after receiving vulgar and threatening telephone calls and having their Facebook pages smeared with gay pornography for merely *saying* that they would not cater a same-sex marriage in a TV interview. The television station labeled Memories Pizza as the "first business to publicly deny same-sex service," in the aftermath Indiana's new Religious Freedom Restoration Act.[15] In fact, Memories Pizza has never turned anyone away from its doors. O'Connor merely said that it would not participate in a gay marriage because to do so would be tantamount to putting his stamp of approval on it. It is cases such as this that make defenders of religious rights feel that what gay activists want is not tolerance, but rather the forced acceptance of their agenda and for the courts to silence and punish anyone who opposes it. This has the potential of leading to a tragic choice society forcing all of us to choose between law and morality. As Frederic Bastiat, a 19th-century French classical liberal pointed out: "When law and morality contradict each other, the citizen has the cruel alternative of either losing his moral sense or losing his respect for the law."[16]

Commenting on the ordeal of the owners of Memories Pizza, Connor Friedersdorf of the left-leaning *Atlantic* magazine doesn't like these hateful gay tactics. While he supports same-sex marriage, he also believes "that the position *I'll gladly serve any gay customers but I feel my faith compels me to refrain from catering a gay wedding* is less hateful or intolerant than *let's go burn that family's business to the ground.*" [17] He goes on to write that the pizzeria owners did not discriminate against anybody but merely said that they would not to serve a gay wedding if they were asked to. He notes that no one asks a small-town pizzeria to cater to any wedding, never mind a gay one? But this is what we have come to in an America whose culture is becoming increasingly dominated by the left.

Service versus Participation

The issue in these cases has been framed as a refusal to serve gays and lesbians. Taylor Flynn finds herself "unnerved by proponents' failure to recognize the dignitary harm at the heart of public *refusals to serve* historically marginalized groups." She sees the issue as analogous to posting a "No gays served here!" sign and sees "Such sign-posting is an embodiment of second-class citizenship."[18] And so it would be, but the issue in each of these cases was not about serving gays and lesbians. Defendants in each of these cases all served homosexuals many times, and Elane Photography has even employed homosexuals.

The issue is more correctly stated as a refusal of these business owners to *actively* participate in the event that contravenes their religious identities, not one of refusing to serve gays and lesbians. A photographer must attend a wedding and participate in it by recording it on film; a baker must decorate the wedding cake with words and images, and a florist must do much the same, and in some cases arrange flowers at the location of the ceremony. All this activity is facilitating or participating in, an event that contravenes deeply held beliefs. In no instance was the issue one of whether a same-sex couple can get married, have flowers, have their photos taken, or obtain a wedding cake. All of these goods and services are available in abundance from people anxious to provide them, so why resort to state tyranny to force people into endorsing a practice they consider wrong? These people are perfectly willing in good conscience to bake cakes, take pictures, and provide flowers to gays and lesbians to celebrate any and all occasions except same-sex marriage because there is no religious reason for not doing so.

LGBT activists refuse to recognize the difference between serving and participating. Businesses owned by devout Christians must either violate their religious identities or face crippling legal penalties and be driven out of business. Conform or withdraw from society was the counsel of Colorado Democratic Senator Pat Steadman when he said of people whose religion forbids them to participate in same-sex weddings: "Get thee to a nunnery and live there then. Go live a monastic life away from modern society."[19] This is the kind of bigoted message that was once aimed at homosexuals—"Live your scandalous life if you must, but live it in the closet outside of mainstream society." Steadman, who is gay, evidently does not see the intolerance in his insistence that religious business people must check their moral principles at the shop entrance or be squeezed out of civic life. For such people, their businesses are an extension of their Christian ministry, and religion is not something just practiced by ordained ministers in a church. These people do not compartmentalize their religious and professional lives, even if the state insists that they must. They believe that right of free exercise is derived from the Creator, not from secular laws. When legislation is passed making compliance impossible for the devout, it is violating Madison's "Universal Sovereign" and discriminating against, marginalizing, and even criminalizing people who take seriously the right to free exercise of religion, free speech, and free association. According to Madison, the state should only interfere with free exercise when it "manifestly endangers" the state. The state is hardly threatened with extinction by bakers, photographers, florists, and owners of public accommodations seeking to live their lives in accordance with their faith.

The Coercion Test: Christian's Need Not Apply

Recall that in *Lee v. Weisman* (the case banning prayers at high school graduations) that Justice Kennedy formulated what is known as the coercion test for deciding if someone is being forced against their conscience to participate in something. Writing about the "burden" Deborah Weisman suffered by being exposed to a non-sectarian prayer, Kennedy proclaimed that she had:

> a reasonable perception that she is being forced by the State to pray in a manner her conscience will not allow...It is of little comfort to a dissenter, then, to be told that for her the act of standing or remaining in silence signifies mere respect, rather than participation. What matters is that, given our social conventions, a reasonable dissenter in this milieu could believe that the group exercise signified her own participation or approval of it.

How is "standing or remaining silent" signifying her participation in, or approval of, the prayer different from saying that providing for flowers, baking a cake, or taking pictures for a same-sex wedding is signifying the florist's, baker's, and photographer's participation or approval of it? It is certainly different by many degrees of magnitude because these business people were unambiguously "forced by the State." Remaining silent is negative non-participation (the person does nothing, thus signaling her disapproval), and the only cross Deborah had to bear is a few moments of discomfort. Being forced under penalty of law to take pictures, bake a cake, or arrange flowers celebrating a same-sex wedding is positive participation because the person actually does something, thus implying approval. If Deborah's case constituted coercion and participation and approval "in a manner her conscience will not allow," then the small business people's ordeal is unambiguously coercion and participation, and signals approval a devout Christian's "conscience will not allow." Furthermore, refusing to cater to such a wedding brings far more grief that a little-supposed discomfort; it may, and has, forced people out of business and brought financial ruin. This is perhaps the reason that the Supreme Court has left rulings of the lower courts to stand without comment when appeals that cite the coercion test from religious dissenters reach its hallowed halls. Legal precedent is supposed to be binding, but we can't have that, so we'll ignore the appeal because it seems that the *statutory* rights of gays and lesbians are more binding than the *Constitutional* rights of Christians.

The Analogy with Jim Crow Laws

LGBT activists like to make the analogy between refusing to facilitate a same-sex wedding with refusing to serve blacks in the old South. Jacquelyn Cooper calls it "modern-day segregation." She reveals that she does not understand the religious objections at all when she writes: "If a liberal chef serves a conservative patron, the chef is not professing 'I support conservative views.'"[20] She also opines that "A florist may detest lilies, but if a customer wants lilies, the florist will provide them."[21] She seems unaware that there are no religious objections to conservative views or lilies. A devout Christian chef will gladly serve a gay couple because there is no moral objection to dining, and a Christian florist who "hates lilies" will sell them to a gay customer because there is no morality attached to loving lilies. Anyone of minimal sense knows that doing so is not analogous to endorsing the gay lifestyle. Her argument is simply a monumental nonsequitur since there is a difference of several orders of magnitude between violating religious conscience and violating political or floral preferences. Cooper also states that "Asking a baker to bake a cake or a florist to make an arrangement does not involve force at all." She is absolutely right at the time that someone merely asks. But it is when they are refused and they run off to Big Brother to use the law to compel them that force comes into play. She also invokes Jesus by pointing out that he fed, healed, and ministered to people whose lifestyle he found distasteful, but she neglects to point out that he told them to "go and sin no more." Jesus did not put his stamp of approval on their behavior, or facilitate it by ministering to them.

Under Jim Crow laws it was the state that was discriminating. It was not religious conscience that motivated Jim Crow practices; it was the racism, which makes a world of difference. White businesses were forbidden by law to serve blacks, or if they did so, such as in restaurants or public transportation, there had to be a separate "colored" section. Even if a white business wanted to serve blacks for financial reasons or any other reason, it could not do so under penalty of law. White businesses were not in a position to say that they would not lend their talents to facilitate a black wedding but are willing serve blacks in all other ways. They could not serve them, period. Religious believers, however, are more than willing to serve gays and lesbians for all occasions except for a same-sex wedding. This one faith-based exception does not remotely compare with refusing service in any form to a group of people because of the color of their skin. Thus the issue is not about discrimination against persons for what they are, but rather about discriminating against an activity that religious believers consider sinful. I have difficulty seeing how anyone of intelligence cannot grasp the difference.

There are principled LGBT people who defend the right to refuse to cater to same-sex weddings on either religious or libertarian grounds; no black person (presumably) would similarly defend government sanctioned Jim Crow practices on any grounds. For instance, Peter Tatchell, a prominent campaigner for gay rights, has noted that "Much as I wish to defend the gay community, I also want to defend freedom of conscience, expression, and religion." Gays such as Tatchell don't want to see the Constitution and the Bible thrown on the trash heap in the name of protecting the rights of a minuscule few to force others into involuntary servitude.[22]

It is difficult to wrap one's mind around the idea of a same-sex couple wanting to do business with someone who has moral objections without believing there is a deeper issue involved. If I am gay and want to marry my partner, there are numerous businesses eager to provide services to facilitate it, so why would I push the issue? I would want someone that supports me and will gladly do their best job. I would not leave any aspect of my wedding to someone that does not agree with my lifestyle. Even though gays and lesbians can acquire these services freely elsewhere, they purposely target those who they know will not in their "take no prisoners" stance toward religion. It has nothing to do with obtaining services; it is all about malevolently destroying anyone who does not approve of their lifestyle and getting themselves in front of the cameras and the courts to advance their message. The cultural Marxist goal of producing an "anti-Christian mind," is riding the coat tails of the LGBT agenda.

In most other instances people can refuse to offer their services if they find that the people who seek them offend their sense of justice, fairness, or morality. For instance, Bruce Springsteen cancelled his concert in in 2016 because he objected to the so-called "Bathroom Law" that denies men the use of a woman's bathrooms. I have no qualms with his decision because he believes the law is "discriminatory." It is, of course, but it is that way we want it because we don't want voyeurs and exhibitionists pretending that they "self-identify" as a woman to spy on young girls and women and parade their stuff in front of them (wouldn't that be discriminating against females by violating their privacy and putting them in danger?). I agree with Springsteen (who wants to remain a darling of the left) because I believe he or any other seller of services has the absolute right not to do business with people with whom they disagree. But if Springsteen can deny services to people with whom he disagrees on principled grounds, why can't Christian business owners? The easy answer is "because Christian business owners are breaking the administrative law; Springsteen is not." But that begs the question of why such laws exist to completely satisfy the principled demands of one group by denying the principled demands of another completely. If Springsteen had refused to perform at a gay wedding, he would be cast as a bigot rather than a hero of the left. I guess Springsteen has rights that Christians do not in LGBT America where the only right Christians have is the right to agree with the LGBT agenda.

The Reason Why: Administrative Law

The role of administrative law is a major reason that LGBT rights are prevailing time after time over the Constitutional rights of Christians. Disputes that fall under the administrative law are adjudicated by administrative commissions, which are distinct from judicial courts in a number of important ways. Disputes between authorities, and contracts between private persons fall into the jurisdiction of the general court system, but administrative acts are about state public powers that are considered binding without the consent of the involved parties. Philip Hamburger writes that because administrative law essentially places executive, legislative, and judicial power in one body: "It revives what used to be called prerogative or absolute power, and it is thus something that the Constitution centrally prohibited."[23] In all same-sex marriage cases discussed in this chapter, as well as the hundreds of others to be found dotting the Internet, the defendants cannot avail themselves of the Fifth and Sixth Amendment rights afforded by the protection of juries as they could in a criminal or non-administrative civil case. Juries composed of one's peers have long been considered in common law to be an essential intermediary between the awesome power of the state and the powerless defendant.

Because there are no juries in administrative hearings, the administrative law judge is both the finder of the law and the finder of facts. In criminal and other civil cases, the judge only rules on the law, and the jury rules on the facts and renders the verdict. If juries were involved in these same-sex cases, the results might have been dramatically different. Jurors would perceive the state bullying involved and may engage their right of jury nullification. Jury nullification occurs when a jury finds a person "not guilty" despite the defendant being guilty "in fact" of the violation charged. By engaging in nullification, the jury is in effect nullifying a law it believes to be immoral or wrongly applied. Administrative court decisions may be appealed to a judicial court, but again there is no jury for such appeals. With no citizen oversight, the state is free to impose its draconian financial penalties on decent religious people guilty only of refusing to partake in what they consider an abomination in the eyes of God.

Some scholars see the battle between religious liberty and LGBT rights as a zero-sum battle: "Once the nation realizes that there will be a winner and a loser, then the only question is whether religious liberties and free speech rights should be repressed to promote legal recognition of same-sex relationships."[24] Thomas Berg sees a way that both rights can be recognized because the same arguments made for recognizing same-sex marriage can be applied to protecting the rights of religious service providers. He argues that "both same-sex couples and religious believers claim that their conduct stems from commitments central to their identity: love and fidelity to a life partner, faithfulness to the moral norms of God—and that they should be able to live these commitments in a public way, touching all aspects of their lives."[25] In other words, gays and lesbians claim a right beyond private behavior; that is, the right to have their love and commitment publicly recognized in marriage and religious people wish to live by the tenets of their faith in their public lives, not just in their homes and churches. However, as long as the state can punish Christians who act on their faith with respect to same-sex marriage can be punished by administrative commissions out of the sight or control of the people we will not have religious liberty as the Founders envisioned.

Justice Alito pointed out religious protections would have been in place if the issue of same-sex marriage had been decided democratically by the people of each state. He notes that some states would have recognized same-sex marriage and others would not, but those who voted to recognize it would likely have tied "recognition to protection for conscience rights." But *Obergefell* decision in 2015 makes the protections Berg wrote about in 2010 highly problematic, as Justice Alito noted: "The majority today makes that impossible. By imposing its own views on the entire country, the majority facilitates the marginalization of the many Americans who have traditional ideas."

Because the Supreme Court used Religious Freedom Restoration Act (RFRA to Protect Hobby Lobby in *Burwell v. Hobby Lobby,* one might ask why the RFRA did not protect the small business owners discussed here. Using the same logic exercised in *Burwell* (the use of the "least restrictive means"), there are obvious ways of accessing photographers, florists, and bakers without restricting the religious liberty of others. Furthermore, these businesses, and numerous other small businesses across the country that have been similarly targeted are "closely held corporations." Indeed, they fit the definition far more closely than the huge Hobby Lobby, but in no instance has the "closely held" or "least restrictive means" criteria applied to their cases. Recall that the Court held that closely held corporations are businesses in which more than 50 percent of the value of its stock is directly or indirectly owned by five or fewer individuals, and owners have religious rights under the RFRA. The reason that the logic articulated in *Burwell* was not applied in these small business cases, you may recall, was that the Supreme Court in *City of Boerne v. Flores* held that the RFRA only applies to the federal government. Responding to this ruling, 21 states passed their own RFRAs, but the states in which these the cases we have been discussing—Colorado, Oregon, Iowa, and Washington—are not among them. New Mexico does have a RFRA, but it did not protect Elane Photography because the New Mexico Supreme Court held that it only applied to disputes in which a government agency is a party, which is almost always the case. People of faith just can't win.

Will Government Tyranny Go all the way to the Altar for LGBT Rights?

But is the free exercise of faith safe in church anymore? Many Christians view the small business owners who have been persecuted as holding the line against what may become an even bigger infringement on religious liberty. During oral arguments in *Obergefell v. Hodges:* "Justice Antonin Scalia repeatedly noted that if the High Court finds same-sex 'marriage' is a constitutional right, then priests, ministers, rabbis, and imams will be required to perform such ceremonies – regardless of their religious beliefs – or face state penalties." He further noted: "I'm concerned about the wisdom of this court imposing through the Constitution a requirement of action which is unpalatable to many of our citizens for religious reasons."[26]

Now that same-sex marriage is the law of the land, churches are increasingly being coerced into abiding by laws affirming it in ways that are reaching within their four walls. The legalization of same-sex marriage could have the effect of criminalizing a church's view on marriage and sexual morality, even if is expressed from the pulpit. Churches are no longer free to operate under their own definition of marriage, and this is in direct violation of that old-fashioned thing we call the United States Constitution. Denmark has already done what Scalia feared. Denmark's parliament has made it mandatory for all churches to conduct gay marriages. In Canada, after 15 years of service, Rev. Jay Brown, a Church of Christ minister, was fired from her post as Cambridge, Ontario, council minister for refusing to officiate at same-sex weddings, and in France, the Constitutional Council, France's Supreme Court, ruled that mayors cannot refuse to carry out same-sex marriages on the grounds of their religious or moral beliefs.

These countries do not have the history of religious liberty that the United States used to enjoy, but we have witnessed something akin to this in Idaho. *Coeur D'Alene Press* reporter Keith Cousins wrote that in this city in 2014, officials told and two ordained ministers that they must perform same-sex ceremonies or face jail time and/or fines. However, faced with public outrage the city relented. Then we have the Iowa Civil Rights Commission declaring that prohibitions against discrimination on the basis of sexual orientation and gender identity "sometimes" apply to churches. The Commission wants to make it illegal to preach views that would "directly or indirectly" make "persons of any particular gender identity" feel "unwelcome" in conjunction "with church services, events, and other religious activities." It also stated that a "church service open to the public" is not a "bona fide religious purpose" that would limit the application of the law. In other words, Iowa's anti-discrimination law is a de facto ban on free speech because it seeks to prevent pastors from preaching about sexual morality.[27] No "separation of church and state" in Iowa.

Another state agency that invaded the sanctuary of the church to forward the LGBT agenda is the Georgia Department of Public Health's (GDPH). This agency fired its director, Eric Walsh, a physician and lay minister in the Seventh Day Adventist Church, because of his church sermons on marriage and homosexuality. The GDPH investigated his sermons and found them to be politically incorrect. Walsh said in an interview that: "If this is allowed to stand it sets an incredibly terrible precedent in this country that's supposed to be founded on certain inherent freedoms and rights. And if this is erased for Eric Walsh, it is erased for generations to come."[28] Walsh's lead attorney in his fight against the GDPH, Jeremy Dys, remarked: "No one in this country should be fired from their job for something that was said in a church or from a pulpit during a sermon. If the government is allowed to fire someone over what he said in his sermons, they can come after any of us for our beliefs on anything." [29]

In effect, Walsh has to give up his religious freedom and free speech rights as a condition of his employment with the GDPH. "Investigating" a pastor's sermons for politically incorrect statements sounds very much like something the Gestapo would have done. The GDPD is also saying that because Walsh's Bible-based sermons were deemed "hateful," the Bible itself must be hateful. As one commentator remarked on television "First, they silenced the sheep [those of us who remain silent about these abominations], and now they are trying to silence the shepherds [such as Eric Walsh]". In the inverted hierarchy of rights, as sexual liberty has expanded religious liberty has narrowed to the confines of Christian homes and churches. It may not be too safe in church either in the not so distant future unless Christians and libertarians, of whatever religious persuasion or sexual orientation, join the fight against this abomination.

Endnotes

1. ACLU. Masterpiece Cakeshop.
2. Crossland. Baker must cater to same-sex weddings, or else.
3. Starns. Baker forced to make gay wedding cakes.
4. Ibid.
5. Cited in ACLU. Colorado Supreme Court refuses to hear case of bakery.
6. Dewart. On Writ of Certiorari to the United States Court of Appeals, pp. 30-31.
7. Free Legal Dictionary, emphasis mine.
8. Legal Information Institute of Cornell University.
9. In Liptak, Weighing free speech.
10. Cited in Anderson and Ford, Protecting religious liberty, p. 4.
11. Alliance Defending Freedom, Wash. floral artist's home, savings at risk.
12. Cited in Backman, Arlene's Flowers response to Attorney General's settlement offer.
13. Cited in Hallowell, Lawyer for Christian bakers.
14. Hamilton, *The Judiciary Department.*
15. Moyer, Indiana Pizza Shop.
16. Bastiat, *The Law,* p. 10).
17. Friedersdorf, Should mom-and-pops that forgo gay weddings be destroyed?
18. Flynn, Clarion call or false alarm, p. 236, emphasis mine.
19. Cited in Laycock, Religious liberty and the culture wars, p. 871.
20. Cooper, Modern day segregation, p. 427.
21. Ibid, p. 427.
22. Tatchell, I've changed my mind on the gay cake row.
23. Hamburger, P. The history and danger of administrative law, p.1
24. Lindevaldsen, Fallacy of neutrality, p. 461.
25. Berg, What same-sex marriage and religious-liberty claims, p. 207.
26. Hodges, States could Force Catholic priests.
27. French, Churches won't perform same-sex weddings.
28. First Liberty Staff Writers, State of Georgia fired doctor.

29. Dys, cited in Conservative Tribune. State officials demand pastor's sermons.

Cases Cited.

Agency for International Development v. Alliance for Open Society International, Inc. 570 U.S. ___ (2013)

Bailey v. State of Alabama, 219 U. S. 219, 241 (1911).

Elane Photography v. Willock, 296 P. 3d 491 - 2012.

Girouard v. United States, 328 U.S. 61 (1946).

United States v. Kozminski, 487 U.S. 931, 942-943 (1988).

Spence v. Washington, 418 U.S. 405 (1974).

Texas v. Johnson, 491 U.S. 397 (1989).

Washington v. Arlenes Flowers, No. 91615-2, Washington Supreme Court (2017).

Wooley v. Maynard, 430 U.S. 705 (1977).

Chapter 11

The Enemies of Christian America: What Motivates Them?

"In its main features the Declaration of Independence is a great spiritual document...They have their source and their roots in the religious convictions... Unless the faith of the American people in these religious convictions is to endure, the principles of our Declaration will perish. We cannot continue to enjoy the result if we neglect and abandon the cause"
Calvin Coolidge--30th President of the United States.

Back to the Past

In 1630, John Winthrop led 1,000 devout Puritans from England to the Massachusetts Bay Colony to escape the tyranny of the state and to establish a "city upon a hill" dedicated to God and to obeying God's laws. The Puritans left England because they wanted to follow their own form of worship and personal intimacy with God, but were compelled to accept, participate, and affirm the prayers and practices of the established Church of England. The goal of these Puritans and other religious dissenters from state interference with religion worked out as well as can be expected in America given the vices and imperfections of human nature until the Supreme Court began meddling in religion in the middle of the twentieth century.

From *Everson* onwards, the state has been functioning as if it wanted to turn Winthrop's city upon a hill into a moral ghetto. Under the guise of advancing statutory rights for homosexuals, the government is stripping the Constitutional liberties of Christians when their faith runs afoul of the LGBT agenda. When these contrary rights butt heads in the courts, the courts have done what ethicists consider the essence of immorality; they have disregarded the needs and demands of one claim entirely to satisfy the needs and demands of another fully. Just as 17th century England tried to force the Puritans to accept, affirm, and participate in the practices of the Church of England, modern America is trying to force Christians to accept, participate in, and affirm same-sex marriage. The state's efforts have been made easier by the slow erosion of religion in public life since the 1940s. There is no new world to escape to this time; now dissenters must accept Huxley's Brave New World of Big Government or face ruin.

The fight against religious freedom is slowly being won by cultural Marxists with the help of unsuspecting dupes on the left who, while not necessarily calling themselves Marxists, are supporters of big government who mock the notion of a moral power higher than the state. They cannot accept this because it would mean respecting "the first liberty" enshrined in the Constitution. If the radical left respected this inalienable right in the way the Founders meant it to be respected, it would stand in the way of Obama's agenda to "fundamentally change" America from Winthrop's "city upon a hill" into a moral cesspit devoid of core truths.

At a time when the plain words of the religious clauses of Constitution were still read as their authors intended, Justice Douglas wrote in *Girouard v. United States* (a 1946 case in which a candidate for naturalization declined to say that he would take up arms in defense of the United States on religious grounds and was refused citizenship. The Court affirmed his right to decline and ruled that his refusal should not bar him from citizenship):

> The struggle for religious liberty has, through the centuries, been an effort to accommodate the demands of the State to the conscience of the individual. The victory for freedom of thought recorded in our Bill of Rights recognizes that, in the domain of conscience, *there is a moral power higher than the State*. Throughout the ages, men have suffered death rather than subordinate their allegiance to God to the authority of the State. Freedom of religion guaranteed by the First Amendment is the product of that struggle.

The modern American state is impervious to the truth stated by Justice Douglas that religious belief is tethered to the idea that there is an allegiance to God that transcends secular politics. There must be a secular rule of law, but it must be consistent with natural law. It is this law that the Founders wrote into the Declaration of Independence's most trenchant passage affirming that all people are "endowed by their Creator with certain inalienable rights." It was partly for this reason that some of the Framers opposed a Bill of Rights, thinking that it might enforce the idea that rights are granted by government, while the Constitution made plain that the government's role is to protect rights, not grant them. Liberty of conscience is the most absolute, sacrosanct, and non-negotiable of inalienable rights. The radical left is contemptuous of such notions, and we want to ask why.

The Left's Animosity toward America

Someone once said that "If America were a house, the left would root for the termites." But the radical left doesn't just root for the termites; they are the termites busily feeding on the rafters and foundations of America's soul in the dark and unseen. We will only spot them scurrying about when the foundations of our magnificent mansion crumble, and we tear the timbers apart, but by then it will be too late. While I believe that most liberals (the weak variety) are patriotic, many on the hard left have a palpable contempt for their country. Dan Flynn relates how he has been physically and verbally attacked and ejected from college campuses and leftist rallies while researching his book *Why the Left Hates America: Exposing the Lies That Have Obscured Our Nation's Greatness.* At one of these rallies, a middle-aged demonstrator remarked that: "We are a terrorist nation; I think the United States is a culturally and emotionally diseased country." At another, a brainwashed student commented: "Who's the real Axis of Evil? If any country's really an Axis of Evil, it's us." Flynn tells us that "Such sentiments are virtually ubiquitous among those attending leftist rallies."[1]

It goes without saying that many on the left clearly do not view the United States as Abraham Lincoln's "Last best hope of Earth." Because progressives are forever harping about changing some aspect or another of America, we can say without fear of contradiction that is they are unhappy with it. That is why they were so excited by Obama's 2007 campaign promise to fundamentally transform the United States. A "fundamental" transformation of anything means it must be gutted and replaced with something quite different, and Obama and his czars and apostles did their best to make this happen during his tenure.

There are some outrageous examples of anti-American hatred coming from our university campuses, which have become leftist politically correct monocultures. For example, ethnic studies professor Ward LeRoy Churchill infamously asserted that the 9/11 victims in the Twin Towers deserved their fate because they were symbols of capitalist and imperialist America: "If there was a better, more effective, or in fact another way of visiting some penalty befitting their participation upon the little Eichmanns inhabiting the sterile sanctuary of the twin towers, I'd really be interested in hearing about it...No matter what its eventual fate, America will have gotten off very, very cheap."[2]

This obnoxious clown is hardly alone in sharing radical Islam's a profound hatred of America. Jonathan Schanzer relates that: "In 2001, Rutgers University English professor Barbara Foley called the 9/11 attacks a legitimate response to the 'fascism' of U.S. foreign policy. In 2006, Noam Chomsky, an M.I.T. linguistics professor, lauded Hezbollah leader Hassan Nasrallah, whose group calls for the destruction of America and Israel."[3] The left's rush to bury Ben Carson in vitriol when he said that Islam and the American Constitution are fundamentally incompatible make clear both its ignorance and anti-American animus. Islamists have made it crystal clear on countless occasions that they agree 100 percent with Carson, but facts make no difference to leftists who seem to have a psychic need to defend Islam no matter what. Barack Obama felt it necessary at the 2015 National Prayer Breakfast to ram it down America's throat that Christians attacked Muslims during the Crusades. Pennsylvania senator Rick Santorum is among those who rebuked Obama for this: "Today's remarks by the President were inappropriate, and his choice of venue was insulting to every person of faith at a time when Christians are being crucified, beheaded, and persecuted across the Middle East."[4]

Someone should have informed Obama that the last crusade ended 725 years ago and that Muslims launched their own crusades against the West 365 years earlier than the first Christian crusade, which began in 1095. After conquering Zoroastrian Persia, Muslims went on to subjugate Christendom from Egypt to Spain, and even plundered the Churches of St. Peter and St. Paul in Rome in 846, two and a half centuries before the first Crusade.[5] Nevertheless, leftists insist on casting the worst light possible on the Christian crusades while ignoring the primacy, longevity, and barbarity of the perpetual Muslim "crusades entirely." They seem to be temperamentally incapable of finding anything good about the West. The Crusades were intended as a "counter-jihad" to stop further Muslim expansion across formerly Christian areas and to recover former Christian territory conquered less than four centuries before. Furthermore, historian Bernard Lewis tells us that, "a substantial proportion of the population of these lands, perhaps even a majority, was still Christian."[6]

Indicative of leftist attempts to acquit the guilty and condemn the innocent are the remarks of gay and lesbian studies professor Jonathan Katz, that conservatives and "the Christian right" are to blame for the horrific radical Islamic terrorist attack at a gay nightclub in Orlando in 2016 which left 49 dead and wounded 53 others. The fact that the attack was carried out by Omar Mateen while pledging allegiance to the Islamic State was entirely discounted by Katz. Katz charged that the focus on ISIS is a "deliberate misdirection" by the homophobic right, which would otherwise find the defense of murdered gays "unpalatable."[7] No wonder, so many of our American youth are coming out of our universities as little lefties. They are being indoctrinated at taxpayer expense by tenured fools like Churchill, Chomsky, Foley, and Katz, who twist the truth beyond recognition to fit their anti-American agenda.

It goes without saying that the left does not respect our foundational documents. In 2015, Project Veritas posted a video on YouTube featuring university administrators and faculty members at Vassar, Cornell, Yale, and Oberlin shredding the Constitution. They did so at the request of a "student" (actually an undercover reporter for Project Veritas) who complained that people were handing out pocket copies of the Constitution on campus. She related that this caused her to panic and hyperventilate because she considered the Constitution to be a "flawed, oppressive, and racist" document. Various academics agreed with her, and shredded or ripped up the copy she brought with her. One bonehead academic remarked: "Like I said before, it is a very flawed document and it is written by flawed individuals," and another said: "I am happy to take it and shred it in my office."[8]

What Animates the Left?

Why do privileged and presumably intelligent people exhibit such animosity toward their country and its foundational principles? They are Americans but believe that America is responsible for just about every evil in the world. They are white, but wallow in guilt about slavery, Jim Crow, and "white privilege." They are human but feel that humans are destroying the planet and that some tiny critter in the bayou is worth protecting more than humans. They love to complain about the one-percent, but on a worldwide scale, they (and most other Americans) are the one-percent. There must be aspects of self-loathing, envy, resentment in the deep recesses of their psyches.

Leftists like to think that they come from their views rationally; after all, they are "intellectuals." But being an intellectual in the humanities and soft sciences often means being cognitively trapped by abstract ideas and emotional convictions, while lacking the ability to engage with reality. They cling to socialism despite the fact that it fails everywhere it has been tried, but for them, the solution is to try again; it's just too beautiful a theory to be wrong.

It would appear that emotion rather than rational meditation leads many people to accept certain ideologies; after all, what rational person would support socialism given its sad and brutal history? Economist David Henderson provides an example of the power of envy and resentment in driving people to embrace Marxism. Henderson tells of a conversation he and a friend had with Will Herberg, a former prominent communist, asking him how he became a Marxist. Herberg informed them that as a young man he felt intense resentment because he had nothing and people who he felt less smart than himself had a lot. He said he became a Marxist because he hated the rich, and that this resentment was a common route to becoming a Marxist: "The number of people who became Marxists by reading Marx "can be counted on the fingers of one hand."[9] It is very likely that most hard leftists have a deep sense of envy and resentment and have temperaments inclining them toward negative emotionality. With Herbert Marcuse, they yearn to throw off "the vexatious authority of logic" and the shackles of morality while yearning for the "ought" of tomorrow and repudiating the "is" of today. For radical leftists, life is one long toothache. After all, if you are constantly complaining about your country, your species, your race, and your finances, when do you have time to contemplate on the bounties they enjoy by virtue of living in the United States?

Personality and Ideology

The left is keen to brand conservatives as a mean-spirited unhappy lot with low self-esteem, "bitter" people "clinging to their religion and their guns," as Obama characterized them, or "irredeemable deplorables" as Hillary Clinton called them. Yet much of this, it turns out, is just the opposite: "In surveys across the globe, conservatives report being more satisfied with their lives than liberals."[10] A Pew Center survey reported that 47 percent of conservative Republicans described themselves as "very happy," compared with 28 percent of liberal Democrats. This result held regardless of income level (poor, middle-income, and rich). According to the report this pattern has been demonstrated consistently since such polls were initiated in 1972.[11] Another study addressed the ideology/happiness issue with four different samples composed of 78,876 respondents and summarized their findings as follows: "Conservatives score higher than liberals on personality and attitude measures that are traditionally associated with positive adjustment and mental health, including personal agency, positive outlook, transcendental moral beliefs, and generalized beliefs in fairness. These constructs, in turn, can account for why conservatives are happier than liberals."[12]

The lower scores on personal agency among leftists may be explained by their consistent belief that every individual's problems are the result of an unjust society and never attributable to personal responsibility and choice. If someone sees life as unfair, they will naturally have a negative outlook because if an abstract force we call "society" is in control of our destinies and is inherently unfair, there is nothing they can do about it except yearn for America's "fundamental transformation." Conservatives, on the other hand, compare America to every other civilization, past and present, and praise the Lord that they live there.

Perhaps the average liberal's low level of life satisfaction can be further accounted for by the fact that they are also less likely to be married and to attend a place of worship. A Pew Research Report found that 79 percent of Republicans versus 59 percent of Democrats were married, and 42 percent of Democrats were divorced versus 22 percent of Republicans.[13] Another Pew report found that 55 percent of conservatives regularly attend a place of worship versus only 27 percent liberals.[14] These figures reflect a relative leftist

estrangement from two of the major institutions of society, but then, alienation from the family ("patriarchal slavery") and religion ("the opiate of the
masses") is part of the cultural Marxist agenda.

Being unhappy increases the probability of developing mental health problems. A Gallup poll found that Republicans (58%) were significantly more
likely than Democrats (38%) to rate their mental health as excellent. The relationship persisted within all categories of income, age, gender, church attendance, and education. The Gallup researchers wrote that: "one cannot say
whether something about being Republican causes a person to be more mentally healthy, or whether something about being mentally healthy causes a
person to choose to become a Republican (or whether some third variable is
responsible for causing both to be parallel)."[15] The elusive third variable is
probably a generally more positive outlook on life; a sense of satisfaction with
was *is* rather than what should be, and a deep sense of self-reliance.

To explore personality differences among conservative and liberals, it is useful to look at studies of the so-called Big Five personality traits (agreeableness,
extraversion, neuroticism, conscientiousness, openness). The Big Five constitute the core dispositional traits of all of us because they "are based on genetic differences and/or early childhood experiences, with limited contextual
influences later in life."[16] These core traits are composed of a number of sub-
traits that provide useful insights into the ways we think and behave. A team
of psychologists surveyed the voluminous literature on political orientation
and personality involving many thousands of people around the globe and
added their own study of 12,472 Americans.[17] Most studies find no difference
between liberals and conservatives on agreeableness (friendly, warm, consid-
erate, trusting, altruistic) although two of the studies found that conserva-
tivism was more strongly associated with agreeableness.

Conservatives are more extraverted (energetic, assertive, sociability, domi-
nant, positive emotionality), which is not surprising since conservatives are
the people who keep the economy humming. Their energy and assertiveness
mean that the get on with life as it is rather than sitting around bemoaning
the "evils" of America. Previous studies have all found that liberals are more
neurotic (uneven tempered, insecure, lacking confidence, low impulse control) than conservatives, and this one replicated that finding, with conservatives being more emotionally stable than liberals. Neither is this too surprising since being tied to family and religion are predictors of both happiness
and positive mental health. Finally, to no one's surprise, all studies find that
the biggest gaps between conservatives and liberals are between conscientiousness (disciplined, reliable, self-control, scrupulous, delayed gratification)
on which conservatives score higher, and openness (intellectual curiosity,
creativity, preference for novelty) on which liberals score higher. This open-

ness to novel ideas among leftists explains why they fall for the emotional allure of socialism, which is a creative and even beautiful idea, but which becomes hell on Earth when put into practice; just ask the people of Venezuela right now.

Political Ideology and Altruism

Liberals believe that because conservatives disavow their ideas of radical redistribution of wealth that they "hate" (liberals love to use this word when talking about conservatives) the poor. Consistent with this liberal belief, and disturbed by the ubiquitous finding that conservatives are happier than liberals, two psychologists tried to prove that the reason conservatives are happier is that they are unconcerned with the plight of the poor. They examined the issue with data from 10 different countries and found the same results, but concluded that liberals are less happy than conservatives "because liberals lack ideological rationalizations that would help them frame inequality in a positive (or at least neutral) light."[18] But why is a belief in meritocratic principles a rationalization, a term that denotes a distortion of reality? The great majority of people the world over and almost all moral philosophers endorse equity as the epitome of fairness. It is far more plausible to argue that liberals rationalize their unhappiness by their distortion of reality when they perpetually accentuated inequities of an actual capitalist society with a hypothetical perfectly egalitarian society they yearn for.

But what about leftist claims that conservatives are mean-spirited toward the poor? The empirical research shows that they are wrong about this also, and it is they who are mean-spirited. This empirical research finds that whether measured in terms of individuals and families, states, or cities, conservatives are found to be more generous with their time (volunteering) and resources (monetary and blood donations) than liberals.[19] Arthur Brooks' book on charitable giving notes that although the average family in San Francisco enjoys 78 percent more household income than South Dakota households: "The average South Dakotan gives away 75 percent more of its household each year." It also notes that a survey conducted by Harvard University's Kennedy School of Government showing that: "Republican households give 30% more to charity than Democratic households."[20] Research comparing average state charitable giving with how it voted in the 2012 Presidential race (Obama vs. Romney). Only one of the top 20 giving states voted for the liberal Obama. Of the bottom 20 giving states, all but 3 voted for Obama.[21]

Commenting on a large number of these studies, *New York Times* columnist Nicholas Kristof, a self-proclaimed liberal, wrote that: "Liberals show tremendous compassion in pushing for generous government spending to help the neediest people at home and abroad. Yet when it comes to individual contributions to charitable causes, liberals are cheapskates."[22] Three marketing professors admitted that: "Households headed by a conservative individual donate more money than households headed by a liberal." They seemed to have found this unpalatable because they added an excusatory "however" to their observation: "when measuring a respondent's support of government spending on social programs, those with a relatively liberal political identity are more generous."[23] It is true that liberals feel that they owe a debt to their fellow man, but they propose to pay it with other people's money. Liberals find it agreeable for the government to be generous with tax payer's money, but are evidently reluctant to dig into their own pockets. Altruistic sentiments are great, but they must motivate altruistic actions if they are to mean anything. Liberals are probably terribly upset that what they give of themselves in the form of protests, rallies, sit-ins, and making everyone feel miserable and victimized does not count as charity.

Perhaps I am being unfair; there are other actions besides giving money, blood, and time to charities that count as altruism. But findings from the General Social Survey's cumulative database found, alas, that liberals fail here also. The survey compared "yes" answers to questions among people identifying themselves as "very conservative" (VC) or "very liberal" (VL) and found the following:

- "Do you get happiness by putting someone else's happiness ahead of your own?" VCs = 55%; VLs = 20%.

- "Would you endure all things for the one you love?" VCs = 55%; VLs = 26%.

- "Are you willing to sacrifice your wishes to let the one you love succeed?" VCs = 57%; VLs = 33%.

- "Is it your obligation to care for a seriously injured/ill spouse or parent?" VCs = 71%; VLs = 46%.[24]

The Growth of the Leviathan

My brief excursion into personality provides some insight into the mindset of those who want to undermine Christianity and to use the power of big government to do so. I do not want to characterize all liberals as unhappy, stingy and anti-Christian. I have known many happy and decent, even churchgoing, liberals, but these are weak liberals who will probably change their ideological stripes as they get older and wiser. French Premier Georges Clemenceau is said to have opined: "Not to be a socialist at twenty is proof of want of heart; to be one at thirty is proof of want of head." I have long been struck with the phenomenon of radical changes in political orientation with age, which is

almost invariably a shift from left to right. There are numerous famous individuals who were former Marxists, socialists, and liberals who became conservatives with maturity. Internet searches will reveal a number of lists of
these people, but I have yet to see a list of famous conservatives who turned
liberal in their older years. I wonder if liberals can provide a reasonably plausible explanation for this.

It is the leftists who continue to support the cultural Marxist agenda of elim-
inating religion and the family by promoting radical sexual liberalism we
should fear. These are the folks with a strong genetic load leading them left-
wards, and they are to be found primarily in the humanities and social science departments in our universities. These tenured radicals conjure crazy
ideas and yearn for the ideal. They suffer from disenchantment and angst
because the world as it exists is never good enough, ought to be better. As
sociologist Lewis Coser puts it: "Intellectuals are men who never seem satisfied with things as they are, with appeals to customs and usage. They question
the truth of the moment in terms of higher and wider truth; they counter
appeals to factuality by invoking the 'impractical ought.'"[25] Another sociologist (and former Marxist), Lewis Feuer, views the alienation of many intellectuals in the "soft" disciplines of academia arising from a subterranean desire
for power: "In the beginning was the emotion; then came the idea and last the
deed. The emotional need for an ideology is the primary theme in the history
of intellectuals; it is their longing for a generational myth of mission, and the
validation of their claim to rule."[26]

Hard leftists need an ideology into which they can immerse their Godless
souls and a mission to make them feel useful, neither of which can be found
within democratic capitalism. They need a revolutionary sort of opposition; a
romantic cause to focus their anger and display their passion. Many Western
intellectuals in the 1930s were fascinated by fascism and Nazism for this very
reason. English socialist H.G. Wells called himself a "liberal fascist," and told
the Young Liberals at Oxford in 1932 that "Progressives must become 'liberal
fascists' and 'enlightened Nazis" [27] Wells also heaped praise on totalitarianism, saying that "I have never been able to escape altogether from its relentless logic."[28] Not to dress all academic liberals in brown shirts, but far too
many of them on the hard left are enthralled by the "relentless logic" of totalitarianism lusting to tear the heart out of American values and freedom under
the guise of supporting rights for segments of the population that have been
discriminated against in the past.

A telling example of this is the 2016 U.S. Commission on Civil Rights report
titled, *Peaceful Coexistence: Reconciling Nondiscrimination Principles with
Civil Liberties.* Despite the positive tone of its title, it comes out forcefully
against religious liberty for Americans in the name of protecting LGBT rights.

We will get the "peace and reconciliation" promised only if we conform to its views. Obama appointee Chairman Martin R. Castro's statement opens with a quote he attributed to President John Adams: "The government of the United States is not, in any sense, founded on the Christian religion." This sets the stage for the Commission's attack while ignoring the fact that this was a phrase of appeasement written in a period of American weakness which was later removed from the Treaty of Tripoli, and not written by Adams, as we saw in chapter 3.

Castro's disdain for religious liberty was clearly in evidence when he wrote (putting the words "religious liberty" and "freedom" in scare quotes):

> The phrases "religious liberty" and "religious freedom" will stand for nothing except hypocrisy so long as they remain code words for discrimination, intolerance, racism, sexism, homophobia, Islamophobia, Christian supremacy or any form of intolerance. Religious liberty was never intended to give one dominion over other religions, or a veto power over the civil rights and liberties of others.[29]

Castro employs the typical liberal strategy of accusing those who disagree of moral venality and hypocrisy and turning something most of us consider a positive thing—religious liberty—into a "code words" for hate. Leftists have honed their skills in demonizing people who disagree with them to a sharp point and have turned them into pitiful objects of fear, hatred, and scorn. On issues with moral content, liberals insist there is no debate and there should not be; there is only liberal "sense" and conservative "nonsense." They are winning the cultural war because they control the language in the national debate through their control of academic and journalistic wordsmiths who get their ideas disseminated. These are clever masters of Orwellian Newspeak with the ability—to quote Marcuse again—to turn "illusion into reality and fiction into truth" while ignoring the "vexatious authority of logic."

Castro accuses people who just want to be left alone to live their lives in accordance with their faith of exercising "dominion" and "veto power" over others, thus refusing to recognize that it is the government's embrace of the LGBT agenda that is exercising dominion and veto power over people of faith, as numerous court cases attest. There is a big difference between the desire not to be coerced by the government to violate one's faith on the one hand, and the desire to enlist to power of the government to coerce people of faith to affirm and participate in something they consider offensive to God, on the other Nowhere in this 306-page document do the commissioners make the distinction between serving gays and lesbians, which all the persecuted small business owners have done on many occasions, and putting their personal stamp of approval on same-sex marriage by lending their services to facilitate one. The majority of the commissioners may fail to see the difference between serving and participating, but there is a world of difference for men and women of faith.

Castro went on to remark that "In our nation's past religion has been used to justify slavery" while ignoring the fact that it was a worldwide phenomenon, and that Christians in the United States and Britain fought costly wars to end it in the West. In another statement authored by three other commissioners, they were adamant that "attempts to place religious liberty above other nondiscrimination laws."[30] must be assiduously avoided. In other words, ancient Constitutional rights of religious expression must be subordinate to novel statutory laws of sexual liberty assuring LGBT people that can demand Christians business people be placed in involuntary servitude to them. The commissioners have employed the cultural Marxist's tactic of shackling discrimination and hate to religion and justice and progress to liberalism.

Commissioner Peter Kirsanow dissented from the majority on the Commission and concluded that the recommendations and findings in the report "should serve as an alarm to liberty-loving Americans."[31] Kirsanow sees the increase in government power, forever expanding into all aspects of public life, leading to conflicts between the dictates of God and the dictates of the state. He quotes Ilya Shapiro on the matter:

> The cultural flashpoint surrounding wedding vendors' pleas for toleration is evidence of a more insidious process whereby the government foments social conflict as it expands its control into areas of life that we used to consider public yet not governmental. Indeed, it's government's relationship to public life that's changing - in the places that are beyond the intimacies of the home but still far removed from the state, like churches, charities, social clubs, small businesses, and even "public" corporations that are nevertheless part of the private sector. Under the influence of the Obama administration, the Left is weaving government through these private institutions, using them to shape American life according to its vision.[32]

The only other dissent came from Commissioner Gail Heriot, who voiced similar fears of big government. Heriot writes: "The bigger and more complex government becomes, the more conflicts between religious conscience and the duty to comply with the law we can expect... The bureaucratic juggernaut thus rolls on."[33] Reading a statement such as this, one wonders at the remarkable foresight contained in the Founder's desire for limited government and the prescience of their warnings about the dire consequences to liberty if the Leviathan to allowed to grow.

Positive and Negative Rights

When the Founders decided to sever their ties with the mother country, it was not because of petulant claims that the British government was not providing them with adequate resources to which they felt entitled. Rather, it charged that the British government was infringing on "certain unalienable rights endowed by their Creator." The Founders wrote of "Life, Liberty and the pursuit of Happiness." By this, they did not mean that the government should provide these things, but rather it should not interfere with individuals pursuing them legitimately. What they did expect from their government was that it should protect their God-given inalienable rights to do so. These natural rights have been rather dissonantly labeled "negative rights."

Herein lies the tension between liberal and conservative thought on rights. A negative right is a right not to be subjected to wants and demands of another person or group, which obliges government inaction. A positive right is a right to demand some action on the part of others to provide you with goods and services despite their objections, which obliges government action to secure them. The Constitution is a document of freedom; if one reads the Bill of Rights, it is full of injunctions against government abuses of negative rights. The only positive rights requiring government action involve such things that protect rights such as the right to counsel (and that came later as an entitlement) and a jury trial in criminal cases.

Gays and lesbians claim the right to be free from sexual discrimination; Christian small business owners claim the right to freedom of religion. The various Human Rights Commissions say these two rights conflict, and only one of them can be granted, and thus the other will necessarily be violated— the Christian's. The concept of rights contained in the Constitution includes the notion of inviolability and universality, something that cannot legitimately be infringed upon by the state. Thus, only claims that can genuinely construe as rights are those that are reciprocal and applicable to all. If everyone claims the same rights, everyone has the same obligation not to violate the rights of others. If I do not have the right to coerce you into involuntary servitude, the same obligation applies reciprocally to you. Constitutionally enumerated negative rights create no conflict between claimants because they are the inalienable right to be left free from coercion. If a person, or the state on behalf of that person, claims that he or she has a positive "right" to coerce another in violation of that person's Constitutional negative right to be left alone to live their life on Christian principles, that statutory positive "right" is both bogus and despotic. The exercise of power by high or petty organs of government must cohere with the Constitution. Whenever statutes they enact do not, they are in violation of the supreme law of the land, and therefore null, and should be treated as such.

Positive rights trump individual freedom by having *enforceable obligations* foisted on people as they are conscripted into involuntary servitude on behalf of others regardless their own beliefs, choices, and goals. Big Government does not discourage positive right dependency because it is the source of the things upon which people depend. If you depend on the state for everything you have, you owe everything to it and must abandon all pretenses of independence and responsibility.

Conclusion

I have provided evidence (it could have been increased a thousandfold) that Christianity is under concerted attack in America. Again, I do not see this as a conspiracy in the traditional sense of the term wherein there is a cabal of secret conspirators directing the attack from the epicenter. It is not a hub-and-spokes conspiracy in which one or more contemporary principal conspirators at the hub have entered into agreements with others at the spokes to take action to achieve their goal. Rather, it is more like a cancer—an unseen and largely undirected conspiracy of the dead Frankfurters—that has spread unknowingly over decades to invade almost every cell in American life. It has led to the tragic disintegration of American values of God, country, and family, and its name is cultural Marxism. To be sure, it is not the only reason for our cultural debasement, but it is an important one. It involves Gramsci's "long march through the institutions" by which new generations were to give their loyalty not to God, country, family, and individualism, but to the almighty State. Beginning slowly with the poisoned pens of cultural Marxist, it metastasized rapidly among the intellectual left.

Italian Renaissance philosopher and diplomat, Niccolo Machiavelli, uses a medical metaphor to make the point that the loss of that virtue begins with slow, imperceptible steps and that it is extremely difficult to stop the rot once it has reached a certain point. At the beginning of a physical disease, it is easy to cure if diagnosed, but the diagnosis is difficult. As the condition goes untreated, it becomes easy to diagnose, it becomes a lot more difficult to cure. Machiavelli says: "This happens in affairs of state, for when the evils that arise have been foreseen (which it is only given to a wise man to see), they can be quickly redressed, but when, through not having been foreseen, they have been permitted to grow in a way that everyone can see them, there is no longer a remedy." [34]

Richard Rorty, a deceased former radical relativist and a true believer in cultural Marxism, offers us an example of this rot. He had contempt for religion and family and desired to rip both apart. He arrogantly "knows" that he is right and feels that stripping children of their faith in God and their parents is a benevolent act: "I don't see anything *herrschaftsfrei* [domination free] about my handling of my fundamentalist students. Rather, I think those students are lucky to find themselves under the benevolent *Herrschaft* [domination] of people like me and to have escaped the grip of their frightening, vicious, dangerous parents.[34]

Little of the cultural Marxist agenda exemplified by Rorty's narcissistic ramblings would have seeped into the public landscape without the Supreme Court's help. As predicted by the dissenting Justices in *Obergefellt*, the legalization of same-sex marriage opened the floodgates to attacks on Christians who exercise their beliefs in the public square. Witness the Commission on Civil Rights calling religious dissenters hypocrites and otherwise demonizing them. The Commission clearly stated on many occasions in its 306-page document that the rights to coerce others to do your bidding laid out in antidiscrimination statutes take precedence over the Constitutional right of free exercise of religion. If the state forbids us the freedom to acknowledge the Creator in the public square according to our consciences, the "first freedom," every other right is vulnerable.

Not so long ago the very notion that religion would be unwelcome in the public square would have been dismissed as unthinkable, but presently it is a fact of life. It is not at all difficult to see a conscious strategy at work to neutralize the influence of religious morality on any moral public policy issue. The Supreme Court's assault began under the pretext of someone, or some group, whining that they were offended by some public sign of devotion to God and that this "right" not to be offended must be protected. Somehow, every snowflake's feelings must be affirmed if Christianity is the source of offense. After every election, from the presidential down to local elections, a significant proportion of the population is "offended" by the outcome. But most of us accept this as the nature of democracy and go about our business. The destructive ongoing shenanigans of many extreme left-wing Democrats after Donald Trump's election is a notable exception, which again serves to emphasize the left's inherent fascist tendencies. These creatures notwithstanding, the outcome of political elections is not appealed to the courts so that they can be overturned, yet if a handful of atheists or non-Christians say they are offended by Christian symbols revered by millions, they demand that the courts step in and order their removal. There is thus one rule in politics where the majority will prevail against a very large minority and another for religion where a numerically insignificant minority prevails against the overwhelming majority. To add insult to injury, the minority prevail by virtue of a reading of the Establishment Clause (and the trashing of the Free Exercise Clause) that its authors and ratifiers would find foreign, abhorrent, and tyrannical.

The left revels in the success of the assaults, but they should be reminded that ultimately we must choose between a society of humans governed by internal or external restraint; rule by conscience or rule by tyrants. We have been reminded multiple times by great minds that it is impossible to have a free and democratic society without the moral foundations of religion. The American Humanists Association's motto, "Good Without God," will only last as long as society has a cadre of men and women raised on Judeo-Christian values remaining on Earth. After they have gone to their Maker and we have citizens who have been raised in a society that has given God the boot, watch out! Robert Winthrop, one time speaker of the House of representative, put it cogently: "Men...must necessarily be controlled, either by a power within them, or by a power without them; either by the Word of God, or by the strong arm of man; either by the Bible, or by the bayonet."[35]

Ronald Reagan's 1984 speech at a Dallas ecumenical breakfast (well worth reading in its entirety) expressed similar sentiments. After decrying Supreme Court decisions banning school prayers and the reading of the Bible in public schools, he went on to say:

> Once religion had been made vulnerable, a series of assaults were made in one court after another, on one issue after another. Without God there is no virtue because there is no prompting of the conscience. Without God there is a coarsening of the society. Without God democracy will not and cannot long endure. If we ever forget that we are one nation under God, then we will be a nation gone forever.[36]

America moral and spiritual soul is well along the path to the point when "there is no longer any cure." America's cultural rot energizing our moral and spiritual decline was activated by the cancerous doctrine of cultural Marxism, first adopted by academic elites and entertainment moguls, and now entrenched in the mainstream. The disease accelerated with Supreme Court rulings that have led to so many Americans abandoning everything that underpinned the values that made us a great nation. If the hard left does not want the rule of tyrants, and I suspect it does not, it will have to seriously rethink its stance on our Christian heritage and join with the faithful in giving voice to our national motto: **In God we Trust**.

Endnotes

1. Flynn, *Why the left hates America.*
2. Churchill, Some people push back.
3. Schanzer, Review of United in Hate, p. 93.
4. Cited in Jaffe, Obama takes fire for Crusades comparison.
5. Durant and Durant. The Age of Faith, p. 290.
6. Lewis, B. Islam and the West, p. 12.
7. Cited in Prestigiacomo, Tenured professor.
8. Project Veritas. Officials at Cornell, Syracuse, and Yale.
9. Henderson, How I fought envy.
10. Schlenker, Chambers & Le, Conservatives are happier than liberals p. 1.
11. Taylor, Funk & Craighill. Are we happy yet?
12. Schlenker, Chambers & Le, Ibid, p.14.
13. Newport, Marriage remains key predictor of party identification.
14. Newport, Americans' church attendance inches up in 2010.
15. Newport, Republicans report much better mental health than others.
16. Ekehammar et al., The generality of personality heritability.
17. Gerber, et al., Personality and political attitudes.
18. Napier & Jost, Why are conservatives happier than liberals? p. 565.
19. Brook, *Who Really Cares.*
20. Ibid, p.32.
21. Chronical of Philanthropy. How states compare.
22. Kristof, Bleeding heart tightwads.
23. Winterich, Zanh and Mittal, How political identity and charity positioning, p. 5.
24. Schweizer, *Makers and Takers*, pp. 30-31.
25. Coser, *Men of ideas*, p. xiii.
26. Feuer, *Ideology and the ideologists*, p. 79.
27. Goldberg, *Liberal fascism*, p. 21.
28. Ibid, p. 21.
29. U.S. Civil Rights Commission. *Peaceful Coexistence*, p. 29.
30. Ibid, p. 35.
31. Ibid, p.108.
32. Ibid, pp. 107-108.
33. Ibid, p. 115.
34. Machiavelli, *The prince*, p. 21.
35. Rorty, Universality and truth, pp. 21-22.
36. *Winthrop, Addresses and Speeches*, p. 172.
37. Reagan, *Remarks at a Dallas Ecumenical Prayer Breakfast.*

References

ACLU (2013). Masterpiece Cakeshop. ACLU http://aclu-co.org/court-cases/masterpiece-cakeshop/

ACLU. (2016). Colorado Supreme Court refuses to hear case of bakery who turned away gay *couple*. https://www.aclu.org/news/colorado-supreme-court-refuses-hear-case-bakery-who-turned-away-gay-couple

Acs, G., Braswell, K., Sorensen, E., & Turner, M. (2013). The Moynihan report revisited. Washington, DC: *The Urban Institute*.

Adams, J. (1798). From John Adams to Massachusetts Militia, 11 October 1798. http://founders.archives.gov/documents/Adams/99-02-02-3102.

Adams, J. (1854). The Works of John Adams, Second President of the United States, Volume 9. Boston: Little, Brown.

Alliance Defending Freedom (2015). Wash. floral artist's home, savings at risk of state seizure after court ruling." http://www.alliancedefendingfreedom.org/News/Detail?ContentID=83837

American College of Pediatricians (nd). What you should know about sexual orientation of youth. http://factsaboutyouth.com/wp-content/uploads/Facts-on-full-sheet-Apr-1.pdf

American Thinker (2008). Obama 2001: Scrap the Constitution, spread the wealth. *American Thinker*, October, 27th http://www.americanthinker.com/blog/2008/10/obama_2001_scrap_the_constitut.html.

Anderson, R. (2014). Marriage, reason, and religious liberty: Much ado about sex, nothing to do with race." *Backgrounder*, 2894, April.

Anderson, R. & Ford, L. (2014). Protecting religious liberty in the state marriage debate. *Backgrounder*, No. 2891, April.

Antieau, C. J., Downey, A. T., & Roberts, E. C. (1964). *Freedom from Federal Establishment: Formation and Early History of the First Amendment Religion Clauses* (No. 1). Milwaukee, WI: Bruce Publishing Company.

Aquilino, W. (1999). Two views of one relationship: Comparing parents' and young adult children's reports of the quality of intergenerational relations. *Journal of Marriage and the Family*, 61:858-870.

American Sexual Health Association (2015). Statistics. http://www.ashasexualhealth.org/ stdsstis/statistics/

Americans United for Separation of Church State (nd). Is America a Christian nation? https://www.au.org/files/christian-nation-pdf.pdf

Association of American Physicians & Surgeons (2015). Amicus Curiae Brief in Little Sisters of the Poor v. Burwell. http://www.scotusblog.com/wp-content/uploads/2015/08/15-105-Little-Sisters-v.-Burwell-amicus-brief-of-AAPS-et-al.pdf

Backman, J. (2015). Arlene's Flowers response to Attorney General's settlement offer. Family Policy Institute. February 20.

http://www.fpiw.org/blog/2015/02/20/barronelle-stutzmans-repsonse-attorney-general/

Barnes, R., P. Calow, P. & P. Olive (2001). The Invertebrates: A New Synthesis (3rd ed.), Blackwell Science Publications.

Bahr, H. & Chadwick, B. (1985). Religion and family in Middletown, USA. *Journal of Marriage and the Family*, 47:407-414.

Ball, H. *Hugo L. Black: Cold steel warrior.* New York: Oxford University Press.

Barton, D. (1992). The origin of the phrase 'Separation of Church and State.' The myth of separation. Aledo, TX: Wallbuilders Press.

Barton, D. (2008). The Founding Fathers on Jesus, Christianity and the Bible. http://allianceforreligiousfreedom.com/educate-yourself/one-nation-under-god/the-founding-fathers-on-jesus-christianity-and-the-bible/ Barton, D. (2016). America's most Biblically-hostile U.S. President. Wallbuilders. http://www.wallbuilders.com/libissuesarticles.asp?id=106938

Bastiat, F. (2006/1850). *The Law.* Minneapolis. MN: Filiquarian.

Bay Area News. (2014). Supreme Court strikes down ObamaCare abortion mandate, June 30th. http://www.yourhoustonnews.com/bay_area/news/supreme-court-strikes-down-obamacare-abortion-mandate/article_bde716e9-2747-51c1-ab5f-63aef1e13353.html

Beard, C. (1912). The Supreme Court--Usurper or Grantee? *Political Science Quarterly, 27:*1-35.

Beckingham, C. (1937). Parallel passages in Bacon and Fuller. *The Review of English Studies,* 52: 449-453.

Bell, A. (2001). God Save This Honorable Court: How current Establishment Clause jurisprudence can be reconciled with the secularization of historical religious expression. *American University Law Review, 50:* 1273-1314.

Benkof, D. (2008). Why California gays shouldn't celebrate state court ruling. *Seattle Post-Intelligence.r* http://www.seattlepi.com/local/opinion/article/Why-California-gays-shouldn-t-celebrate-state-1273942.php

Bennett, W. (1992). The de-valuing of America: The fight for our culture and our children. New York: Touchstone.

Bennetts, M. (2014). Who's 'godless' now? Russia says it's U.S. Washington Times, January 28. http://www.washingtontimes.com/news/2014/jan/28/whos-godless-now-russia-says-its-us/?page=all

Bernstein, D. (2003). Defending the First Amendment from antidiscrimination laws. *North Carolina Law Review,* 82: 1-32.

Berg, T. (2010). What same-sex marriage and religious-liberty claims have in common. *Northwestern Journal of Law and Social Policy, 5:* 206-235.

Black, J. (1994). When Nations Die: Ten Warning Signs of a Culture in Crisis. Wheaton, IL: Tyndale House.

Boller, P. F. (1960). George Washington and Religious Liberty. *The William and Mary Quarterly, 17*(4), 486-506.

Botham, F. (2009). *Almighty God created the races: Christianity, interracial marriage, and American law.* Chapel Hill, NC: University of North Carolina Press.

Brennan, P. (2015).Hillary's infamous women in the world talk isn't quite as awful as you've heard (Though it's still awful). National Review, April 24th. http://www.nationalreview.com/corner/417460/hillarys-infamous-women-world-talk-isnt-quite-awful-youve-heard-though-its-still-awful.

Brook, A. (2006). *Who Really Cares: The surprising truth about compassionate conservatism.* New York: Basic Books.

Brown, B. (2007). Pornography and feminism: Is law the answer? *Critical Quarterly*, 34:72-82.

Burk, R. (2014). Cardinal Burke on faith, the right to life, and the family: English exclusive. Lifesite. https://www.lifesitenews.com/news/english-exclusive-cardinal-burke-on-faith-the-right-to-life-and-the-family

Butler, P. & Scanlan, A. (1961). Wall of Separation--Judicial gloss on the First Amendment. *Notre Dame Law Review, 37:* 288-308.

Calabresi, S. G., & Lindgren, J. (2005). Term limits for the Supreme Court: Life tenure reconsidered. *Harvard Journal of Law & Public Policy, 29,* 769-876.

Call, V. & Heaton, T. (1997). Religious influence on marital stability. *Journal for the Scientific Study of Religion,* 36:382-392.

Cameron, P., Playfair, W.., & Wellum, S. (1994). The longevity of homosexuals: Before and after the AIDS epidemic. *OMEGA-Journal of Death and Dying, 29*(3), 249-272.

Catholic Answers (nd). Abortion. http://www.catholic.com/tracts/abortion

Catechism of the Catholic Church (nd). Matrimony. http://www.vatican.va/archive/ccc_css/archive/catechism/p2s2c3a7.htm

Center for Disease and Prevention (2010). HIV Cost-effectiveness. http://www.cdc.gov/hiv/programresources/guidance/costeffectiveness/index.html

Central Intelligence Agency (2008) The World Factbook: United States; People; Religions.: https://www.cia.gov/library/publications/the-world-factbook/geos/us.html).

Chesterton, G. (2001). The Collected Works of G.K. Chesterton, Vol. 20. San Francisco: Ignatius Press.

Christenson, G. (2012). Liberty of the exercise of religion in the Peace of Westphalia. *Transnational Law & Contemporary Problems, 21:* 721-761.

Chronical of Philanthropy (2014). How states compare and how they voted in the 2012 election. https://philanthropy.com/article/How-States-CompareHow/152501

Churchill, W. S. (2012). What good's a Constitution? In Hillsdale College Political Science Department (Ed.), *The U.S. Constitution: A reader,* pp. 737-743. Hillsdale, MI: Hillsdale College Press.

Churchill, W. L. (2005) "Some people push back": On the justice of roosting chickens. *Democracy Now,* February 18. http://www.kersplebedeb.com/mystuff/s11/churchill.html

Clinton, W. (1997). *Public Papers of the Presidents of the United States: William J. Clinton, 1995.* Washington, DC: United States Government Printing Office.

Congressional Record (2000). Congressional Record, vol. 146. Washington, DC: United States Printing Office.

Congressional Record (2001). Congressional Record, vol. 147. https://www.congress.gov/congressional-record/2001/12/10/daily-digest

Conservative Tribune (2016). State officials demand pastor's sermons in massive breach of his rights. Conservative Tribune, October 27. http://conservativetribune.com/state-demand-pastor-give-in/

Coolidge, C. (1926). Speech on the 150th Anniversary of the Declaration of Independence. http://teachingamericanhistory.org/library/document/speech-on-the-occasion-of-the-one-hundred-and-fiftieth-anniversary-of-the-declaration-of-independence/

Cooper, J. (2014). Modern day segregation: States fighting to legally allow businesses to refuse service to same-sex couples under the shield of the First Amendment. *Rutgers Journal of Law and Religion, 15*: 413-432.

Corbin, A., & Walsh, A. (1988). The U.S. Supreme Court and value legitimacy: An experimental approach with older Americans. *Sociological Inquiry, 58,* 75–86.

Coser, L. (1965). *Men of ideas: A sociologist's view.* New York: Free Press.

Crossland, K. (2013). Baker must cater to same-sex weddings, or else. *The World.* http://www.worldmag.com/2013/12/baker_must_cater_to_same_sex_weddings_or_else

Davies, P. (2007). Taking science on faith. *New York Times*, November 24th. http://www.nytimes.com/2007/11/24/opinion/24davies.html?pagewanted=all

Day, R. D., & Acock, A. (2013). Marital well-being and religiousness as mediated by relational virtue and equality. *Journal of Marriage and Family, 75:* 164-177.

Dean, J., Folsom, G., Shea, J., Stiles, H. & Dawson, B. (1861). *The Historical Magazine: And notes and queries concerning the antiquities, history, and biography of America* (Vol. 5). New York: Charles Richardson & Co.

Dedert, E., Studts, J., Weissbecker, I., Salmon, P., Banis, P., & Sephton, S. (2004). Religiosity may help preserve the cortisol rhythm in women with stress-related illness. *The International Journal of Psychiatry in Medicine, 34*(1), 61-77.

Degeneffe, C. (2003). What is Catholic about Catholic charities? *Social Work, 48*: 374-383.

DeMar, G. (1995). *America's Christian History: The Untold Story.* Atlanta, GA: American Vision.

De Tocqueville, A. (1994). *Democracy in America*, Bradley, P. (ed.). New York: Alfred A. Knopf.

De Toledano, R. (2002). What the ACLU doesn't want you to know. Insight on the News, 18.

Dewart, D. (2012). On Writ of Certiorari to the United States Court of Appeals for the Ninth and Second Circuits: Brief of Liberty, Life and Law Foundation, and North Carolina Values Coalition as amici curiae in support of Hollingsworth and bipartisan legal advisory group addressing the merits and supporting reversal. American Bar Association. https://www.glad.org/uploads/docs/cases/windsor-v-united-states/amicus-brief-of-liberty-life-and-law-foundation.pdf.

Dilley, S. (2012). Charles Darwin's use of theology in the Origin of Species. *The British Journal for the History of Science, 45:* 29-56.

Dobzhansky, T. (1973). Nothing in biology makes sense except in light of evolution. *The American Biology Teacher,* 35:125-129.

Dolan, T. (2012). Wall Street Journal op ed on religious freedom. http://www.usccb.org/about/media-relations/resources/wall-street-journal-op-ed-on-religious-freedom.cfm

Dollahite, D. & Thatcher, J. (2005). How family religious involvement benefits adults, youth, and children and strengthens families. Salt Lake City: *The Sutherland Institute.*

Donohue, W. (1985). *The politics of the American Civil Liberties Union.* New Brunswick, NJ: Transaction.

Dreisbach, D. & Hall, M. (2009). *The Sacred Rights of Conscience: Selected Readings on Religious Liberty and Church–State Relations in the American Founding.* Indianapolis: Liberty Fund Press,

Dreher, R. (2015). Traditional Christians under siege. *Time,* April 13, 185: 13.

Duigon, L. (2012). The push is on! Canadian, U.S. public schools continue to promote homosexuality. *Chalcedon.* http://chalcedon.edu/research/articles/the-push-is-on-canadian-u-s-public-schools-continue-to-promote-homosexuality/

Durant, W. (1935). *Our Oriental Heritage.* New York: Simon & Schuster.

Durant, W. (1952). *The story of philosophy.* New York: Simon and Schuster.

Durant, W. & Durant, A. (1965). *The Age of Voltaire.* New York: Simon and Schuster.

Durant, W. & Durrant, A. (1968) *The Lessons of History,* New York: Simon and Schuster.

Dworkin, R. (2005). *Freedom's Law: The Moral Reading of the American Constitution.* Oxford: Oxford University Press.

Easton, J. (205). Survey on physicians' religious beliefs shows majority faithful Medical Center Public Affairs, University of Chicago Chronicle. July 14. http://chronicle.uchicago.edu/050714/doctorsfaith--.shtml

Ecklund, E. & Park, J. (2009). Conflict between religion and science among academic scientists? *Journal for the Scientific Study of Religion, 48:* 276-292.

Edmunds, D. (2014). Britain is sleepwalking into losing religious freedoms. *Breitbart,* November 26th. http://www.breitbart.com/london/2014/11/26/britain-is-sleepwalking-into-losing-religious-freedoms-says-christian-leader/

Edwards, C. (1971). *Hammurabi, King of Babylonia.* Port Washington, New York: Kennikat Press.

Einstein, A. (2010). *The ultimate quotable Einstein.* A. Calaprice (ed.), Princeton, NJ: Princeton University Press.

Ekehammar, B., Akrami, N., Hedlund, L., Yoshimura, K., Ono, Y., Ando, J., & Yamagata, S. (2010). The generality of personality heritability: Big-Five trait heritability predicts response time to trait items. *Journal of individual differences, 31*:209-214.

Ellis, M., Vinson, D., & Ewigman, B. (1999). Addressing spiritual concerns of patients. *Journal of Family Practice, 48:* 105-106.

Epstein, S. (1996). Rethinking the constitutionality of ceremonial deism. *Columbia Law Review, 96:*2083-2174.

Easton, J. (2005). Survey on physicians' religious beliefs shows majority faithful. Medical Center Public Affairs, University of Chicago Chronicle. July 14.

Executive Office of the President (2013). Statement of Administration Policy. https://www.whitehouse.gov/sites/default/files/omb/legislative/sap/113/saphr1960r_20130611.pdf

Federer, W. (1994). *America's God and Country: Encyclopedia of Quotations.* St. Louis, MO: Amerisearch, Inc..

Feuer, L. (1975). *Ideology and the ideologists.* New York: Harper & Row.

First Liberty (2015). Federal court declares historic World War I Veterans Memorial Constitutional, American Humanist Association Appeals. http://firstliberty.org/cases/bladensburg/

First Liberty (2016). State of Georgia fired doctor and lay pastor for content of Sermons; First Liberty files lawsuit. https://firstliberty.org/newsroom/state-of-georgia-fired-doctor-and-lay-pastor-for-content-of-sermons-first-liberty-files-lawsuit/

First Liberty (2017). Supreme court justice says hostile wind is blowing against religious freedom, April, 14th. http://firstliberty.org/newsroom/supreme-court-justice-says-hostile-wind-is-blowing-against-religious-freedom/

Flynn, D. (2002). Why the left hates America. *Frontpagemag,* October 18. http://archive.frontpagemag.com/readArticle.aspx?ARTID=21706.
Flynn, T. (2010). Clarion call or false alarm: Why proposed exemptions to equal marriage statutes return us to a religious understanding of the public marketplace." *Northwestern Journal of Law and Social Policy, 5:* 236-259.

Ford, P. (1892). *The Writings of Thomas Jefferson,* vol. IX. New York: Putnam.

Fox News (2011). Houston veterans claim censorship of prayers, including ban on 'God' and 'Jesus.' http://www.foxnews.com/us/2011/06/29/houston-veterans-claim-censorship-prayers-ban-on-god-and-jesus.html.

Fragile Families Research Brief (2005). Religion and marriage in urban America. Bendheim-Thoman Center for Research on Child Wellbeing, Princeton University Social Indicators Survey Center, Columbia University.

Friedersdorf, C. (2015). Should mom-and-pops that forgo gay weddings be destroyed? http://www.theatlantic.com/politics/archive/2015/04/should-businesses-that-quietly-oppose-gay-marriage-be-destroyed/389489/

Free Legal Dictionary (nd). http://legal-dictionary.thefreedictionary.com/Involuntary+Servitude. Legal Information Institute of Cornell University (nd). https://www.law.cornell.edu/uscode/text/22/7102

Freedom House (2015). *Freedom in the World Index.* https://freedomhouse.org/report/freedom-world/freedom-world-2014.

French, D. (2015). Churches won't perform same-sex weddings: Insurance begins to look iffy. National Review, July 8th. http://www.nationalreview.com/article/420928/churches-wont-perform-same-sex-weddings-insurance-begins-look-iffy-david-french

Frisch, M., & Brønnum-Hansen, H. (2009). Mortality among men and women in same-sex marriage: a national cohort study of 8333 Danes. *American Journal of Public Health,* 99: 133-137.

Garrow, D. (1998). *Liberty and sexuality: The right to privacy and the making of* Roe v. Wade. Berkeley: University Of California Press.

Gate, G. & Newport, F. (2012). Special Report: 3.4% of U.S. Adults Identify as LGBT. http://www.gallup.com/poll/158066/special-report-adults-identify-lgbt.aspx

George, F. (2012). What are you going to give up this Lent? *Catholic New World,* February 26. http://www.catholicnewworld.com/cnwonline/2012/0226/cardinal.aspx.

George, R. (2005) Judicial Usurpation and the Constitution: Historical and Contemporary Issues.

Gerber, A., Huber, G., Doherty, D., Dowling, C., & Ha, S. (2010). Personality and political attitudes: Relationships across issue domains and political contexts. *American Political Science Review, 104*:111-133.

Gilman, S., Cochran, S., Mays, V., Hughes, M., Ostrow, D., & Kessler, R. (2001). Risk of psychiatric disorders among individuals reporting same-sex sexual partners in the National Comorbidity Survey. *American journal of public health, 91*:933-939.

Glied, S. (2012). The cost of covering contraceptives through health insurance. U.S. Department of Health & Human Services. https://aspe.hhs.gov/basic-report/cost-covering-contraceptives-through-health-insurance.

Gold, S. (2009). *Loving v. Virginia: Lifting the ban against interracial marriage.* New York: Cavendish Square.

Goldberg, J. (2007). *Liberal fascism: The secret history of the American left, from Mussolini to the politics of meaning.* New York: Doubleday.

Goodrich, L. (2011). The health care and conscience debate. *Engage,* 12:121-127.

Gross, N., & Simmons, S. (2009). The religiosity of American college and university professors. *Sociology of Religion,* 70:101-129.

Guiso, L., Sapienza, P., & Zingales, L. (2003). People's opium? Religion and economic attitudes. *Journal of monetary economics, 50*: 225-282.

Grant, J. (2010). The rise of the juristocracy. *The Wilson Quarterly,* Spring: 16-22.

Hall. D. (2006). Religious attendance: More cost effective than lipitor? *Journal of the American Board of Family Practice,* 19:431-433.

Hall, M. (2011). Did America Have a Christian Founding? Lecture #1189 on Political Thought. http://www.heritage.org/research/lecture/2011/06/did-america-have-a-christian-founding

Hallowell, B. (2015). Lawyer for Christian bakers who were forced to pay nearly $137,000 to lesbian couple reveals most shocking element of the case. *The Blaze*, December 31st. http://www.theblaze.com/stories/2015/12/31/lawyer-for-christian-bakers-who-were-forced-to-pay-nearly-137000-to-lesbian-couple-reveals-most-shocking-element-of-the-case/

Hamburger, P. (2014). "The history and danger of administrative law," *A Publication of Hilldale College, (speech transcript) Impris*, Vol. 23, September.

Hamilton, A. (1788). *The Judiciary Department. Federalist Papers No 78.* http://www.constitution.org/fed/federa78.htm.

Hamilton, A. (2012). The farmer refuted. In *The U.S. Constitution: A Reader*, pp. 95-98.

Hillsdale, MI: Hillsdale College Press.

Hammer, S. (2013). Feds establishing religion? DOJ defunds "Young Marines" that reference God. Freedom Outpost. http://freedomoutpost.com/feds-establishing-religion-doj-defunds-young-marines-that-reference-god/

Hannam, J. (2009) *God's Philosophers: How the Medieval World Laid the Foundations of Modern Science*. London: Icon Books.

Harris Interactive, Inc. and Gay, Lesbian & Straight Education Network (2005). From teasing to torment: School climate in America. *New York: Gay, lesbian, and straight education network*.

Harrison, P. (2012). Christianity and the rise of western science. *ABC Religion and Ethics*. http://www.abc.net.au/religion/articles/2012/05/08/3498202.htm

Hatch, V. & Walsh, A. (2016). *Capital punishment: The theory and practice of the ultimate penalty.* New York: Oxford University Press.

Hazard, J., Butler, W. & Maggs, P. (1977). *The Soviet legal system.* Dobbs Ferry, NY: Oceana.

Hazelton, J. (1970). The Declaration of Independence: Its history. New York: Da Capo Press.

Heise, M., & Sisk, G. (2012). Religion, schools, and judicial decision making: an empirical perspective. *The University of Chicago Law Review*, 79:185-212.

Henderson, D. (2011). How I fought envy. *Library of Economics and Liberty*, August 16. http://econlog.econlib.org/archives/2011/08/how_i_fought_en.html

Heritage Foundation. http://www.heritage.org/research/lecture/judicial-usurpation-and-the-constitution-historical-and-contemporary-issues.

Heyer, W. (2011). Public school LGBT programs don't just trample parental rights. They also put kids at risk. The Witherspoon Institute. http://www.thepublicdiscourse.com/2015/06/15118/

Hodges, M. (2015). States could Force Catholic priests to perform same-sex 'marriages' or lose Legal Status: Justice Scalia. *Lifesite News*. https://www.lifesitenews.com/news/states-could-force-catholic-priests-to-perform-same-sex-marriages-or-lose-l

Hogg, R., Strathdee, S., Craib, K., O'Shaughnessy, M, Montaner, J., & Schechter, M. (1997). Modelling the impact of HIV disease on mortality in gay and bisexual men. *International Journal of Epidemiology*, 26:657-661.

Holt, J. (1997). Science resurrects God. *Wall Street Journal,* December 24. http://www.wsj.com/articles/SB882911317496560000.

Hosking, G. (1985). The First Socialist Society: A History of the Soviet Union From Within. Cambridge: Harvard University Press.

Hummer, R., Rogers, R. Nam, C. & Ellison, C. (1999). Religious Involvement and U.S. Adult Mortality. *Demography* 36:273–285.

Hunnicutt, G. & L. Broidy (2004). Liberation and economic marginalization: A reformulation and test of (formerly?) competing models. *Journal of Research in Crime and Delinquency,* 41:130-155

Hurley, L. (2015) Americans favor Supreme Court term limits - Reuters/Ipsos poll http://www.reuters.com/article/us-usa-court-poll-idUSKCN0PU09820150720

Hazard, J., Butler, W., & Maggs, P. (1977). *The Soviet legal system.* Dobbs Ferry, NY: Oceana.

International Christian Concern (2017). *2016 hall of shame.* Washington, DC: ICC.

Isaacson, W. (2007). Einstein: His life and universe. New York: Simon and Schuster.

Jaffe, A. (2015). Obama takes fire for Crusades comparison. CNN Politics. February 6. http://www.cnn.com/2015/02/06/politics/obama-isis-crusades-comparison/

Jal. M. (2010), Interpretation as phantasmagria: Variations on a theme on Marx's Theses on Feuerbach. *Critique,* 38: 117-142.

Jay, J. (1822). John Jay, *The Correspondence and Public Papers of John Jay, vol. 4 (1794-1826)* Address to the American Bible Society May 9. http://oll.libertyfund.org/titles/jay-the-correspondence-and-public-papers-of-john-jay-vol-4-1794-1826

Jefferson, T. (1804). From Thomas Jefferson to Ursuline Nuns of New Orleans, 13 July 1804. Founders Early Access. http://rotunda.upress.virginia.edu/founders/default.xqy?keys=FOEA-print-04-01-02-0068

Jefferson, T. (1784). Notes on the State of Virginia, Amendment I: Religion. http://press-pubs.uchicago.edu/founders/documents/amendI_religions40.html.

Jefferson, T. (1809). From Thomas Jefferson to Richard Douglas, 4 February 1809. Founders Online. http://founders.archives.gov/documents/Jefferson/99-01-02-9714

Jefferson, T. (1818). Report of the Commissioners for the University of Virginia, August 4, 1818, *The University of Virginia.* http://etext.virginia.edu/etcbin/toccer-new2?id=JefRock.sgm&images=images/modeng&data=/texts/english/modeng/parsed&tag=public&part=1&division=div1.

Jefferson, T. (1820). Thomas Jefferson on judicial tyranny. The 10th Amendment Center. http://tenthamendmentcenter.com/2012/06/04/thomas-jefferson-on-judicial-tyranny/

Jefferson, T. (1904). *The Writings of Thomas Jefferson,* vol. X1X. A. Lipscomb (ed.). Washington DC: The Thomas Jefferson Memorial Association.

Jefferson, T (1998). Jefferson's letter to the Danbury Baptists. The Library of Congress. https://www.loc.gov/loc/lcib/9806/danpre.html

Jeffries, J., & Ryan, J. (2001). A political history of the Establishment Clause. *Michigan Law Review, 100:* 279-370.

Johnson, H. (2006). The rule of law in the realm and the province of New York: Prelude to the American Revolution. *History* 91:3–26.

Judicial Watch (2011). President Obama's Czars. Judicial Watch Special Report. Washington, DC: Judicial Watch, Inc.

Kainz, H. P. (2010). *The Existence of God and the Faith-instinct.* Selinsgove, PA: Susquehanna University Press.

Kaminski, J. (2002). Religion and the Founding Fathers. *Annotation: the Newsletter of the National Historic Publications and Records Commission,* 30:1-20.

Kaye, J. (1998). Commentaries on Chancellor Kent. *Chicago.-Kent Law Review, 74:* 11-29.

Kennedy, D. (1907). St. Albertus Magnus. In *The Catholic Encyclopedia.* New York: Robert Appleton Company. Retrieved January 4, 2009 from New Advent: http://www.newadvent.org/cathen/01264a.htm. p. 265.

Keirsey, D. (1998). Please Understand Me II: Temperament Character Intelligence by David

Keirsey. Del Mar, CA: Prometheus Nemesis.

Kenyon, D. (2002). *Unlocking the mystery of life:* Script draft of video. http://www.divinerevelations.info/documents/intelligent_design/unlockingthemysteryoflifescript.pdf.

King, V., Ledwell, M., & Pearce-Morris, J. (2013). Religion and ties between adult children and their parents. *The Journals of Gerontology Series B: Psychological Sciences and Social Sciences,* 68: 825–836.

Klukowski, *K. (2013) Symposium: Time to restore longstanding meaning – and sanity – to the Establishment Clause in Town of Greece v. Galloway,* SCOTUSblog, Oct. 3, 2013. http://www.scotusblog.com/2013/10/symposium-time-to-restore-longstanding-meaning-and-sanity-to-the-establishment-clause-in-town-of-greece-v-galloway/

Koenig, H., Cohen, H., George, L., Hays, J., Larson, D., & Blazer, D. (1997). Attendance at religious services, interleukin-6, and other biological parameters of immune function in older adults. *The International Journal of Psychiatry in Medicine, 27:* 233-250.

Kolakowski, L. (1981). *Main currents of Marxism: Volume III, the breakdown.* Oxford: Oxford University Press.

Koppelman, A. (2015). Theorists, get over yourselves: A response to Steven D. Smith. *Pepperdine Law Review,* 41: 937-942.

Krauthammer, C. (1993). Defining deviancy up. *The New Republic, 22:* 20-25.

Kristof, N. (2008). Bleeding heart tightwads. *New York Times,* December 20th. http://www.nytimes.com/2008/12/21/opinion/21kristof.html.

Kruk, E. (2012). Arguments for an equal parental responsibility presumption in contested child custody. *The American Journal of Family Therapy,* 40:33-55.

Kuhn, D. (2012). The Incredible Polarization and Politicization of the Supreme Court. *The Atlantic, June 29.* http://www.theatlantic.com/politics/archive/2012/06/the-incredible-polarization-and-politicization-of-the-supreme-court/259155/.

Kuntzman, G. (2016). Major League Baseball must permanently retire 'God Bless America,' a song that offends everyone. New York Daily News. June 30. http://www.nydailynews.com/sports/baseball/major-league-baseball-permanently-retire-god-bless-america-article-1.2693228

Lambert, F. (2005). *The Barbary wars: American independence in the Atlantic world.* London: Macmillan.

Larson, D., Larson, S. & Gartner, J. (1990)., in D. Wedding, (ed.), *Behavior and Medicine,* pp. 135-147. St. Louis: MO: Mosby.

Laycock, D. (1990). The Supreme Court's assault on Free Exercise, and the amicus brief that was never filed. *Journal of Law and Religion, 8*(1-2), 99-114.

Laycock, D. (2014). Religious liberty and the culture wars. *University of Illinois Law Review, 14:839-880*

Laycock, D. (2016). Religious Liberty for Politically Active Minority Groups: A Response to NeJaime and Siegel. *Yale Law Journal Forum, 125:369-416.*

Leiter, B. (2014). *Why tolerate religion?* Princeton, NJ: Princeton University Press.

Legal Information Institute of Cornell University (nd). https://www.law.cornell.edu/uscode/text

Lenz, R. (2012) American College of Pediatricians defames gays and lesbians in the name of protecting children. Southern Poverty Law Center.https://www.splcenter.org/fighting-hate/intelligence-report/2012/american-college-pediatricians-defames-gays-and-lesbians-name-protecting-children.

Levin, J. (2010). Religion and mental health: Theory and research. *International Journal of Applied Psychoanalytic Studies, 7:* 102-115.

Lichtblau, E. (2009). Questions raised anew about religion in military. *The New York Times,* March. 1, p. 14;

Levin, Y. (2016). The Perils of Religious Liberty. *First Things,* 260:29-36.

Lim, C., & Putnam, R. (2010). Religion, social networks, and life satisfaction. *American Sociological Review, 75:* 914-933.

Lincoln, A. (1861). Lincoln's first inaugural address. Historical Documents. http://www.ushistory.org/documents/lincoln1.htm.

Lindevaldsen, R. (2010). Fallacy of neutrality from beginning to end: The battle between religious liberties and rights based on homosexual conduct. *Liberty University Law Review, 4:* 425-463.

Liptak, A. (2013). Weighing free speech in refusal to photograph lesbian couple's ceremony. *New York Times,* Nov. 18. http://www.nytimes.com/2013/11/19/us/weighing-free-speech-in-refusal-to-photograph-ceremony.html

Lipson, J. (2001). *Hostile hallways: Bullying, teasing, and sexual harassment in school.* AAUW Educational Foundation, 1111 Sixteenth Street, NW, Washington, DC 20036.

Lively, S. (2009). Redeeming the Rainbow. Springfield MA: Veritas Aeterna Press

Locay, A. (2008). *Unveiling the Left.* Xulon Press.

Loewy, A. (2003). The positive reality and normative virtues of a 'neutral' Establishment Clause. *Brandeis Law Journal,* 41:533-543.

Machiavelli, N., & Viroli, M. (2008). *The prince* (Vol. 43). Oxford University Press.

Madison, J. (1785) Memorial and Remonstrance against Religious Assessments. http://press-pubs.uchicago.edu/founders/documents/amendI _religions43.html.

Madison, J. (1792). Property. National Gazette, March 29. http://www.constitution.org/jm/17920329_property.txt.

Madison, J. (1904). *Writings of James Madison, G. Hunt ed. Philadelphia: Putnam and Sons.*

Madison, J. (nd). The Founder's Constitution: Virginia Ratifying Convention http://press-pubs.uchicago.edu/founders/documents/amendI_religions 49.html.

Malachi, M. (2008). *Keys of This Blood: Pope John Paul II Versus Russia and the West for Control of the New World Order.* New York: Simon and Schuster.

Marcuse, H. (1966). *Eros and Civilization: Philosophical inquiry into Freud.* Boston: Beacon.

Marcuse, H. (1969). *An essay on liberation.* Boston: Beacon Press.

Marcuse, H. (2002). *One dimensional man.* New York: Routledge.

Maringoff, L. & Carvallo, B. (2017). *Religious liberty and the Supreme Court, 2017.* Poughkeepsie, NY: Marist College Institute for Public Opinion.

Marsh, J. (2012). *The Liberal Delusion: The Roots of Our Current Moral Crisis.* Bury St. Edmunds, England: Arena books.

Mathisen, R. (2014). *The Routledge Sourcebook of Religion and the American Civil War: A History in Documents.* New York: Routledge.

Matthew, H. (1997). *Gladstone 1809-1898.* Oxford: Oxford University Press.

Masci, D. (2009). Scientists and belief. Pew Research Center. http://www.pewforum.org/2009/11/05/scientists-and-belief/

McGonnigal, J. (2011). Catholic Charities abandons thousands of children instead of adopting to LGBT parents. Gay voices, Huffington Post. http://www.huffingtonpost.com/jamie-mcgonnigal/catholic-charities-adoption_b_1095396.html

McConnell, M. (1985). Accommodation of religion. *The Supreme Court Review,* 1985:1-59.

McDowell, J. & Hostetler, B. (1998). *The new tolerance: How a cultural movement threatens to destroy you, your faith, and your children.* Carol Stream, IL: Tyndale House Publishers.

Mercer, C., Fenton, K., Copas, A., Wellings, K., Erens, B., McManus, S., & Johnson, A. (2004). Increasing prevalence of male homosexual partnerships and practices in Britain 1990–2000: evidence from national probability surveys. *Aids, 18,* 1453-1458.

Miller, M (2010) *The Book and The Right: The Roots of America's Greatness.* Maitland, Fl: Xulon Press.

Miniter, F. (2011). *Saving the Bill of Rights: Exposing the left's campaign to destroy American exceptionalism.* New York: Regnery Publishing.

Minnicino, M. (1992). The Frankfurt School and 'Political Correctness.' *Fidelio,* I: 4-27.

Moyer, J. (2015). Indiana Pizza Shop won't cater gay wedding, Gets over $50K from supporters." *Washington Post,* April 2nd. http://www.washingtonpost.com/news/morning-mix/wp/2015/04/02/indianas-memories-pizza-wouldnt-cater-gay-wedding-gets-40k-in-crowdfunding/

Moynihan, D. P. (1993). Defining deviancy down. *The American Scholar, 62:* 17-30.

Mua, K. (2016). Religion as a Tool for Economic/Political Transformation. *Political Transformation, Working Paper, 1-22.*
Mueller, P., Plevak, D, & Rummans, T. (2001). Religious involvement, spirituality, and medicine: implications for clinical practice. *Mayo clinic proceedings,* 76: 1225-1235.

Muñoz, V. (2008). The original meaning of the Free Exercise Clause: The evidence from the First Congress. *Harvard Journal of Law and Public Policy, 31:* 1083-1120.

Meyer, S. (2003). DNA and the origin of life: Information, specification, and explanation. In J. Campbell & S. Meyer (eds.), *Darwinism, design, and public education,* pp. 223-284. Lansing, MI: Michigan State University Press.

Napier, J. & J. Jost (2008). Why are conservatives happier than liberals? *Psychological Science,* 19:565-572.

Natelson, R. (2005). Original meaning of the Establishment Clause. *The William & Mary Bill Rights Journal,* 14:73-140.

New York Times obituary (1955). Dr. Albert Einstein Dies in Sleep at 76; World Mourns Loss of Great Scientist. April 19. http://www.nytimes.com/learning/general/onthisday/bday/0314.html

Newport, F. (2007). Republicans report much better mental health than others, Gallup Poll. http://www.gallup.com/poll/102943/Republicans-Report-Much-Better-Mental-Health-Than-Others.aspx

Newport, F. (2009). Marriage remains key predictor of party identification. Pew Report, http://www.gallup.com/poll/121571/marriage-remains-key-predictor-party-identification.aspx.

Newport, F. (2010). Americans' church attendance inches up in 2010. Pew Report, http://www.gallup.com/poll/141044/americans-church-attendance-inches-2010.aspx

Ngun, T. & Vilain, E. (2014). The biological basis of human sexual orientation: Is there a role for epigenetics. *Advance in Genetics,* 86:167-184.

Noll, M. (1988). *One Nation Under God?: Christian Faith and Political Action in America.* New York: HarperCollins.

Nowlan, R. (2012). *The American Presidents, Washington to Tyler: What they did, what they Said, what was said about them, with full source notes.* Jefferson, NC: McFarland.

Obama, B. (2004). *Dreams from My Father: A Story of Race and Inheritance.* New York: Three Rivers Press.

Olsen, B. (2013). *Future Esoteric: The Unseen Realms.* San Francisco: CCC Publishing.

Olson, C. (2012). Cardinal George criticizes Sebelius' declaration of "war on citizens." The Catholic World Report. http://www.catholicworldreport.com/Blog/1429/cardinal_george_criticizes_sebelius_declaration_of_war_on_citizens.aspx.

Oneil, T.(2006). *The Student manifesto.* Valley, AL: Liberty international Ministries Publishing.

Painter, G. (2005). The sensibilities of our Forefathers: The history of Sodomy Laws in the United States. Retrieved from http://www.glapn.org/sodomylaws/sensibilities/introduction.htm

Paulsen, M. (2015) Why the Supreme Court should take up the Bronx Household of Faith case. *National Review,* February 19.

Peabody, B. G. (2007). Legislating from the Bench: A Definition and a Defense. *Lewis & Clark Law Review, 11*:185-232.

Pepper, S. (1986). Taking the Free Exercise Clause Seriously. *Brigham Young University Law Review,* 1986:299-336.

Perkins, T. & Boykin, W. (2014). *Clear and present danger: The threat to religious liberty in the military.* Washington, DC: Family Research Council.

Pilon, R. (2013-2014). Long view: Toward restoring the Constitution. *Cato Supreme Court Review,* vii-xxiii.

Planck, M. (1949). *Religion and natural science: Scientific autobiography and other papers.* New York: Philosophical Library.

Powel, S. (2009). Judge Kent reports to prison hospital in Massachusetts. *Houston Chronical,* June 15th. http://www.chron.com/news/houston-texas/article/Judge-Kent-reports-to-prison-hospital-in-1673073.php.

Posner, R. (2016). The academy is out of its depth. Supreme Court breakfast table. http://www.slate.com/articles/news_and_politics/the_breakfast_table/features/2016/supreme_court_breakfast_table_for_june_2016/law_school_professors_need_more_practical_experience.html?wpsrc=sh_all_mob_tw_top

Prestigiacomo, A. (2016). Tenured professor: 'The Christian Right' caused Orlando but blame ISIS because they hate gays. http://www.dailywire.com/news/6694/tenured-professor-christian-right-caused-orlando-amanda-prestigiacomo

Project Veritas (2015) Officials at Cornell, Syracuse, and Yale destroy U.S. Constitution http://www.projectveritas.com/posts/news/officials-cornell-syracuse-and-yale-destroy-us-constitution

Pulliam, M. (2015). The quandary of judicial review. National Review, April 8th. http://www.nationalreview.com/article/416590/quandary-judicial-review.

Raehn, R. V. (2004). The Historical Roots of Political Correctness. In *Political Correctness: A short history of an ideology. Alexandria, VA: Free Congress Foundation.*

Reagan, R. (1984). *Remarks at a Dallas Ecumenical Prayer Breakfast.* American Rhetoric Online Speech Bank. http://www.americanrhetoric.com/speeches/ronaldreaganecumenicalpray er.htm

Reisman, J. & Eichel, E. (1990). *Kinsey, sex and fraud: The indoctrination of a people.* Lafayette, LA: Huntington House Publishers.

Reston, J. (1969). Faith of Our Fathers, living still? Eugene Register-Guard, April 3, p. 12a.

Rodell, F. (1955). *Nine men: A political history of the Supreme Court from 1790 to 1955.* New York: Random House.

Rorty, R. (200). Universality and truth. In R. Brandom (ed.), *Rorty and his Critics,* pp. 1-30. Oxford, Blackwell.

Rosenberg, G. (1991). *The hollow hope: Can courts bring about social change?* Chicago: University of Chicago Press.

Rutledge, C. (2008). Caught in the crossfire: How Catholic Charities of Boston was victim to the Clash between Gay Rights and Religious Freedom." *Duke Journal of Gender, Law. & Policy, 15:* 297-314.

Ryan, C. (2009). Helping families support their lesbian, gay, bisexual, and transgender (LGBT) children. Washington, DC: National Center for Cultural Competence, Georgetown University Center for Child and Human Development.

Sampson, R. (2005). *The Heart of Wisdom Teaching Approach: Bible Based Homeschooling.* Merritt Island, FL: Heart of Wisdom Publishing.

Sanburn, J. (2014). Houston's pastors outraged after city subpoenas sermons over transgender bill." *Time Magazine,* Oct. 17. http://time.com/3514166/houston-pastors-sermons-subpoenaed/

Saewyc, E., Poon, C., Wang, N., Homma, Y., & Smith, A. (2007). Not yet equal: The health of lesbian, gay, & bisexual youth in BC. Vancouver. British Columbia: McCreary Centre Society.

Sandfort, T., de Graaf, R., Bijl, R., & Schnabel, P. (2001). Same-sex sexual behavior and psychiatric disorders: Findings from the Netherlands Mental Health Survey and Incidence Study (NEMESIS). *Archives of general psychiatry, 58:* 85-91.

Schanzer, J. (2010). Review of *United in Hate: The Left's Romance with Tyranny and Terror. Middle East Quarterly, 17:* 93.

Schlenker, B., J. Chambers & B. Le (2012). Conservatives are happier than liberals, but why?

Political ideology, personality, and life satisfaction. *Journal of Research in Personality.* Doi:10:1016/jrp.2011.12.009.

Schwartzman, M. (2012). What if religion is not special? *The University of Chicago Law Review,* 79: 1351-1427.

Schweizer, P. (2008). *Makers and Takers: How Conservatives Do All the Work While Liberals Whine and Complain.* New York: Doubleday.

Sheehan, C. (2009). *James Madison and the spirit of republican self-government.* Cambridge University Press.

Shrader, D. (2005). Thou shalt not: Supreme Court rulings concerning public displays of religious symbols. In *Proceedings of the Fourth Annual Hawaii International Conference on Arts and Humanities* (pp. 5564-5608).
Setari, A., & Setari, R. (2016). Trends in Catholic School minority enrollment and higher education entrance over the recession. *Journal of Catholic Education, 19*: 4-19

Shackelford, K. (2016). Undeniable: The Survey of Hostility to Religion in America. First Liberty Institute, Plano: TX. https://firstliberty.org/wp-content/uploads/2016/02/2016_Undeniable.pdf

Sheen, F. (1948). *Communism and the Conscience of the West.* Indianapolis and NY: Bobbs-Merrill.

Shrader, D. (2005). Render Unto Caesar. In *Proceedings of the Third Annual Hawaii. International Conference on Arts and Humanities.*

Skousen, W. C. (1958). *The Naked Communist.* Pleasant Grove, UT: Verity Publishing.

Smith, S. (2013) *Town of Greece v. Galloway symposium: The end of "no endorsement"?*, SCOTUSblog, Oct. 2, http://www.scotusblog.com/2013/10/town-of-galloway-v-greece-symposium-the-end-of-no-endorsement/

Sørensen, T., Danbolt, L., Lien, L., Koenig, H., & Holmen, J. (2011). The relationship between religious attendance and blood pressure: the HUNT study, Norway. *The International Journal of Psychiatry in Medicine, 42:* 13-28.

Sowell, T. (2016). Supreme Hypocrisy. http://townhall.com/columnists/thomassowell /2016/03/29/supreme-hypocrisy-n2139969?utm_source=thdaily&utm_medium=email&utm

Sprig, P. (2006). *Homosexuality in your child's school.* Washington, DC: Family Research Council

Stark, R. (2005). *The Victory of Reason: How Christianity Led to Freedom, Capitalism, and Western Success.* New York: Random House.

Stark, R. (2012). *America's Blessings: How Religion Benefits Everyone, Including Atheists.* West Conshohocken, PA: Templeton Foundation Press.

Starns, T. (2014). Baker forced to make gay wedding cakes, undergo sensitivity training, after Losing Lawsuit." *Fox News,* June 3. http://www.foxnews.com/opinion/2014/06/03/baker-forced-to-make-gay-wedding-cakes-undergo-sensitivity-training-after.

Steffensmeier, D., B. Feldmeyer, C. Harris, & J. Ulmer (2011). Reassessing trends in black violent crime, 1980–2008: Sorting out the "Hispanic effect" in Uniform Crime Reports arrests, National Crime Victimization Survey offender estimates, and US prisoner counts, *Criminology, 49:* 197-251.

Stevenson, B., & Wolfers, J. (2009). *The paradox of declining female happiness* (No. w14969). Cambridge, MA: National Bureau of Economic Research.

Story, J. (1833). Commentaries on the Constitution of the United States. Boston: Hilliard, Gray and Company. Cambridge: Brown, Shattuck, and Co. Volume III, page 728,

Stormer, J. (1964). *None Dare Call It Treason.* New York: Buccaneer Books

Strawbridge, W., Cohen, R., Shema, S., & Kaplan, G. (1997). Frequent attendance at religious services and mortality over 28 years. *American Journal of Public Health, 87:* 957-961.

Straumann, B. (2008). The peace of Westphalia as a secular constitution. *Constellations, 15:* 173-188.

Strobel, L. (2004). *The case for a creator.* Grand Rapids, MI: Zondervan.

Stuntz, W. 2000. Self-defeating crimes. *Virginia Law Review* 86:1871–99. Substance Abuse and Mental Health Services Administration (2015). *Behavioral Health Trends in the United States: Results from the 2014 National Survey on Drug Use and Health.* Washington, DC.

Suicide Resource Prevention Center (2008). Suicide prevention for lesbian, gay, bisexual, and transgender youth. Newton, MA: Education Development Center.

Tatchell, P. (2016). I've changed my mind on the gay cake row. Here's why. *The Guardian,* February 1. https://www.theguardian.com/commentisfree/2016/feb/01/gay-cake-row-i-changed-my-mind-ashers-bakery-freedom-of-conscience-religion

Taylor, R. (1990). The American judiciary as a secular priesthood. *Free Inquiry, 10,* 37–43.

Taylor, P., C. Funk & P. Craighill (2006). Are we happy yet? Pew Research Center. http://pewresearch.org/assets/social/pdf/AreWeHappyYet.pdf.

Thomas, E (2016) Air Force veteran removed from colleague's ceremony after referencing 'God' in speech. ABC News, June 23rd. http://abc7news.com/news/air-force-veteran-removed-from-ceremony-after-referencing-god-/1399165/

Throckmorton, W. (2012). Alan Chambers: 99.9% have not experienced a change in their orientation. Patheos. http://www.patheos.com/blogs/warrenthrockmorton/2012/01/09/alan-chambers-99-9-have-not-experienced-a-change-in-their-orientation/

Time Magazine (2007). Person of the year: Putin Q&A. *Time Magazine.* http://content.time.com/time/specials/2007/personoftheyear/article/0,28 804,1690753_1690757_1695787-3,00.html

Tocqueville, A. (2006). *Democracy in America.* Harper Perennial Modern Classics, p. 444.

Trigg, R. (2011). Freedom of religion. *Ars Disputandi Supplement Series, 5:* 109-124.

United States Congress (March 27, 1854), received the report of Mr. Meacham of the House Committee on the Judiciary: Congressional Record of the 108th Congress p. 1226. https://www.congress.gov/bill/108th-congress/house-bill/2622

United States Conference of Catholic Bishops (2016). Letter, March 31. http://www.usccb.org/issues-and-action/religious-liberty/conscience-protection/upload/Conscience-Protection-Act-Dolan-Lori-Ltr-to-Congress-03-31-16.pdf

U.S. Census Bureau, *Statistical Abstract of the United States (2015).* Washington, DC, http://www.census.gov/compendia/statab/.

U.S. Civil Rights Commission. (2016). Peaceful Coexistence: Reconciling non-discrimination Principles with civil liberties. Washington, DC: U.S. Commission on Civil Rights.

U.S. Department of Health and Human Services (2011). *Births: Preliminary data for 2010.* Washington, DC: U.S. Government Printing Office.

U.S. Department of Health & Human Services (2014). AIDS.gov. https://www.aids.gov/hiv-aids-basics/hiv-aids-101/statistics/

U.S. History/Valley Forge, George Washington's Earnest Prayer. http://www.ushistory.org/valleyforge/washington/earnestprayer.html

U.S. Congress (1998). Title 22 - Foreign relations and intercourse: Chapter 73-International religious freedom. https://www.law.cornell.edu/uscode/pdf/uscode22/lii_usc_TI_22_CH_73_SE_6401.pdf

Vickers, A. (2002). *The New Nation.* Westport, CN: Greenwood Press.

Waldron, J. (2006). The core of the case against judicial review. *The Yale Law Journal,* 1346-1406.

Waldron, J. (2014). Five to Four: Why Do Bare Majorities Rule on Courts? *The Yale Law Review,* 123: 1692-1730.

Walpin, G. (2015). Five justices have transformed the First Amendment's freedom of religion to freedom from religion. *Touro Law Reviw, 31*:187-1089.

Walsh, A. (1998). Religion and hypertension: Testing alternative explanations among immigrants. *Behavioral Medicine,* 24:122-130.

Walsh, A. & Hatch, V. (2017). Ideology, race, and the death penalty: "Lies, damn lies, and statistics" in Advocacy Research. *Journal of Ideology,* 37:1-34.

Walsh, A. & Hemmens, C. (2016). *Law. Justice, and society (4th ed.).* New York: Oxford University Press.

Walsh, M. (2015). *The Devil's pleasure palace: The cult of critical theory and the subversion of the west.* New York: Encounter Books.

Washington, G. (1789). From George Washington to the Society of Quakers, 13 October 1789. http://founders.archives.gov/documents/Washington/05-04-02-0188

Washington, G. (1796). Washington's farewell address, 1796. The Avalon Project, http://avalon.law.yale.edu/18th_century/washing.asp.

Weber, M. (1930). *Protestant Ethic and the Spirit of Capitalism;* T. Parsons (trans.). New York: Charles Scribner.

Weitoft, G., A. Hjern, B. Haglund, & M. Rosén (2003). Mortality, severe morbidity, and injury in children living with single parents in Sweden: a population-based study. *The Lancet, 361:* 289-295.

Wiker, B. (2005). How the world's most notorious atheist changed his mind. *Strange Notions.* http://www.strangenotions.com/flew/

Wilcox, B. (2004). *Soft patriarchs, new men: How Christianity shapes fathers and husbands.* Chicago: University of Chicago Press.

Winterich, K., Zanh W. & Mittal, V. (2012). How political identity and charity positioning increase donations: Insights from moral foundations theory. *International Journal of Research in Marketing.* Doi.org/10.1016/j.ijres.2012.05.002.

Winthrop, R. (1852). *Addresses and Speeches on Various Occasions, Boston: Little, Brown.*

Witte, J. (1996). The essential rights and liberties of religion in the American Constitutional experiment. *Notre Dame Law Review,* 71:371-445.

Wolpert, L. (1998). *The unnatural nature of science.* Cambridge, MA: Harvard University Press.

Wood, R., Goesling, B., & Avellar, S. (2007). The effects of marriage on health: a synthesis of recent research evidence. *Washington DC: Mathematical Policy Research.*

Yale Law School (nd). Northwest Ordinance; July 13, 1787, Avalon Project. http://avalon.law.yale.edu/18th_century/nworder.asp

Yates, R. (1788a). *Anti- Federalist Paper No. 11:* http://www.constitution.org/afp/brutus11.htm

Yates, R. (1788b). *The Power of the Judiciary.* http://www.thisnation.com/library/antifederalist/78-79.html

Index